Grid and Services Evolution

Proceedings of the
3rd CoreGRID Workshop on
Grid Middleware
June 5-6, 2008, Barcelona, Spain

Grid and Services Evolution

Proceedings of the
3rd CoreGRID Workshop on
Grid Middleware
June 5-6, 2008, Barcelona, Spain

Edited by

Norbert Meyer
Poznań Supercomputing and Networking Center
Poznań, Poland

Domenico Talia
University of Calabria
Rende, Italy

Ramin Yahyapour
Dortmund University of Technology
Dortmund, Germany

Springer

Editors:
Norbert Meyer
Poznan Supercomputing & Networking Centre
ul. Noskowskiego 10
61-704 Poznan, Poland
meyer@man.poznan.pl

Domenico Talia
Università Calabria
Dipto. Elettronica Informatica
Sistemistica (DEIS)
via P. Bucci,41 c
87036 Rende, Italy
talia@deis.unical.it

Ramin Yahyapour
Universität Dortmund
IT und Medien Centrum (ITMC)
44221 Dortmund, Germany
ramin.yahyapour@udo.edu

ISBN-13: 978-1-4419-4678-2 e-ISBN-13: 978-0-387-85966-8

Printed on acid-free paper

springer.com

Contents

Foreword

This proceedings is the newest of a series of books that have been edited by researchers to disseminate the results of their joint research activities carried out within CoreGRID, the only one Network of Excellence in Grid and P2P technologies funded by the EU 6th Framework Programme. The mission, assigned to CoreGRID by the European Commission (EC), was to build a research community in Europe to gather the expertise and the know-how of researchers in various research fields related to Grid and P2P computing into a single entity. After fours years of existence, I am proud to say that CoreGRID has fully met its objectives as defined five years ago in the proposal submitted to the sixth Framework Programme funded by the European Union. CoreGRID acts as the main portal providing researchers worldwide with the latest results from their European colleagues. It has established a solid research community covering various aspects in Grid research. After a period of four years funded by the EC, the network is now entering another phase of its existence: to be sustainable for the years to come. This is the objective of the newly formed ERCIM Working Group, that uses the same brand name - CoreGRID. Additionally to Grid and P2P computing, this working group will also cover service computing.

One of the main activities of CoreGRID is to ensure a proper dissemination of its research results. The organization of workshops, linked with highly visible events, is the main strategy of the network. This book is the proceedings of the 3rd edition of the CoreGRID Grid Middleware Workshop that was held in conjonction with OGF23. I would like to take this opportunity to express my gratitude to the organizers of those workshops as well as to all contributors. I wish you a good reading.

Thierry Priol, CoreGRID Scientific Co-ordinator

Preface

The CoreGRID Network of Excellence includes a large number of European scientists working to achieve high-level research objectives in Grid and P2P systems. CoreGRID brings together a critical mass of well-established researchers from more than forty European institutions active in the fields of distributed systems and middleware, models, algorithms, tools and environments.

Grid middleware and Grid services are two pillars of Grid computing systems and applications. Currently a large number of Grid researchers and developers are providing solutions in both those areas. The marriage of the Grid computing model with SOA enlarged the application arena of Grids and, at the same time, put in place new technological solutions in the world of service oriented architectures. Service oriented Grids are becoming effective solutions in science and business because they offer interoperable high-performance systems for handling data- and compute-intensive distributed applications.

This book is the eleventh volume of the CoreGRID series and it brings together scientific contributions by researchers and scientists working on knowledge and data management on Grids, Grid resource management and scheduling, Grid information, resource and workflow monitoring services. The book includes contributions presented at the workshop organized in Barcelona on June 5th and 6th, 2008. This is the third workshop of its kind. The first two workshops took place in Dresden, 2006 and 2007.

The goals of these workshops is to:

- to gather current state of the art and new approaches in the areas mentioned above

- to include work-in-progress contributions, e.g. as short papers

- to provide a forum for exchanging the ideas between the users' community and Grid middleware developers

- to collect requirements towards the middleware from application's perspective

- to disseminate existing results and provide input to the CoreGRID Network of Excellence

This book contains 15 chapters. The first one considers task execution in commodity Grids. The second chapter deals with the evaluation of Grids storage elements either using custom technology or commodity-based. The third chapter addressed the modeling of non functional properties of Grid resources. The fourth chapter discusses a Grid checkpointing service and the integration of lower level checkpointing packages.

Chapter five proposes an extending of GWORKFLOWDL as a multi-purpose language for workflow enactment.The sixth chapter considers workflow monitoring and analysis tool for the Askalon project. Chapter seven presents the approach to implement a secure intensive care Grid system based on gLite. Chapter eight discusses workflow management for automatic performance analysis of massive parallel applications.

In chapter nine fault detection, prevention and recovery techniques on Grid workflow systems are analyzed. Chapter ten considers self-healing by a self-adaptable monitoring framework. Chapter eleven summarizes the performance monitoring of Grid superscalar. Chapter twelve addresses the problem of authorizing Grid resource access and consumption.

Chapter 13 covers an all-in-one graphic tool for Grid middleware management. The 14th chapter proposes an efficient protocol for reserving multiple grid resources in advance. Chapter 15 presents experimental results for scalable concurrency control in a dynamic membership.

Chapter 16 discusses improvements in peer-to-peer rings for building fault-tolerant Grids. This content was presented at the CoreGRID workshop on Grid Programming Model, Grid and P2P Systems Architecture Grid Systems, Tools and Environments in Crete, June 12-13, 2007.

The Programme Committee who made the selection of the chapters included: Artur Andrzejak, ZIB, DE
Alvaro Arenas, CCLRC-RAL, UK
Angelos Bilas, FORTH, GR
Maciej Brzezniak, PSNC, PL
Marco Danelutto, University of Pisa, IT
Marios Dikaiakos, UCY, CY
Ewa Deelman, Information Sciences Institute, Marina Del Rey, US
Vivi Fragopoulou, Foundation for Research and Technology - Hellas, GR
Vladimir Getov, University of Westminster, UK
Antonia Ghiselli, INFN Bologna, IT
Sergei Gorlatch, University of Münster, DE
Anastasios Gounaris, UoM, UK
Pierre Guisset, CETIC, BE
Domenico Laforenza, ISTI/CNR, IT
Philippe Massonet, CETIC, BE
Salvatore Orlando, CNR-ISTI, IT
Thierry Priol, INRIA, FR
Yves Robert, CNRS, FR
Paolo Trunfio, UNICAL, IT
Rizos Sakellariou, UoM, UK
Frederic Vivien, CNRS, FR
Paul Watson, UNCL, UK
Roman Wyrzykowski, Technical University of Czestochowa, PL
Wolfgang Ziegler, Fraunhofer-Institute SCAI, DE

We would like to thank all the participants for their contributions to making the two workshops a success, the workshop program committees for reviewing the submissions, and all the authors that contributed chapter for publication in this volume. A special thank to the Springer staff for their assistance in editing the book.

Our thanks also go to the European Commission for sponsoring under grant number 004265 this volume of the CoreGRID project series of publications.

Norbert Meyer, Domenico Talia, Ramin Yahyapour

Contributing Authors

Javier Alonso Technical University of Catalonia, ES

Ali Asim University of Paris Sud-XI, FR

Rosa M. Badia Universitat Politècnica de Catalunya, ES

Daniel Becker Forschungszentrum Jülich, DE; RWTH Aachen University, DE

Angelos Bilas Foundation for Research and Technology – Hellas (FORTH), GR

Maciej Brzezniak Poznan Supercomputing and Networking Center, PL

Marian Bubak Institute of Computer Science, AGH, PL; Academic Computer Centre - CYFRONET, PL

David Buján-Carballal University of Deusto, ES

Eddy Caron Université de Lyon, FR

Augusto Ciuffoletti INFN-CNAF, IT

Oscar Corcho-García Polytechnic University of Madrid, ES

Frederic Desprez Université de Lyon, FR

Josuka Díaz-Labrador University of Deusto, ES

Marios D. Dikaiakos University of Cyprus, CY

Erik Elmroth Umeå University, SE

Thomas Fahringer University of Innsbruck, AT

Michail Flouris Foundation for Research and Technology - Hellas (FORTH), GR; University of Toronto, CA

Włodzimierz Funika Institute of Computer Science, AGH, PL

Julius Gehr Technische Universitaet Berlin, DE

Vasil Georgiev University of Sofia 'St. Kliment Ohridski', BG

Francesco Giacomini INFN-CNAF, IT

Harald Gjermundrod University of Cyprus, CY

Rean Griffith Columbia University, US

Donatien Grolaux Universite Catholique de Louvain, BE

Alexandru Iosup Delft University of Technology, NL

Gracjan Jankowski Poznan Supercomputing and Networking Center, PL

Michał Jankowski Poznań Supercomputing and Networking Center, PL

Radoslaw Januszewski Poznań Supercomputing and Networking Center, PL

Péter Kacsuk MTA SZTAKI Computer and Automation Research Institute, HU

Gail Kaiser Columbia University, US

Attila Kertész MTA SZTAKI Computer and Automation Research Institute, HU

Lazar Kirchev Bulgarian Academy of Sciences, BG

Jozsef Kovacs MTA SZTAKI Computer and Automation Research Institute, HU

Barry Linnert Technische Universitaet Berlin, DE

David Loureiro Université de Lyon, FR

Jesus Luna University of Cyprus, CY

Piotr Machner Institute of Computer Science, AGH, PL

Manolis Marazakis Foundation for Research and Technology - Hellas (FORTH), GR; University of Crete, GR

Boris Mejias Universite Catholique de Louvain, BE

Luis Moura Silva University of Coimbra, PT

Norbert Meyer Poznań Supercomputing and Networking Center, PL

Simon Ostermann University of Innsbruck, AT

Simone Pellegrini INFN-CNAF, IT

Kassian Plankensteiner University of Innsbruck, AT

Radu Prodan University of Innsbruck, AT

Morris Riedel Forschungszentrum Jülich, DE

Thomas Röblitz Zuse Institute Berlin, DE

Peter Van Roy Universite Catholique de Louvain, BE

Jörg Schneider Technische Universitaet Berlin, DE

Raül Sirvent Universitat Politècnica de Catalunya, ES

Achim Streit Forschungszentrum Jülich, DE

Jordi Torres Technical University of Catalonia, ES

Felix Wolf Forschungszentrum Jülich, DE; RWTH Aachen University, DE

Shenol Yousouf Bulgarian Academy of Sciences, BG

A JAVA TASK EXECUTION MANAGER FOR COMMODITY GRIDS*

Shenol Yousouf, Lazar Kirchev
Institute on Parallel Processing
Bulgarian Academy of Sciences
25A, Acad. G. Bonchev str., 1113 Sofia
Bulgaria
Shenol@acad.bg
lkirchev@acad.bg

Vasil Georgiev
Faculty of Mathematics and Informatics
University of Sofia 'St. Kliment Ohridski'
5, J. Bourchier blvd., 1164 Sofia
Bulgaria
v.georgiev@fmi.uni-sofia.bg

Abstract Remote execution of applications is used in many distributed systems, including grid systems, volunteer computing networks, peer-to-peer networks, etc. In this paper we describe a software module, which executes Java code remotely. It runs on the remote host and makes its resources available for executing applications on them. Its basic characteristics are its flexibility, extensibility and minimal requirements to the host it runs on. This module executes arbitrary Java applications, both in the form of Java .class files or archived in .jar files. It may execute not only main methods, but also any other public method in the program. The input to the executed method, as well as the output, unlike many other similar components, may be not only based on files, but also values of arbitrary type.

Keywords: distributed computing, task execution, java applications, grid systems

*This work is supported by CoreGRID Network of Excellence (Project No. FP6-004265) and SUGrid (Project No. VU-MI-110/2005)

1. Introduction

Most grid systems provide some software component, module or daemon, which is constantly running on the nodes, constituting the grid and is responsible for making available their hardware resource to the grid platform. This component of the system has a very important role, because it is only through it that the corresponding resource may be used for computations or completion of other tasks.

We are currently building a prototype of the hierarchical general purpose service-centric grid system GrOSD (Grid-aware Open Service Directory)[1]. One of the goals is any user over the Internet to be able to use resources of the system, and to provide own resources to it. The platform is designed to be simple and easy to use and administer, with its own middleware services and not relying on complex middleware tools, such as Globus. GrOSD is built up of connected "virtual clusters", which logically group computers together. Thus the cluster is the unit for organizing nodes, resources and users. The platform provides middleware system services for security, resource management, scheduling, monitoring, information storage.

One of the system services of GrOSD is a task execution service, which we call Node Service and which is responsible for local management of the nodes that are part of the GrOSD system. While the other system services do not reside, in the general case, on the grid resources, the Node Service is located there. The main responsibility of the Node Service is to execute tasks, which the scheduler of the GrOSD system sends to it. It provides a considerable flexibility regarding the tasks, which it may execute. Actually, it may execute arbitrary java code - applications in the form of compiled .class files or .jar archives with a main method in some of the classes, as well as executing methods, different from the main methods. Moreover, the Node Service is very flexible as for the input parameters of the executed method and the results returned. Many grid systems restrict the code that they can execute to units, which receive their input through files and write their output to files. Our Node Service allows the input arguments to have even user-defined types, and the methods may return results of arbitrary type. The task execution is asynchronous to the request and the user is notified when a task finishes through an events mechanism. The different tasks are executed in different threads, thus allowing more than one task to be handled by the Node Service at a time. Node Service also provides support for uploading code which is persistently available to answer requests with different input.

The architecture of the Node Service is modular and extensible. The implementation of one module may be easily changed with another, without affecting the rest of the system. The Node Service may easily be extended to execute new types of tasks. The Node Service is accessed through an Application Programming Interface (API), which encapsulates all the details of the communication between the clients of the Node Service (which in the context of GrOSD are the other middleware services of the platform) and the Node Service itself.

Although, as mentioned before, the Node Service is designed and implemented in the context of the GrOSD system, it is not constrained to be used only in it. Due to the API, it may equally well be used separately from this grid platform, either as a complete manager for remote execution of applications, or as a building block for other grid systems.

The paper is organized as follows. Section 2 makes a short overview of related work. In Section 3 we present the architecture of the Node Service. Section 4 describes the most important features of the Node Service and give examples how it is used. In Section 5 we present our future plans and Section 6 makes a conclusion.

2. Related work

All grid systems provide some service or module, responsible for the local management of resources in the system. Many systems are based on complex grid middleware such as the Globus toolkit [2]. Since we aim at developing a system with minimal requirements to the environment, where it will be used, these are not a solution for us. Following are presented several grid systems with a description of their task execution facilities.

H2O [3]is a component-based and service-oriented framework, intended to provide lightweight and distributed resource sharing. It is based upon the idea of representing the resources as software components, which offer services through remote interfaces. Resource providers supply a runtime environment in the form of component containers (kernels). These containers are executed by the owners of resources and service components (pluglets) may be deployed in them not only by the owners of the containers, but also by third parties, provided that they possess the proper authorization. The pluglets are executed by the containers and answer user requests, but they should implement H2O specific interfaces. Actually, they are used by remotely instantiating the pluglet classes and using the remote objects.

JGrid [4]is a Java-based, service-oriented grid platform. The Compute Services in the system export JVMs of remote computers in the grid infrastructure and are responsible for the execution of tasks. The tasks are in the form of Runnable Java Objects, which are executed in a thread. But these tasks, in order to be executed by the Compute Service, should implement JGrid specific interface, containing an execute() method which will be called by the system.

Triana [5], [6]is a Java-based graphical problem solving environment, which is mainly used for construction and execution of workflows. It has a component called Triana service daemon, which resides on each node, which is part of Triana. This daemon is responsible for execution of the tasks, which compose the workflow. These tasks may be local as well as remote and in the Triana context they are called tools. The tools are actually Java classes, which implement a specific interface.

Condor [7]is a workload management system, or batch system, for compute-intensive jobs. It offers facilities for the management of resources in computing clusters and execution of jobs on these resources. The jobs, which are supported by the system, must receive their input from and write their output to files. The input may also be in the form of command line arguments. Java applications may be executed, but only execution of main methods is supported.

Taverna [8], [9]is a workflow environment, which is oriented towards biology workflows. The Freefluo enactment engine is responsible for execution of the workflow components. These are the processors, which abstract services, with inputs and outputs, and data and coordination links, connecting them. Different processor types are presented, thus enabling the use of different types of services - Web Services, services, provided by local Java classes, and different types of biology services. The local Java classes should comply with a specific Java interface.

ALiCE [10]is a software technology aimed at developing and deploying general-purpose grid applications and systems. On each machine, which volunteers cycles to run ALiCE applications, is running a component called producer. It receives tasks from the system's broker in the form of serialized objects, loads them, executes them and returns the result. The tasks, which are executed by the platform, comply with a specific interface, and the system even provides templates for facilitating the programming of grid tasks.

The **BOINC** [11], [12]is a software platform for volunteer computing. The infrastructure of a project using BOINC includes several servers with different functionality and a large number of client. The client modules work on the hosts which perform the computations. The applications, which they execute are not restricted to a specific interface. Applications in C/C++ and FORTRAN are supported. The input is through command arguments and input files.

Tables 1 and 2 summarize the features of the presented systems.

Some of the existing grid platforms support only execution of tasks with file-based input and output, with no input parameters and return results. We considered this functionality important for our platform. Also, in some systems the available tasks for execution are represented in the form of Web or Grid Services. While this conforms to standards, it requires that the host, where the task will be executed, run a Web service engine. Since we wanted to impose minimum burden upon the executing machines, this is not suitable for us. Some systems provide execution facilities for java applications, but the classes representing the tasks should implement some system-specific interface. In

Table 1. Comparison of task execution in different systems.

System	*Execution of Java code*	*Input/Output*
H2O	yes	Files/objects
jGrid	yes	Files/objects
Triana	yes	Files/objects
Condor	yes	Files
Taverna	yes	Files/objects
ALiCE	yes	Files, arbitrary output
BOINC	no	-

Table 2. Comparison of task execution in different systems.

System	*Arbitrary method execution*	*Specific interface implementation*
H2O	yes	yes
jGrid	no	yes
Triana	no	yes
Condor	no (only main)	no
Taverna	no	yes
ALiCE	no	yes
BOINC	-	-

developing our Node Service we tried to avoid imposing such a constraint. In most systems the task execution component is tightly integrated in the system and cannot be used separately from it. All of the above considered systems possess one or more of the mentioned drawbacks. That gave us motivation to develop our own task execution component, instead of using an existing one.

3. Architecture of the Node Service

Node Service is composed of three main components, as can be seen on figure 1. These are Node Service API, the Node Service core and the Node Service Task Framework.

3.1 Node Service API

The Node Service API implements a communication layer between the clients and the Node Service itself. It provides an abstraction of the logical connection with the component, working on the remote node. The API is

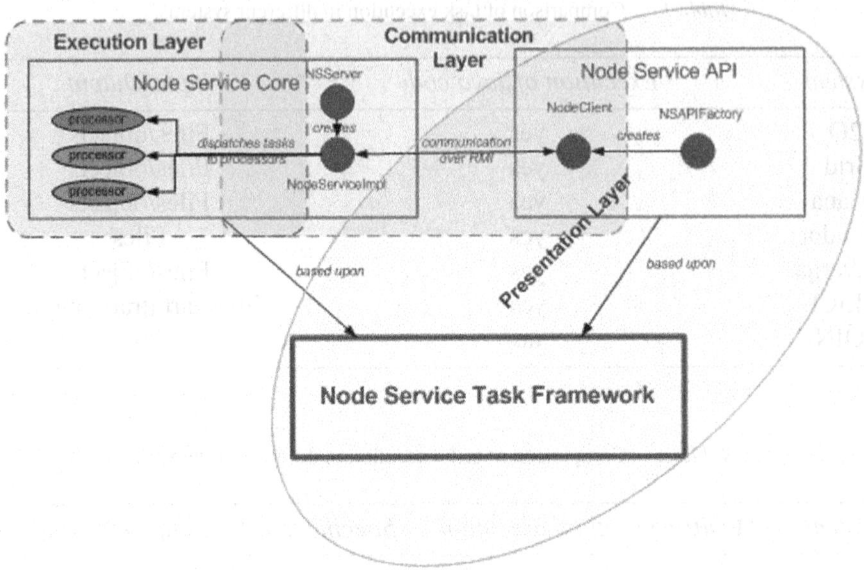

Figure 1. Architecture of the Node Service.

physically located at the machine, where the clients of the Node Service are - in the context of GrOSD these are the Resource Management Service and the Monitoring Service. The API hides the actual details of the communication with the remote node, which are performed with RMI calls. It acts as a proxy of the Node Service core to the rest of the system.

For sending a request for task execution to the remote node, there are a number of actions that have to be performed first. The client should designate the code of the task (in the form of .class files or .jar archives), should provide input parameters (if any), should designate which method and of which class should be called, as well as some additional files that may be needed by the application. All these actions are performed with methods of the API, and it takes care of the transmission of files, passing of parameters and all other details that should otherwise be done by the client itself. All objects, needed for the composition of the request are created through factory methods of the API.

The Node Service API provides the complete set of operations, needed for communication with the Node Service core and sending of requests and any client may use it for this purpose.

3.2 Node Service core

This is the actual Node Service - i.e., the part of the Node Service, and therefore of GrOSD, which works on each node of the grid platform and makes its resources available to the system by executing tasks on them. It forms the execution layer of the Node Service by providing the whole logic for executing applications. The core receives tasks from the Resource Management Service (sent through the Node Service API) and executes them. The Node Service core contains a server module, which exports the remote object through which the Node Service API accesses the functionality of the core. Therefore, the Node Service may be considered also as a server.

Although the connection from the clients of the Node Service to the core is not direct, but goes through the API and thus is one-way, the core is not completely separated from its clients. During the execution of a task the core should be able to “talk” back to the client in two situations - to send events for changes in the status of the executed task, and for the file transfers. Both the transfer of the files which come with the request, and the transfer of the resulting files are performed by the core. For the transfers a remote callback object, located on the client machine, is used. For the state change events propagation listener objects, located on the client machines, are provided to the core.

Currently the Node Service defines three types of tasks. These are Java task, service upload task and service invocation task.

The Java task is a task containing Java code for execution. After it is received by the core, it is executed and the result, if any, is returned to the client.

The service upload task is used to upload a service on the node. The services, unlike standard Java tasks, are persistent - their code is uploaded once on the node and after that it is always running, waiting for requests. Thus a service may be executed many times with different input parameters. These services may be stopped and started, as well as removed from the node. All persistent tasks, uploaded on a Node Service, are started when the Node Service core starts, and if not explicitly stopped by a client, are running until the core itself stops.

A service invocation task is used to invoke an already uploaded service. It does not include the code, since it is already on the node, but only the input parameters and eventually the method to be executed.

The core provides specific processing modules for each of the above described task types. These are actually classes, which know how to handle the particular task. Upon arrival of a task for execution, the core instantiates a processor of the type needed for the type of the task and starts it in a separate thread, passing to it the task object and a callback object. The task type is determined by the API method, which the client called to send the task (different type of tasks are sent through different methods), as well as by a parameter of the call, identifying the type. In order for the core to preserve control over the tasks, executed in their own threads, when starting each processor registers its task in a special task registry, from which the executing task may be accessed.

After a task execution finishes, the client is notified through an event, which also caries an object, containing the result of the execution. This object may contain two types of results - file results and object results. The object results may be directly used by the client, while the file results are actually references to output files, which are transferred to the client only when it tries to use them. In case of task failure the client is notified through an event. Clients may stop their tasks, which are already started, by calling methods on the API. The tasks are identified by a unique identifier, which is created when a task is uploaded and is returned to the client as a result of the method call with which the task is uploaded.

3.3 Node Service Task Framework

This component may be considered as the connection between the core and the API of the Node Service. Actually, both of them are based on it, and it determines the design of the requests to the core and the overall functionality of the core. It forms the presentation layer of the Node Service. It completely defines the interface of the core, the structure of the tasks and the requests and provides an isolation layer between the implementations of the core and the API, since it does not contain any implementation details. The interfaces are implemented by the core and the API. The framework also defines specific interfaces, which, if implemented by the client task, provides processing for specialized tasks.

3.4 Security considerations in the Node Service

Initially the Node Service was developed as part of a grid platform and most security issues are dealt with on a higher level. Generally, this grid system has registered users and only these users may submit tasks for execution, after receiving proper rights from the administrator. Therefore, we assume that the code, submitted by authenticated and authorized users of the system is secure and may be executed. The Node Service does not make further secure checks upon the tasks it executes. This is a disadvantage if the Node Service is to be used in other systems, or independently. We plan as part of our future plans to include in the Node Service some form of sandboxing mechanism to restrict what the executed code does - e.g. using a specific security manager, defining security policy, etc.

4. Features and usage of the Node Service

As a general-purpose node manager, the Node Manager Service is very likely to be run on commodity computers, by ordinary users, therefore it should be simple and easy to use and administer. It should have as minimal requirements as possible to the host it runs on. Therefore it is implemented in pure Java and its only requirement to each one, who wants to volunteer resources, is to have a JVM installed.

The Node Service was designed and implemented with the idea of extensibility and flexibility in mind. This section discusses some of the most important features of the Node Service.

4.1 Adding new types of tasks

The Node Service core may easily be extended to perform other types of tasks, which are not currently supported. This is allowed by the architecture, which provides different processor for each type of task. Thus it is enough to implement and add a new processor in order to provide support for new types of requests. We consider this an important feature for a general purpose grid system, because the types of tasks may be different for the different purposes, for which the system is used.

4.2 Use of factory classes and methods

At the API level, most of the objects, needed for construction of a request, are not instantiated directly, using the constructor of the corresponding class, but through object factories, which create the objects through factory methods. These factory methods return objects of types, defined by the interfaces in the Node Service Task Framework. For example, a task for upload is created by invoking the *NSTaskFactory.createNSJavaTask(...)* method, the real constructor of the task class being inaccessible for the client. The purpose is to screen the implementation of the actual meta-components of the request for the task execution from client code, thus allowing a completely transparent customization of future versions of the API, without changes in client code. Moreover, extending the API may concern only addition of new factories, or new factory methods to an existing factory.

4.3 Changing the implementation

The architecture of the Node Service even allows to completely substitute the API, or the core, ore both, with other implementations, and that will not affect the other component. This is due to the isolation of these two components, provided by the Node Service Task Framework. In this way the Node Service may be adjusted for use in other grid systems, different fro GrOSD, or as an independent manager for remote execution of tasks.

4.4 Adding specific task interfaces

Currently the Node Service provides facilities for execution of arbitrary java applications. Although this is the most user-friendly approach, it imposes some restrictions on the functionality of the system. For example, the Node Service would be able to provide more thorough lifecycle management to applications, which implement a specific interface. The architecture of the framework may easily be extended with such specialized interfaces for applications which require a different kind of processing from the system.

4.5 Support for execution of arbitrary Java code

One of the most important features of the Node Service is the support for execution of both compiled Java classes and jar archives, which represent arbitrary Java applications. It does not require the classes to be executed to implement a specific interface, as is the case in many other grid systems. This makes it more or less universal for execution of Java code.

Some grid systems, which allow execution of Java applications, support only execution of main methods. We considered this to be an unnecessary constraint and designed our Node Service to be able to execute arbitrary methods of Java applications. When the client constructs the request through the API, the client specifies which method of the class should be executed. This may be the main method, or any other public method of the class. Also, the client specifies the class, whose method should be called. In this way when the application code is contained in a jar archive with many classes, methods of an arbitrary class from the archive may be invoked.

The benefit of executing arbitrary public method, different from the main, is that in this way jar archives may be used as libraries of functions, which may be loaded as services on a node, and after that requests for specific methods to be sent to them. In addition, this feature may be useful in building workflow applications. The output of one workflow component may be directly used as input for another by calling its method, which receives as input this value. This is directly connected with the next point, which is

4.6 Support for arbitrary input and output for the executed tasks

Unlike other systems, which support only file-based input and output for the applications they are able to execute, our Node Service allows methods, which it will execute, to have input arguments, and to produce and return a result. In additionIt supports file-based input and output. The input arguments of a method, that is to be called, are specified when constructing the request. The API provides special methods for creating a list of arguments. Here the client may also specify the classes of each argument, in a separate list, but this is not mandatory. The implementation offers this flexibility - if argument types are not specified, the Node Service performs matching with the types of the arguments of all methods in the code with the same name. Even if no exact match is found, it further tries to perform some inexact matching using promotions of types. The types of input parameters may be arbitrary classes, not only primitive types, or standard Java classes, but also user-defined types. In this case it is necessary the classes of the arguments to be included in the jar archive, containing the class whose method will be called.

4.7 Flexible request formation

When the client constructs the request, the client may specify, in addition to the files containing classes and the input files, additional files, which are needed by the application, e.g. configuration files. But all these are optional, what actually is completely necessary for execution, are the class or jar file, the target class, the target method, and its input parameters. In this way the API implements significant flexibility of the construction of the request. All objects, needed for constructing the request - binary, input and auxiliary files, target class, target method, method parameters - are created by specific factory classes and methods. Following is a code snippet, which shows construction and upload of a task.

```
//initialize classFile with the binaries of the class
//whose method will be executed
//...

//create a proxy for the Node Service core
NodeServiceClient client = NSAPIFactory.
createNodeServiceClient("localhost");

//create an object identifying the class whose method
// will be executed
NSTaskTargetClass targetClass = NSTaskTargetClassFactory.
  createNSTaskTargetClass(args[0],
  new NSTaskArgument[] {});

//create an object which wraps the binaries of the
// class which will be executed
FileArgument fileArgument = NSTaskArgumentFactory.
```

```
  createFileArg(classFile, true);

//create an list with the arguments of the method,
//which will be executed
NSTaskArgument[] taskArgsList = NSTaskArgumentFactory.
  createArgsList(3, 4);

//create an object for the method to be executed
NSTaskMethod taskMethod = NSTaskMethodFactory.
  createNSTaskMethod("compute", taskArgsList);

//create the task object
NSJavaTask task = NSTaskFactory.createNSJavaTask(
  targetClass, taskMethod, new FileArgument[]{
  fileArgument});

//save task's id to be able to stop it later if needed
String taskId = task.getTaskID();

//... do some more work here, like creating file
//locator and event listeners

//upload the task to the Node Service Core
client.uploadJavaTask(task);

//... do more work here
```

The code above creates a task by specifying the .class file, which contains the class whose method will be executed, the method, which will be executed, and with what parameters. This is the least information needed to create and upload a task.

4.8 Persistent task upload

The upload of persistent tasks, which are to be executed as services, offers some additional flexibility. When initially uploading the task, the client has to specify its binary files and also a default method, which will be called when a request to the service is made. The parameters of the method are also specified. This facilitates the following calls to the service, since in the request the client need not specify which method should be called. But the API offers the option a method different from the default to be called. In this case when constructing the request to the service the client should specify the method that should be invoked. All features, regarding parameter passing and type matching, which are used for execution of transient tasks, are also valid for executing requests to persistent tasks.

4.9 Task results

Similar to the passing of input parameters, the return of a result from the method call provides certain flexibility. The method may write its output to a file, or may return the result as a value, or both.

If the result is a value, it is encapsulated in the result object, returned to the client. This result object provides a number of methods which return the value, cast to different primitive types. In this way, if the client knows the type of the output in advance, which is the common case, may extract the value as having the type that is needed and expected.

The result may also be in the form of one or more files. In this case the result object contains a list of the URLs of the files and the client is free to request them or not. Actually, the transfer happens transparently for the client. When the client tries to use a file, it is transferred to the client machine. This is done to minimize the traffic between the client and the Node Service machine.

The handling of the result is performed in a user-defined listener, implementing the *NSTaskLifecycleListner*. This interface has two methods - *taskAported()*, which is called with an *NSTaskAbortedEvent* parameter in case the task aborted for some reason, and *taskFinished()*, where the client places the result-handling code.

The client has the option to specify what files should be returned as a result of the execution of the task. This is done when constructing the request through passing a special result locator object, which contains a user-defined file locator object. In this way it is possible the task to produce a large number of files as a side effect of its work, but if the client is interested only in a particular file or files, the client may specify them so that only they are returned in the result object.

4.10 Asynchronous task execution

Additional flexibility for the clients is the asynchronous mode, in which tasks are executed. It is enabled through the use of an event mechanism. The client may register two types of listeners - for task status change events, and for task lifecycle events. The Node Service Task Framework provides the interfaces for the listeners, and the client should provide implementations for the listeners of the events the client is interested in. The listeners are registered at request construction time. The result from the execution of a task is returned with a lifecycle event.

4.11 Multithreaded execution

The tasks, sent to the Node Service core for execution are started in separate threads. This multithreading of the Node Service provides additional flexibility to the way it is used, because in this way a single computing node may run more than one task at a time, which may be very useful, especially for multiprocessor machines. Moreover, another advantage of the multithreading of the Node Service is that in this way a certain level of fault tolerance is achieved. A task, which fails or blocks during execution, does not stop the work of the Node Service, but only of the thread, it is executed in. Failures in the execution of a task are reported to the client through exceptions and the event mechanism.

4.12 Node monitoring

The Node Service, in addition to executing tasks, performs some basic monitoring of the node it is working on. It regularly acquires information about the working parameters of the node and sends it to a special GrOSD service, responsible for monitoring the system. The Node Service, when starting, retrieves the node hardware parameters - hard disk data, network interfaces, CPU, RAM, VGA adaptor, Operating system, and sends it to the GrOSD monitoring service. After that it regularly retrieves the dynamic parameters - CPU load, hard disk free space and RAM free space and sends it them to the monitoring service.

5. Future work

We tried to design and implement the Node Service with maximum flexibility and with a large number of useful features. We have some very preliminary experimental results about the functioning and overall performance of the execution manager, but since this is work in progress we still have a lot of work to do on it. We have to fix bugs, improve parts of the manager, and what is more important - complete our work on the whole grid system, a part of which is the Node Service. We need a fully functioning version of the whole system in order to be able to test the Node Service in real scenarios. In addition, there are several aspects, in which we want to improve the execution manager.

One important extension of the Node Service will be with processors for applications, written is C/C++ and sent in the form of executable files. Since the GrOSD is developed as a general purpose grid system, and there are a lot of applications in the form of executables, we consider this a significant feature of the Node Service.

Currently the Node Service may collect monitoring data only from nodes running a version of the Windows OS. Support for parameter collection from

UNIX-based OS's should be provided and we plan to add a module to the Node Service which performs this retrieval.

There are security considerations regarding the Node Service, especially if it is used outside of the GrOSD platform. Restrictions on what the executed code may do should be added, e.g. using Java sandboxing.

Another possible direction for the further development of the Node Service is as an independent component for remote execution of applications. As such it may be used as part of other grid systems. Actually, this is facilitated by the comprehensive interface of the API.

6. Conclusion

In this paper we presented the architecture and features of the task execution component of the GrOSD grid platform. Our major concerns when developing it were the complete set of features it offers to the rest of the system, its flexibility and extensibility, and the minimal set of requirements it imposes on the machines, where it runs. We consider that its ability to run arbitrary java programs, with arbitrary methods and input parameters, and the flexibility it offers for request construction make it very useful building block for commodity grid systems, and provide many opportunities for its utilization.

References

[1] M. Blyantov, L. Kirchev, V. Georgiev and K. Boyanov. A hierarchical architecture supporting services in grid. in *Proc. Automatics and Informatics'05*, Sofia, Bulgaria, 2005, pages 186-192.

[2] I. Foster. Globus toolkit version 4: software for service-oriented systems. In *Proc. IFIP International Conference on Network and Parallel Computing*, pages 2-13, Springer-Verlag LNCS 3779, 2006.

[3] D. Kurzyniec, T. Wrzosek, D. Drzewiecki and V. Sunderam. Towards self-organizilng destributed computing frameworks: the H2O approach.*Parallel Processing Letters* **13**(2):273-290, 2003.

[4] Z. Juhasz, K. Kuntner, M. Magyarody, G. Major and S. Pota. *JGrid design document.* Parallel and Distributed Systems Department, University of Veszprem, Hungary.

[5] I. Taylor, R. Philip, M. Shields, O. Rana and B. Schutz. The consumer grid. *Presented at the Global Grid Forum (2002)*, Toronto, Canada, February, 17 - 20, 2002.

[6] I. Taylor, M. Shields and I. Wang. Resource management of triana P2P services.*Grid Resource Management.* Kluwer, Netherlands, 2003.

[7] Condor User Manual. Available: http://www.cs.wisc.edu/condor/

[8] T. Oinn, M. Addis, J. Ferris, D. Marvin, M. Senger, M. Greenwood, T. Carver and K. Glover, M.R. Pocock, A. Wipat and P. Li. Taverna: a tool for the composition and enactment of bioinformatics workflows. *Bioinformatics* **20** (17):3045-3054, Oxford University Press, 2004.

[9] T. Oinn, M. Greenwood, M. Addis, J. Ferris, K. Glover, C. Goble, D. Hull, D. Marvin, P. Li, Ph. Lord, M. R. Pocock, M. Senger, A. Wipat and C. Wroe. Taverna: Lessons in

creating a workfow environment for the life sciences. *Concurrency and Computation: Practice & Experience* **18** (10):1067-1100, 2006.

[10] Y. Teo and X. Wang. AliCE: a scalable runtime infrastructure for high performance grid computing, in *Proc. IFIP International Conference on Network and Parallel Computing*, 2004, pages 101-109.

[11] D. Anderson. BOINC: A System for Public-Resource Computing and Storage. In *Proc. 5th IEEE/ACM International Workshop on Grid Computing*, November 8, 2004, Pittsburgh, USA.

[12] D. Anderson, C. Christensen and B. Allen. Designing a Runtime System for Volunteer Computing. In *Proc. Supercomputing '06 (The International Conference for High Performance Computing, Networking, Storage and Analysis)*, Tampa, November 2006.

PRACTICAL EVALUATION OF CUSTOM TECHNOLOGY-BASED VS COMMODITY TECHNOLOGY-BASED STORAGE ELEMENTS*

Maciej Brzezniak, Norbert Meyer
Poznan Supercomputing and Networking Center
61-704 Poznan, Noskowskiego 10, Poland
maciekb@man.poznan.pl
meyer@man.poznan.pl

Michail Flouris, Angelos Bilas
Institute of Computer Science (ICS)
Foundation for Research and Technology – Hellas (FORTH),
P.O. Box 1385, Heraklion, GR-71110, Greece
flouris@ics.forth.gr
bilas@ics.forth.gr

Abstract

Scalable and cost-effective Storage Elements are essential components of Grid systems. Scaling the capacity and performance of the Grid storage infrastructure in an economical manner is an important research goal, due to an increasing number of data-intensive Grid applications and services. In this paper we present practical performance evaluation of two classes of storage systems: an aggressive commercial Fibre Chanel SATA disk matrix and a commodity-based research prototype – Violin. We use a block-level benchmark to examine the performance limits and scalability features of both classes of systems.

Keywords: Grid Storage Elements, storage architectures, storage systems, storage performance, I/O performance.

*This research work is carried out under the FP6 Network of Excellence Core-GRID funded by the European Commission (Contract IST-2002-004265).

1. Introduction

Scaling the capacity and performance of Storage Elements while reducing their costs is an important issue in Grid systems, due to an increasing number of data-intensive Grid applications and services. Storage Elements traditionally rely on DAS (Directly Attached Storage), NAS (Network Attached Storage) or SAN (Storage Area Network) architectures. To satisfy application requirements on performance and capacity scalability, Grid Storage Elements are traditionally built using specialised, aggressive SAN-based storage systems. At the same time, the DAS and NAS-based storage become less popular mainly due to their capacity and performance scalability limits.

Custom SAN-based storage systems are to a large extent centralised solutions. Multiple disk drives are typically connected to one or more central matrix controllers, which process I/O requests coming from user applications and implement various storage virtualisation functions, such as RAID structures and snapshots. This centralised controller-based architecture facilitates providing strong reliability guarantees as well as simplifies system management, including planning, deployment and day-to-day maintenance. However, centralisation induces scalability limitations in terms of both capacity and performance.

Another important feature of custom storage systems is that they use specialised devices optimised for I/O processing purposes. Similarly, the communication protocols used in these systems (mainly the Fibre Channel protocol) are designed for transferring I/O traffic through a dedicated low-latency SAN. This guarantees high performance and reliability of particular components and end-to-end system operation, but it results in high costs both due to technology and market reasons.

An emerging trend is to exploit numerous, low-cost, commodity-based components for building scalable storage systems. In this approach, storage nodes built out of dozens of disks connected to PCs act as storage controllers. They are interconnected with a general-purpose, low-cost network, e.g. 1-10 GBit/s Ethernet. Key features of this approach are (1) the decentralisation of storage I/O processing and (2) the ability to follow technology curves for general-purposes systems (CPUs, memory and interconnects) and thus, achieve high cost efficiency. However, several challenges must be addressed before commodity-based storage systems are used transparently in real applications. Open issues include seamless integration, interoperability, automated management tools, strong reliability guarantees over a distributed system, and robust security mechanisms in decentralised architectures.

In our previous work [3][2] we performed a qualitative analysis of the two approaches (FC-based and commodity-based systems). Our results show that commodity storage systems can scale both capacity and performance at lower cost compared to custom systems, mainly by using a larger number of components.

In this work we quantitatively examine the performance of two such systems. We use two setups, an FC-based setup and a commodity-based research prototype, and measure block-level performance using a simple microbenchmark. We find that performance of processing the sequential and random I/O in both examined systems is similar.

The rest of this paper is organised as follows. Section 2 discusses the methodology we use in our evaluation. Section 3 presents our experimental results and their analysis. Section 4 discusses the related work. Finally, Section 5 shows our conclusions.

2. Methodology

The two systems we use in this work are: (a) Nexsan SATABeast [9], FC-to-SATA matrix that belongs to a low-end segment of custom storage (b) The Violin research prototype [5] of commodity-based storage components.

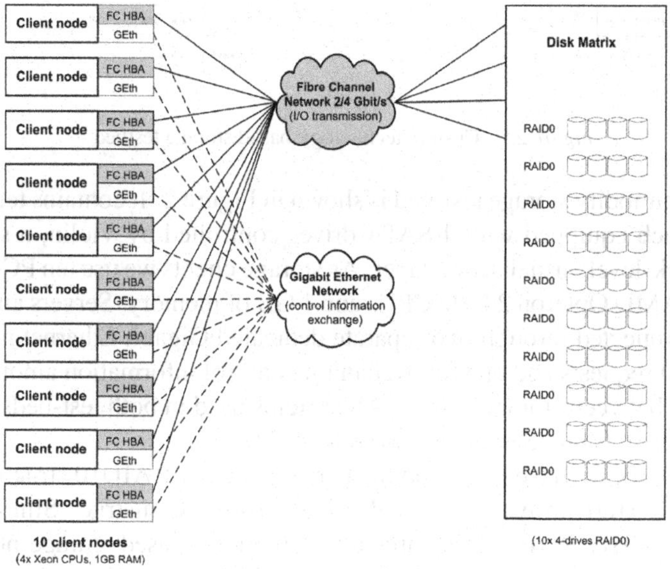

Figure 1. Custom technology-based storage testbed

Figure 1 presents the configurations of the custom storage test-bed. It contains the Nexsan SATABeast matrix equipped with 42 SATA drives (500 GB of capacity each, 40 drives used for testing), two RAID controllers (each has 1 GB of cache memory), and 4 Fibre Channel front-end ports. The matrix is connected to a 4 Gbit/s FC switch using four FC links working in 2 Gbits/s mode (due to a matrix ports speed limitation). As storage clients we use ten PCs, each equipped with four Xeon 3GHz CPUs, 4GB of RAM and ona Fibre Channel 4Gbit HBA. A separate Gigabit Ethernet network is used for coordinating the benchmark operation in the client nodes. The matrix operation mode is set to active-active (both controllers active). We enable cache mirroring between controllers and set the cache optimisation policy to *mixed sequential/random.*

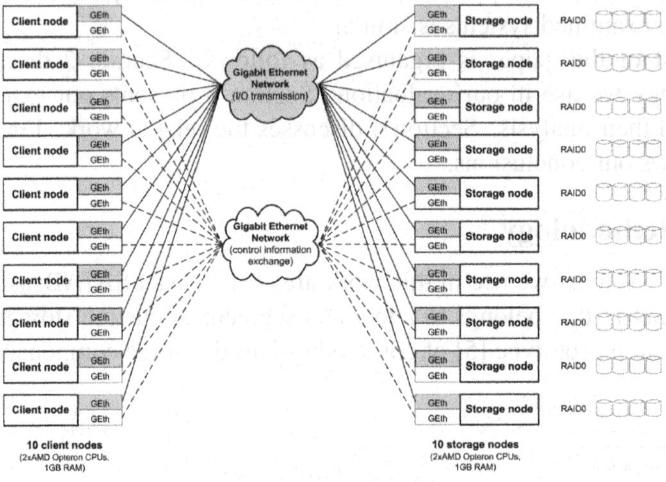

Figure 2. Custom technology-based storage testbed

The commodity storage test-bed is shown in Figure 2. It contains ten storage servers, each equipped with 4 SATA drives controlled by Violin, a software-based block-level virtualisation layer. As storage clients we use ten PCs equipped with two AMD Opteron 2 GHz CPUs and 1 GB of memory. Servers and clients are interconnected through two separate dedicated Gigabit Ethernet networks: one for I/O requests and one for exchanging control information among Violin nodes and between storage clients. All systems used in both test-beds run Red Hat Enterprise Linux Server system (release 5).

In this work we have evaluated the performance of RAID10 structures. We configure RAID1 arrays on every 4 drives in the FC matrix. Similarly, we configure 4-drive RAID1 structures on each Violin-based storage node. We then stripe the RAID1 arrays (10 for each test-bed) on the client side using the Linux MD mechanism (RAID0). Thus, each system is configured with five 8-drive RAID10 structures.

In each test-bed we use a load-balancing mechanism. In the FC setup, distribution of I/O requests over matrix controllers and front-end links is guaranteed by an appropriate assignment of RAID arrays to matrix controllers and a relevant addressing the logical volumes on the client side. In the Violin setup, load-balancing of the storage nodes is performed in the Violin middle-ware, both on the server and the client side.

In our micro-benchmark tests we use xdd [6] for generating the test I/O traffic, including both sequential and random reads and writes. In our experiments we vary the number of outstanding IOs per client (from 1 to 8) and the I/O request size (between 4kB-1024kB). We run xdd in direct I/O mode, where requests are sent directly to a block device, by-passing the file system layer. This eliminates potential influence of the Linux file system caching on the test results.

3. Results

Figure 3 shows the results from both our experimental setups. Throughput values refer to the overall achieved throughput as measured on the client side. Each curve refers to different parameters.

The results of sequential workloads show that performance trends are similar in both classes of storage systems. Sequential I/O throughput grows with an increasing block size and, in most cases, reaches its maximum for block sizes larger than 512kB.

Sequential write throughput in the FC-based setup is limited to a maximum of about 150MB/s, as shown in the top right graph of Figure 3. The observed CPU loads in the client machines were low and the distribution of the I/O traffic among the client-matrix FC links and the balancing of the load of the matrix controllers showed that these components have not reached their maximum potential. Thus our conclusion is that the bottleneck in this case is the internal connectivity of the matrix. On the top left graph, the commodity-based storage system is able to reach the maximum write performance at 219MB/s for small queue depths, which is better than the matrix result. Violin achieves this performance due to the system decentralisation and the fact that it has multiple, independent RAID controllers. The bottleneck in this case is the high latencies of the TCP/IP protocol over the Gigabit Ethernet links. Note, however, that Violin does not always perform well in writes. When using increased I/O queue depths and large block sizes the benchmark performance drops under 150MB/s (block size larger than 512kB for QD=4 and block size larger than 256kB for QD=8). We attribute this behavior to the current I/O queue implementation in Violin.

On the other hand, the centralised architecture of the matrix facilitates effective read-ahead caching for a small number of I/O threads, resulting in higher read throughput, up to 460MB/s. However, for a high number of concurrent I/Os, read operations in the matrix perform similarly (QD=2) or even worse (QD=3, QD=4) compared to the commodity-based setup. This is due to the centralised architecture of the FC-based setup and the inability to distribute I/O traffic among multiple controllers.

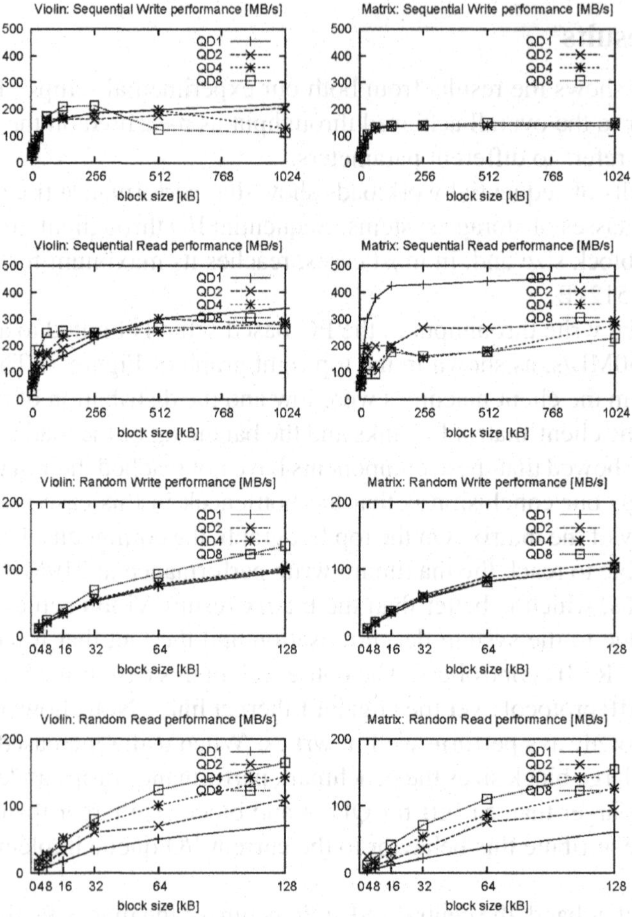

Figure 3. Performance results from the two experimental setups

Measurements with random I/O (read or write) show similar trends in both classes of storage systems. In the results shown in Figure 3, both systems perform within 10% of each other between 4kB and 128kB request sizes. Random read performance drops to under 100MB/s for block sizes smaller than 64kB in most our tests. The main trend is that small blocks sizes result in reduced performance in both setups, and performance improves with a request size. This is expected because of the disks' poor performance in small, random I/O, which is better for the larger requests. Overall, in most random I/O tests, the commodity-based setup performs slightly better than the FC-based setup.

4. Related work

Traditionally, building scalable storage systems that provide storage sharing for multiple applications relies on layering a distributed file-system on top of a pool of block-level storage, typically a SAN. This approach is dictated by the fact that block-level storage has limited semantics that do not allow for performing advanced storage functions, and in particular, they are not able to support transparent sharing without application support. Recently, there has been a lot of research work in enabling cluster-based networked storage systems.

In our previous work [3] we identified potential performance bottlenecks of custom centralised storage architectures. We also examined the potential of commodity-based systems in terms of performance scalability, due to the distributed nature of their architecture. Our cost analysis suggests that the price-performance ratio is significantly better for commodity-based storage than for FC-based systems. This work performs a preliminary performance evaluation of the two base approaches.

Efforts in this direction include distributed *cluster file systems* often based on VAXclusters [7] concepts that allow for efficient sharing of data among a set of storage servers with strong consistency semantics and fail-over capabilities. Such systems typically operate on top of a pool of physically shared devices through a SAN. However, they do not provide much control over the system's operation. Modern cluster file-systems such as the Global File System (GFS) [12] and the General Parallel File System (GPFS) [11] are used extensively today in medium and large scale storage systems for clusters. However, their complexity makes them hard to develop and maintain, prohibits any practical extension to the underlying storage system, and forces all applications to use a single, almost fixed, view of the available data. The Federated Array of Bricks (FAB) [10] discusses how storage systems may be built out of commodity storage nodes and interconnects and yet compete (in terms of reliability and performance) with custom high-end solutions for enterprise environments. Ursa Minor [4], a system for object-based storage bricks coupled with a central manager, provides flexibility with respect to the data layout and the fault-model (both for client and storage nodes). These parameters can be dynamically adjusted on a per data item basis, according to the needs of a given environment. Such fine grain customisation yields noticeable performance improvements.

Previous work also investigated a number of issues raised by the lack of a central controller and the distributed nature of cluster-based storage systems, e.g. consistency for erasure-coded redundancy schemes [1] and efficient request scheduling [8].

5. Conclusions

Traditionally, scalable storage systems are being built using custom SAN-based technologies. An alternative approach is to use commodity components interconnected with commodity networks, such as 1 or 10 GBit/s Ethernet and provide storage virtualisation functionality in the software I/O path. In this work we perform a preliminary evaluation of the two approaches. Although systems perform comparably, there are certain observations to make: we see that in the custom FC-based system, the centralised matrix controller is a major performance bottleneck. At the same time, a heavy communication protocol (TCP/IP), even at the kernel level, is an important factor limiting the performance of I/O in the commodity-based Violin research prototype. Another aspect of performance scalability in the compared systems is the granularity of the available scaling options. In the FC-based system only adding matrix controllers or whole matrices can improve performance, which results in poor cost scalability. Instead, in the commodity-based prototype, performance scaling is possible by adding low-cost, commodity storage components, such as disk drives, memory modules, or CPUs.

Overall, given the price difference between FC-based and commodity-based systems (about ten times higher) and the experimental results we observe, we believe that commodity-based systems have a lot of potential in cost-sensitive environments and applications.

In the future, we plan to examine larger setups for both systems. The matrix we examine in this work belongs to a low-end segment of custom storage market; it is implemented in FC-to-SATA technology (FC front-end ports, SATA disk drives). A further step is to examine the mid-range-class disk matrix implemented in FC-to-SATA or in FC-to-FC (FC front-end ports, FC disk drives). Similarly, it is important to examine larger-scale commodity-based system. Finally, we plan to use file system and application-level benchmarks in both classes of storage systems to examine their behavior in more realistic setups.

Acknowledgments

We thankfully acknowledge the support of the European Commission under the Sixth Framework Program through the Network of Excellence CoreGRID, Contract IST-2002-004265.

References

[1] K. A. Amiri, G. A. Gibson, and R. Golding. Highly Concurent Shared Storage. In IEEE, editor, *Proceedings of* 20th *International Conference on Distributed Computing Systems (ICDCS'2000)*, pages 298–307, Taipe, Taiwan, R.O.C, April 2000. IEEE Computer.

[2] M. Brzezniak, T. Makiela, N. Meyer, R.Mikolajczak, M. Flouris, R. Lachaize, and A.Bilas. An Analysis of GRID Storage Element Architectures: High-end Fiber-Channel vs Emerging Cluster-based Networked Storage. Technical Report 0088, CoreGRID, May 2007.

[3] M. Brzezniak, N. Meyer, M. Flouris, R. Lachaize, and A.Bilas. An Analysis of GRID Storage Element Architectures: High-end Fiber-Channel vs. Cluster-based Networked Storage. In *Proceedings of the CoreGRID Workshop on Grid Middleware. Dresden, Germany. Held with the International Supercomputing Conference (ISC07)*, June 2007.

[4] M. Abd-El-Malek et al. Ursa Minor: Versatile Cluster-Based Storage. In *Proceedings of the 4th USENIX Conference on File and Storage Technology*, San Francisco, CA, USA, December 2005.

[5] Michail D. Flouris, Renaud Lachaize, and Angelos Bilas. A Framework for Extensible Block-level Storage. In *D. Talia, A. Bilas, M. Dikaiakos (eds.): Knowledge and Data Management in Grids*, CoreGRID series, Vol. 3, pages 83–98. Springer Verlag, 2007.

[6] I/O Performance Inc. The xdd. http://www.ioperformance.com/products.htm.

[7] Nancy P. Kronenberg, Henry M. Levy, and William D. Strecker. Vaxcluster: a closely-coupled distributed system. *ACM Transactions on Computer Systems*, 4(2), 1986.

[8] C. R. Lumb, R. Golding, and G. R. Ganger. D-SPTF: Decentralized Request Distribution in Brick-Based Storage Systems. In *Proceedings of the 11th ACM ASPLOS Conference*, Boston, MA, USA, October 2004.

[9] Nexsan Technologies. SATABeast. http://www.nexsan.com/satabeast.php.

[10] Y. Saito, S. Frolund, A. Veitch, A. Merchant, and S. Spence. FAB: Enterprise storage systems on a shoestring. In *Proc. of the ASPLOS 2004*, October 2004.

[11] Frank Schmuck and Roger Haskin. GPFS: A Shared-disk File System for Large Computing Centers. In *USENIX Conference on File and Storage Technologies*, pages 231–244, Monterey, CA, January 2002.

[12] S. Soltis, G. Erickson, K. Preslan, M. O'Keefe, and T. Ruwart. The Global File System: A File System for Shared Disk Storage, October 1997.

A MODEL OF NON FUNCTIONAL PROPERTIES FOR GRID RESOURCES

David Buján-Carballal
Department of Software Engineering, Faculty of Engineering, University of Deusto
Avenida de las universidades 24, 48007 Bilbao, Vizcaya (Spain)
dbujan@eside.deusto.es

Oscar Corcho-García
Department of Artificial Intelligence, Faculty of Informatics, Polytechnic University of Madrid
Campus de Montegancedo s/n, 28660, Boadilla del Monte, Madrid (Spain)
ocorcho@fi.upm.es

Josuka Díaz-Labrador
Department of Software Engineering, Faculty of Engineering, University of Deusto
Avenida de las universidades 24, 48007 Bilbao, Vizcaya (Spain)
josuka@eside.deusto.es

Abstract So far, Grid information providers basically give functional values about resources, although some of them also provide aggregated information. Therefore, existing Grid information models essentially represent this syntactic information and also propose different taxonomies of resources. Hence, Grid information consumers commonly use functional properties to select resources in order to send jobs to a Grid. There are some approaches that try to use isolated techniques to take into consideration some QoS properties, like performance. In this paper, we propose a unified model for representing Grid resources and their non functional properties, adding semantics to Grid information systems. On one hand, this model is an ontology-based model developed to integrate existing approaches of Grid information models and non functional properties representations in general. But on the other hand, our model also proposes a measuring system - currently in development - for some non functional properties like reliability, availability and performance. Here we only present an overview about how to represent and measure reliability information of resources in Grids. This example is used to illustrate our work in progress.

Keywords: Semantic Grid, Grid Information Systems, Non functional properties, Ontology-based models, Measuring systems.

1. Introduction

One of the open issues in the Grid is the discovery of services and resources when Grid users or applications send jobs to the Grid in order to be executed. Most of the approaches are based on the analysis of functional properties about resources, that is, those characteristics that define what is what the resource makes or offers. However, there are non functional properties (like reliability, availability, performance and so on) that can be used in this context. Non functional properties specify global restrictions that must be satisfied [1], indicating how the resource operates or how it exposes its functionality [13].

Sometimes the jobs sent to the Grid fail because the assigned resources to them were not available or had fallen. In these cases, sequential or parallel jobs must be sent back again to the Grid. It implies a new selection and allocation of resources, as well as a waste of time, work and resources, that increases the global time to carry out a job.

On one hand, there are Grid tools for resuming some kind of jobs from the point of failure, but this is not a general case and besides it does not solve the problem of wasting time and work. And on the other hand, fault-tolerant systems based on recovery techniques are very costly in distributed systems, so those jobs that have not finished after a time out are cancelled and sent back again to the Grid. Therefore, one of the most used solutions consists in monitoring the resources that fail and putting them manually as requirements for the job sent to the Grid. Thus, the job is never sent to those bad resources. It is usually also specified an expected time for carrying out the job. This requirement let a job to be assigned a resource of which response time is smaller than expected time to finish for the given job. Besides, it is usually applied the same idea to other concepts like the size of files used by a job or its expected output, regarding the available physical memory space into the storage elements resources.

However, previous solutions are ad-hoc and we think that non functional properties could be useful in these cases. This is an issue in the field of the Grid that has not been studied in depth yet.

Many Grid middleware services (aka Grid information consumers) require knowledge about the behavior of Grid resources in order to effectively select, compose, and execute jobs in dynamic and complex Grid systems. To provide QoS or non functional information about resources for building such knowledge, Grid tools (aka Grid information providers) have to select, measure, and analyze various QoS metrics of resources (about their behavior executing jobs, storing data, etc.). However, there is a lack of a comprehensive study of QoS metrics which can be used to evaluate the QoS of a resource (its non functional properties).

Moreover, given the complexity of both Grid systems and QoS concepts, semantics of existing Grid resources and their essential QoS-related concepts and relationships should be well described. There are several efforts in order to classify resources in the Grid and QoS concepts in SOA, but there is no link among them.

On the one hand, existing Grid information models don't use the same language to represent the same concepts about resources, although some research groups have detected a need for integrating and making their models interoperable. Besides, there is a lack of representation of non functional properties about resources. At best, some models try to represent performance measures about resources, but there is a lack of details about non functional properties in general. Some Grid information consumers and providers use isolated techniques to deal with this information.

On the other hand, most existing work in QoS models concentrates on business workflows and Web services processes in SOA, but several metrics targeted in these models are not valid for Grid environments because Grid resources and their non functional properties are more diverse, dynamic, and inter-organizational. That's why a new model with new metrics is needed.

However, we can learn good lessons from these two groups of models in order to aggregate isolated techniques used by information providers and consumers in both fields. Some of the goals of our future work are to integrate existing approaches into Grid information systems and to enrich the discovery and selection of resources in the Grid using semantic information associated to them [2]. We want to contribute to the Semantic Grid idea: the Semantic Grid is an extension of the current Grid in which information and services are given well-defined meaning through machine-processable descriptions which maximize the potential for sharing and reuse [17][5].

2. Background

2.1 Grid information consumers

So far, most of these Grid information consumers commonly use functional properties to select resources in order to send jobs to a Grid. For example, many Grid tools or applications that carry out functions of planning, selection and/or resource management in the Grid (schedulers, meta-schedulers, resource brokers and so on) discover resources using properties like characteristic of the processor, size of the memory, space of available storage, software that is found installed, response time to the requests of service and so on.

Some of the following initiatives could be good candidates for using non functional properties in their algorithms of selection: Meta-scheduler GridWay, GridARM, LCG/g-LITE, Nimrod-G, EUROGRID/GRIP, SRB, NGS Resource Broker, Moab Grid Scheduler (aka Silver), EGEE WMS, GRMS, Gridbus Grid Service Broker, NorduGrid's ARC. Other Grid middleware that could consume non functional properties would be: WebMDS, Grid User Interfaces (Grid Portals like P-GRADE), Grid tools based on CSF, N1 Grid Engine, WebCom-G, GPT, HPC4U Middleware, or any WSRF client looking for resources (like GEMLCA or the NWS).

There are some approaches that try to use isolated techniques to take into consideration some QoS properties, like performance. Other approaches are still investigating how to incorporate non functional properties in their algorithms of selection.

2.2 Grid information providers

Nowadays, Grid middleware is abundant and there are many monitoring tools that can be used as providers of information about Grid resources: Globus middleware (WS GRAM, MDS4, RFT, RLS, CAS), monitoring systems (Ganglia, Hawkeye, Inca, MonALISA, GEMLCA-GMT, GridICE, GRASP, CluMon, SCALEA-G and other Askalon monitoring tools for their Resource Broker and Scheduler), queueing systems (Condor-G, Sun Grid Engine, Torque/PBS, LSF, Maui) or any other WSRF service that publishes resource properties.

2.3 Grid information models

Regarding the representation and use of quality of service in general, there are some references that describe general and philosophical aspects to be considered, but don't provive a model: MOQ [16]; QoS with QoE and QoBiz [18]; Tosic et al [19]. But there are also other works that have implemented ontologies to represent QoS information: FIPA-QoS [8]; WS-QoS [10]; Zhou Chen's OWL-QoS (previously DAML-QoS) [4]; Maximilien and Singh's OWL-QoS [12]; QoSOnt [7] is trying to unify all the previous initiatives.

As far as Grid is concerning, there are some OGF research groups [14]dealing with aspects related to the representation of information about the Grid: GLUE-WG, EGA-RM, OGSA-WG, RM-WG, OGSA Basic Execution Services WG (OGSA-BES-WG), JSDL-WG, Information Modelling in OGSA, CGS-WG, GOM [11][20], Grid Ontology [15]. There are other OGF's groups of which work could be useful in this area, but their activity has no repercussions yet or has just began: OGSA-RSS-WG, SRM, GRIDREL-RG, TC-RG, NM-WG, GB-RG, RUS-WG, UR-WG, GCE-RG, SEM-RG.

Some of these research groups suggested in the past Open Grid Forums the need of unifying criteria and developments to make these different models interoperable or, at least, to converge in a same more generic specification, since every group tackle the modelling from its own cases of use and goals. Next, we describe most significant information models briefly.

Table 1. Comparison framework for existing information models – comprehensiveness and measurement

Information Models	*Comprehensiveness*	*Measurement*
GLUE 1.1	Good taxonomy of resources, but not enough. There is no reference to non functional properties, except for some isolated QoS values.	None. Only define basic types (int, float, string) for properties.
GLUE 1.3	Extended taxonomy of resources. There are new QoS values, but nothing else.	None. Only define basic types for new properties.
GLUE 2.0	Some useful properties to represent some non functional values, but there is still no reference to a formal schema.	None. Only define basic types for new properties.
OGSA-BES	No taxonomy of resources. Some useful properties, but not a formal schema.	None.
JSDL	No taxonomy of resources. It describes resource requirements of the Grid jobs, but there is no significant reference to non functional properties.	None.
CIM	No taxonomy of resources. No formal description of non functional properties.	None.
UR	No taxonomy of resources. Some properties about how the jobs use the resources that can be useful to calculate non functional properties.	Some ideas about how to measure them, but there is no proposal about how to do it in practice.
EGA	No taxonomy of resources. No formal description of non functional properties.	The model only gives slightly some ideas about how to measure in general some non functional properties.
RM	No significant work done yet after EGA Reference Model and OGSA Glossary.	No significant work done yet.
GOM	Useful taxonomy of resources and services. Performance property is defined.	Focus on performance only. We have no access to it yet.
GRO	Useful Grid foundational ontology. Bad and basic taxonomy of resources. Some references to QoS concepts.	None.
QoSOnt	No taxonomy of resources. No reference to the Grid. Useful taxonomy of QoS concepts and metrics.	None.

2.3.1 An analysis framework for resources and non functional properties models. So far, previous approaches have some limitations that make it difficult to adopt them directly into our model. Despite providing mechanisms for QoS specification, these models lack the flexibility provided by an

Table 2. Comparison framework for existing information models – standards and applications

Information Models	*Standards or Technologies*	*Supporting application*
GLUE 1.1	UML diagrams, XML schema, Xpath 2.0	Integrated into GT 4.0.3. Ganglia and Hawkeye provide an output using this XML schema.
GLUE 1.3	UML diagrams, XML schema, Xpath 2.0	It can be integrated into GT 4.0.x and Grid monitoring tools.
GLUE 2.0	UML diagrams, XML schema, Xpath 2.0	It can be integrated into GT 4.0.x and Grid monitoring tools.
OGSA-BES	UML diagrams, Port-types. GLUE schema is generally considered as a specialisation of BES.	None.
JSDL	XML schema. Informed by DRMAA, CIM, and POSIX.	Core vocabulary informed by Condor, GT, LSF, PBS, SGE, and Unicore.
CIM	UML diagrams.	None.
UR	Usage properties and XML infoset representation.	None.
EGA	Reference CIM or OGSA. There is an opportunity for the EGA to either unify models or at least make them consistent with each other.	None.
RM	This approach will try to use OWL, SML, XML Schemas.	None.
GOM	OWL.	Performance tools from Askalon framework and K-Wf Grid project.
GRO	OWL.	None.
QoSOnt	OWL.	None.

ontology for dealing with the semantic meaning of QoS constraints. In many cases they are not extensible or adaptable to the Grid. In other cases, they are not comprehensive solutions, focusing on functional properties only or providing an ad-hoc solution for some isolated QoS properties. In these cases, some of them don't suggest how to measure the non functional properties or they use very trivial and random criteria. In general, there is no schematic or detailed analysis of Grid resources and their non functional properties. Besides, there is no common Grid information model yet.

We summarize the analysis done using the comparison framework shown in Table 1 and Table 2: Comprehensiveness (detail level representing types of Grid resources and non functional properties), Measurement (methods used for measuring non functional properties, if represented), Standards / Technologies (how the model is implemented), Supporting application (information consumers or providers ready to use the model).

3. Our model

In Software Engineering, an ontology may be described as a specification of a conceptualization or a description of the concepts and relationships that may exist for an agent or a community of agents. Ontologies allow the sharing and reuse of knowledge. Software applications can be written according to the commitment of using the vocabulary defined by an ontology for a particular domain. That way, agents that share the same ontology can communicate among themselves since their vocabulary is understood by everyone.

In our approach, we propose a detailed classification of resources and services that can exist in the Grid, paying attention to multiple levels of abstraction. Taking into account models and specifications given by previous work groups, we propose an ontology for describing Grid resources and the most important non functional properties referenced in previous works: performance, availability and reliability. When different monitoring tools support a common ontology, the Grid users and applications can benefit from having a common understanding of Grid resources and their QoS behavior given by these tools. Our model - currently in development - also needs a formal measuring system for non functional properties. Each one has different characteristics (complexity of calculation, parameters of relevance, etc.).

We are defining, collecting and associating various metrics with relevant QoS concepts about resources in Grids. We are also designing a range for several metrics in order to make possible a comparison. Our study considers QoS metrics for software and hardware resources in many levels of detail such as systems, services, applications/programs, nodes, networks, hosts, etc., following a Grid resource model classification. So far, we only can present an overview about how to represent and measure reliability in Grids. We also introduce how the ontology can be utilized for representing and analyzing non functional properties of Grid resources.

3.1 Representing Grid resources and non functional properties

The ontology we are introducing in this paper is available from [3]for public inspection, use and comment. We have integrated some ideas from different ontologies and reused / extended some classes and created new ones to develop our own ontology. GOM Resource ontology (ResourceOntology.owl), GOM Service ontology (ServiceOntology.owl), Grid Foundational Ontology (Base.owl), Globus Ontology (Globus.owl) have been used as starting point for designing a more detailed and multilevel classification of Grid resources and services, taking into account the roles that can be associated to them in a Grid environment. Since these ontologies have a poor definition of non functional properties, we have used the QoSOnt ontology (QoSOnt2.owl) as starting point to develop our model. Here, due to space requirements, we present just a partial overview of it using the following partial figures. You can navigate all the classes consulting NFP4Grid.owl file.

Figure 1. Partial diagram of classes related to non functional properties.

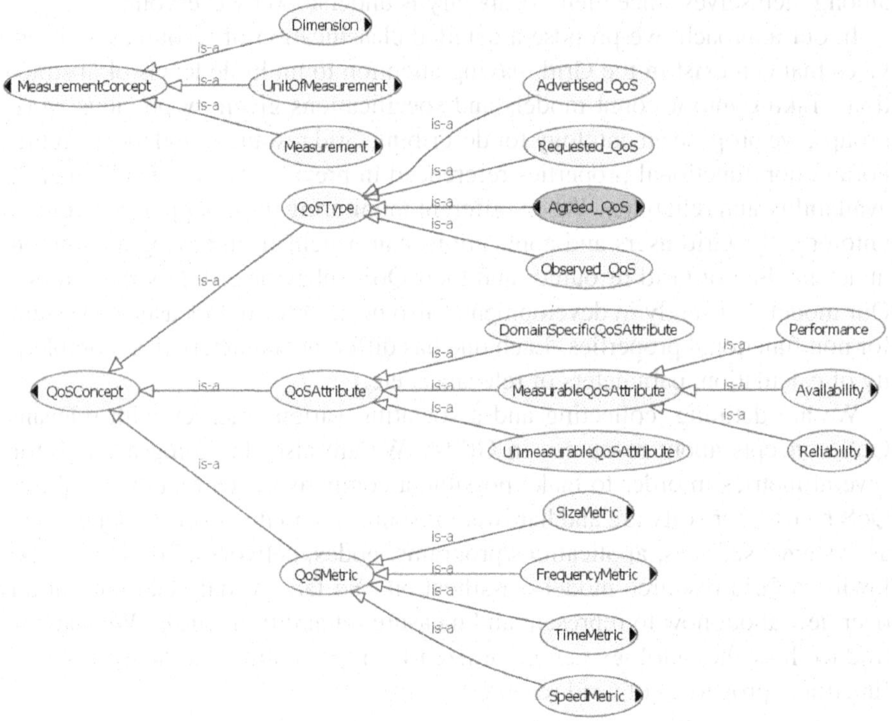

Numerical information about non functional properties will be represented directly into the ontology, but also associated with some ranges of possible values, since languages as OWL cannot handle them directly. Thus, information consumers could extract values of these non functional properties of different represented resources in order to compare them. So our model has a hybrid approach, as it is based on an ontology and other techniques at the time of selecting the resources.

Figure 2. Partial diagram of classes related to resources.

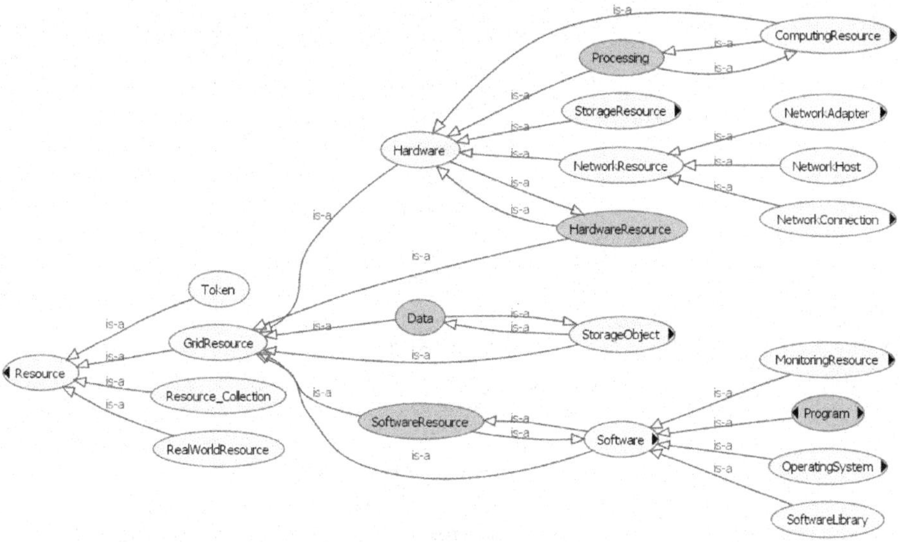

Figure 3. Partial diagram of classes related to services.

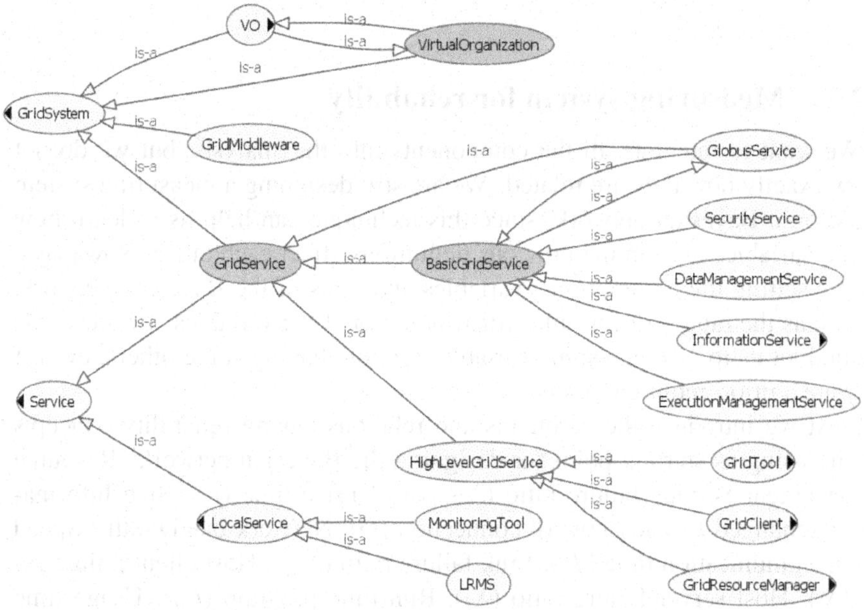

Figure 4. Partial diagram of classes related to roles.

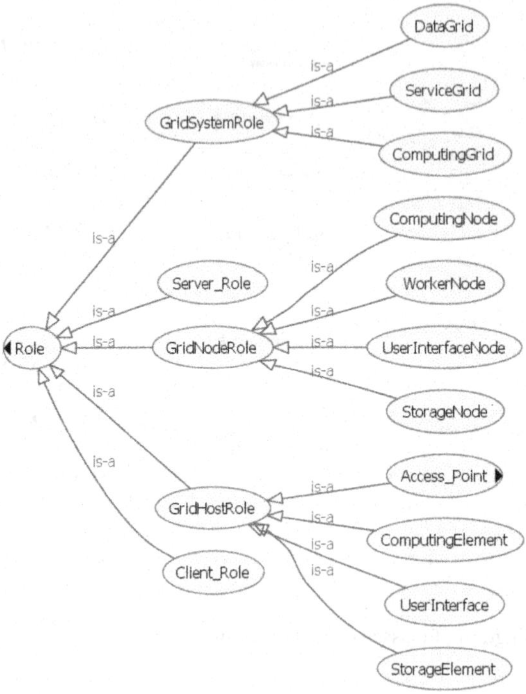

3.2 Measuring system for reliability

We want to integrate all the components into the analysis, but we do not know exactly how they are related. We are still designing a measuring system based on a Bayesian network, since this technique can help us to learn how all the variables used in the previous definitions affect each other. Nowadays, we are setting the assumptions, variables and links of the Bayesian network, as well as the ranges or formulas (distributions) of the variables. Besides, this method let us to estimate some variables without having some others, even if they are a priori required inputs.

Next we introduce the acronyms and relations among reliability concepts we are using as starting point for designing the Bayesian network: Resource Management Service failure ratio (λ_{RMS}), Service time (t_s), Size Information Exchanged / Load network connection (D), Network bandwidth / Speed (S), Communication time (T_c), Link failure ratio ($\lambda_{i,j}$), Host client failure ratio (λ_i), Host server failure ratio (λ_j), Run time program (t_m), Usage time program (t_u), RMS reliability (R_{RMS}), Link reliability (R_L), Communication reliability (R_c), Host program reliability (R_{prog}), Host resource reliability

(R_{res}), GridResource program reliability (R_{GPR}), GridNode system reliability (R_S), GridResource program reliability with RMS reliability ($R_{GPR-RMS}$), GridNode system reliability with RMS reliability (R_{S-RMS}).

Figure 5. Relations among reliability concepts.

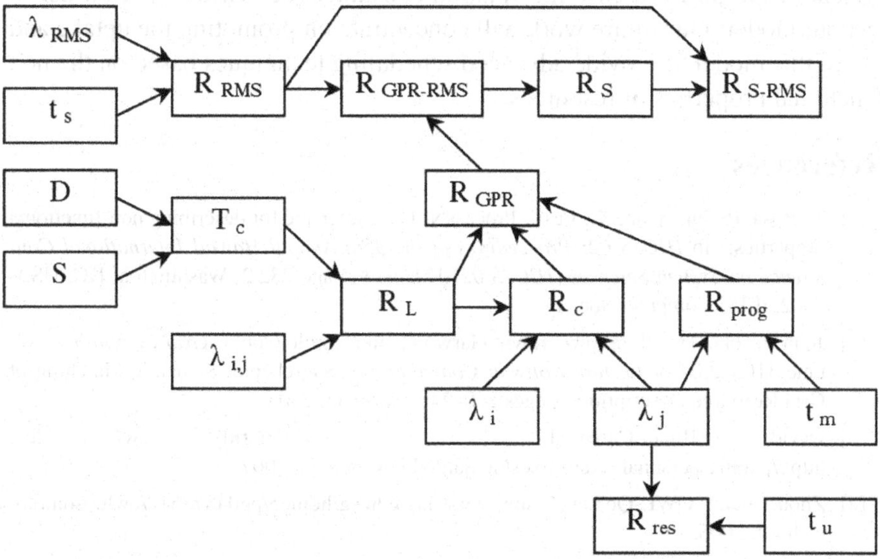

4. Conclusions and future work

This work has briefly presented a model and reference ontology of non functional properties for Grid resources that not only capture concepts such as Grid resources and services but also non functional properties about them. We also introduce how they can be obtained from Grid information providers and used by Grid information consumers, using reliability as a proof of concept - currently in development. By taking this novel perspective of the non functional properties for Grid resources we have provided the foundations for describing Grid resources and their non functional properties.

Many QoS concepts are not considered in our approach yet. We observed a number of works building Grid information models and QoS metrics for Web services separately. Some of them have concepts and metrics in common with our model.

Some of the Grid tools mentioned before in section 2.2 can be used to develop our measuring system of not functional properties, although we will develop our own scripts as well. We will aggregate or process given data by these providers in order to calculate our target non functional properties and to represent them in our model. In fact, we are planing to design an aggregator resource source script. Its implementation will be based on MDS4 to collect, store and index information about resources, respond to queries concerning the stored information using the XPath language, and control the execution of testing and information retrieval tools built as part of the GT4 Basic Services Monitoring Toolkit. Afterwards, we are planning to develop a prototype system or plugin for a Grid information consumer (i.e. GridWay) in order to test our model. Our future work will concentrate on promoting the uptake and use of this model to provide advanced scheduling techniques based on the non functional properties of resources.

References

[1] N. Rosa, P. Cunha, and G. Justo. ProcessNFL: A language for describing non-functional properties. In *HICSS 02: Proceedings of the 35th Annual Hawaii International Conference on System Sciences (HICSS 02)-Volume 9*, page 282.2, Washington, DC, USA, 2002. IEEE Computer Society.

[2] John Brooke, Donal Fellows, Kevin Garwood, and Carole Goble. *Grid Computing*, volume 3165/2004 of *Lecture Notes in Computer Science*, chapter Semantic Matching of Grid Resource Descriptions, pages 240–249. Springer, 2004.

[3] David Buján-Carballal. NFP4Grid owl file, http://paginaspersonales.deusto.es/dbujan/NFP4Grid.owl, 2007.

[4] Zhou Chen. OWL-QoS web site, www.ntu.edu.sg/home5/pg04878518/owlqosontology.html, 2005.

[5] Oscar Corcho, Pinar Alper, Ioannis Kotsiopoulos, Paolo Missier, Sean Bechhofer, and Carole Goble. An overview of s-ogsa: A reference semantic grid architecture. *Web Semantics: Science, Services and Agents on the World Wide Web*, 4(2):102–115, June 2006.

[6] Y.S. Dai, M. Xie, and K.L. Poh. *Computing System Reliability*, chapter Reliability of Grid Computing Systems, pages 179–205. Springer US, 2004.

[7] Glen Dobson, Russell Lock, and Ian Sommerville. QosOnt: A QoS ontology for service-centric systems. In *EUROMICRO 05: Proceedings of the 31st EUROMICRO Conference on Software Engineering and Advanced Applications*, pages 80–87, Washington, DC, USA, 2005. IEEE Computer Society.

[8] FIPA. FIPA-QoS web site, www.fipa.org/specs/fipa00094, 2002.

[9] Imperial-College-London. Free on-line dictionary of computing, 2007.

[10] Shonali Krishnaswamy. Ws-qos web site, www.csse.monash.edu.au/ shonali/ws-qos/, 2003.

[11] KWfGrid. Gom grid ontologies, http://gom.kwfgrid.net/web/space/grid+ontologies, 2007.

[12] E. Michael Maximilien and Munindar P. Singh. Toward autonomic web services trust and selection. In *ICSOC 04: Proceedings of the 2nd international conference on Service oriented computing*, pages 212–221, New York, NY, USA, 2004. ACM.

[13] J. Mylopoulos, L. Chung, and B. Nixon. Representing and using nonfunctional requirements: A process-oriented approach. *IEEE Trans. Softw. Eng.*, 18(6):483–497, 1992.

[14] OGF. Ogf work groups web site, http://forge.ogf.org/sf/projects/, 2007.

[15] M. Parkin, S. van der Berghe, O. Corcho, D. Snelling, and J. Brooke. Knowledge of the grid: a grid resource ontology. In Marian Bubak, Michal Turala, and Kazimierz Wiatr, editors, *CGW 06 Proceedings*, 2006.

[16] Robert M Pirsig. Moq web site, www.moq.org, 2007.

[17] David De Roure and York Sure. Semantic grid-the convergence of technologies. *Journal of Web Semantics*, 4(2):82–83, 2006.

[18] Alfonso Sánchez-Macián, Luis Bellido, and Encarna Pastor. Ontologías para la medida de la calidad de servicio percibida. In *Libro de Ponencias de las V Jornadas de Ingeniería Telemática (Jitel 2005)*, pages 693–700, 2005.

[19] Vladimir Tosic, Kruti Patel, and Bernard Pagurek. WSOL - A language for the formal specification of classes of service for web services. In CSREA Press, editor, *Proceedings of the 2003 International Conference on Web Services (ICWS03)*, pages 375–381. CSREA Press, 2003.

[20] Hong-Linh Truong, T. Fahringer, F. Nerieri, and S. Dustdar. Performance metrics and ontology for describing performance data of grid workflows. In *CCGRID 05: Proceedings of the Fifth IEEE International Symposium on Cluster Computing and the Grid (CCGrid 05) - Volume 1*, pages 301–308, Washington, DC, USA, 2005. IEEE Computer Society.

GRID CHECKPOINTING SERVICE – INTEGRATION OF LOW-LEVEL CHECKPOINTING PACKAGES WITH THE GRID ENVIRONMENT*

Gracjan Jankowski, Radoslaw Januszewski
Poznan Supercomputing and Networking Center
61-704 Poznan, Noskowskiego 12/14, Poland
gracjan@man.poznan.pl
radekj@man.poznan.pl

Jozsef Kovacs
MTA SZTAKI Computer and Automation Research Institute Hungarian Academy of Sciences,
1111 Budapest Kende u. 13-17. Hungary
smith@sztaki.hu

Abstract There is no doubt that the fault-tolerance and load-balancing capability benefit the Grids. The technology that significantly supports these capabilities is the job's checkpointing. Nevertheless, contemporary Grid environments distinctly lack the possibility of integration with the low-level processes' checkpointers. Nowadays, some Grids support the checkpointing of applications which internally implement this functionality and that additionally adhere to the imposed interface. Contrary, the paper describes the Grid Checkpointing Service, which is the prototype design and implementation of Grid-level service which makes it possible to utilize low-level or legacy checkpointing packages in Grids. In fact, the presented service is a proof-of-concept implementation of the part of the Grid Checkpointing Architecture (GCA). Nevertheless, the way the GCS was implemented allows it to be installed and utilized independently of the other parts of the GCA.

Keywords: Grid Resource Management, checkpointing, load-balancing, fault-tolerance, Grid Checkpointing Architecture.

*This research work is carried out under the FP6 Network of Excellence Core-GRID funded by the European Commission (Contract IST-2002-004265).

1. Introduction

In short, the checkpointing mechanism provides the functionality of storing the state of computing processes into images. The data stored in the image can be used to resume the computing process to the same state as the process had when the image was created.

To allow the Grid Resource Broker to take advantage of the checkpointing functionality, the checkpointing tools have to be integrated with the Grid environment. The Grid Resource Broker has to be aware of which jobs can be checkpointed while the checkpointing tools have to expose the Grid level interface. Additionally, the storage and accessibility of the created images have to be managed.

In general, there are two most common approaches to integrating the checkpointing functionality with the Grid. The first one is to embed the checkpointing functionality within the computing process and additionally provide it with some well-defined Grid-level interface that would allow external services to utilize this functionality. The second one is to provide the Grid-level service which would act as a kind of a driver to underlying low-level checkpointing tools, including those based on user- and application-level approach. The former approach is addressed by the OGF's GridCPR [1] [14] [15] group while the latter is the one that the GCA [2] [3] [16] and the present paper deal with.

The aforementioned GCA architecture has been designed within one of the Virtual Institutes of the CoreGRID Network of Excellence [4]. The architecture specifies the set of Grid Services, design patterns and tools that make it possible to integrate the already existing [5] [6] as well as the future checkpointing packages with the Grid-oriented computing environment. The underlying checkpointing package can be of almost any kind, i.e. cooperation with kernel-level, user-level and application-level checkpointers is possible. Cooperation with the VMMes (Virtual Machine Manager) that allows suspending and resuming the state of the whole virtual machine has also been taken into account.

To validate the feasibility and sanity of the GCA's assumptions, the selected parts of the architecture have been developed in a form of proof-of-concept implementations. The paper presents one of such implementations named Grid Checkpointing Service (GCS). It is important to understand that the GCS is not the exact implementation of a part of the GCA. The GCS validates mainly the key assumptions of the GCA's component named Checkpoint Translation Service (CTS); however, as such it is implemented in a form of an independent system that can be deployed and utilized within the GRMS [7] and Globus [8] based environments.

Please note that owing to a number of abbreviations and terms used in the paper, the most important ones are collected and briefly defined in the Appendix at the end of the paper.

2. Architecture

This section discusses the architecture of proof-of-concept implementation of the GCA.

2.1 Architecture's outline

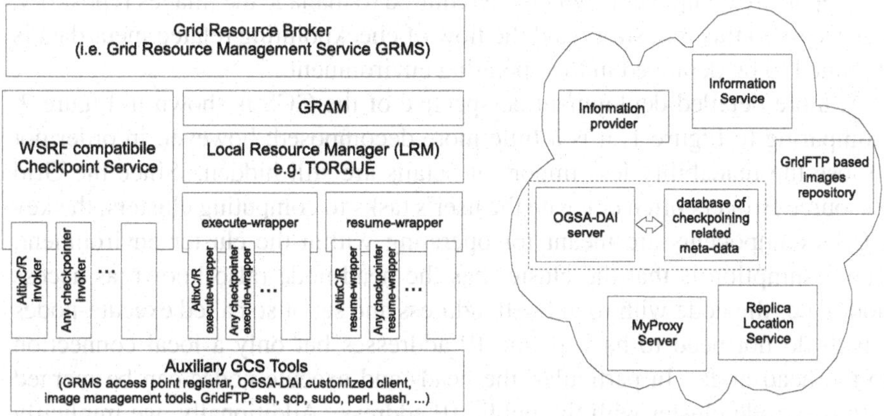

Figure 1. Logical perspective of the GCS architecture

The overall, logical perspective of the presented system is depicted in Figure 1. The main elements that comprise the GCS are: the WSRF [9] based checkpointing service and execute- and resume-wrapper. These tree components form the backbone of the architecture. Both wrappers are intended to be executed by the Grid Resource Broker in place of the original computing tasks. The wrappers perform some preliminary work and then execute or resume the original computing job. Most of the work performed by the wrappers is the same for all types of checkpointers and the checkpointer-dependent scripts are executed at the end of the wrappers. The actual Grid Resource Broker used in the presented implementation is GRMS. The GRMS submits the execute- or resume-wrapper on a destination cluster with the help of the GRAM service which in turn executes the wrapper on assigned execute-node using the underlying Local Resource Manager (LRM). More information concerning wrappers responsibility is presented in sections 4.1 and 4.3. The component that receives and then forwards the Grid Resource Broker's checkpoint requests is WSRF-compatible Checkpoint Service (in short Checkpoint Service). The way the GRMS acquires the information about the location of the adequate Checkpoint

Service is presented in section 4.1. For now it is important that the service is able to forward the checkpoint-request to the checkpoint-invoker that is dedicated to a particular underlying low-level checkpointer. After the checkpoint is taken, the Checkpoint Service is in charge of storing the checkpoint image in an external repository and remembering the location of the image with the help of Replica Location Service (RLS) [10]. The aforementioned wrappers and the Checkpoint Service utilize the set of auxiliary tools (see the lowest rectangle in Figure 1) which comprise both, the ones implemented especially for GCS as well as the common pre-existing grid-level (e.g. GridFTP [11], OGSA-DAI [12]), and system-level tools (e.g. ssh, sudo). Additionally, the set of supporting components which are required to manage the images repository, the access to this repository and the flow of checkpointing related meta-data is assumed to be deployed in the operating environment.

A more detailed deployment perspective of the GCS is shown in Figure 2. Comparing to Figure 1, it is a little more decomposed; however, in order not to lose the readability less important details are still hidden. Since the Grid Resource Brokers often delegate the user's tasks to computing clusters, the key GCS's components are meant for operating within the cluster environment. The assumption is that the cluster has the head-node (also known as access node), i.e. the node with routable IP address and set of so called execute-nodes which do not need to have public IP addresses but only a local connection to the head-node. In particular, the head- and execute-nodes can be merged into one-node cluster with the public IP address. Additionally, we implicitly assume that each individual cluster consists of homogeneous nodes.

As it is shown in Figure 2, the components involved in GCS-related environment can be divided into four categories. The components marked with light grey colour constitute the GCS backbone. They provide a kind of framework that is independent of the actual underlying low-level checkpointers but lets them be integrated with the Grid. To make that framework operational, some auxiliary tools and services have to be properly configured. For example, to allow actions delegation and checkpoint images copying between nodes the ssh has to be configured to accept the host-based authentication policy. These auxiliary components are marked with thin mesh in the background in Figure 2. The final integration with the low-level checkpointer takes place by providing the components especially dedicated to this particular checkpointer. In Figure 2, these components are marked with dark grey colour. In order to incorporate the new checkpointer, the integrator has to provide the customized execute- and resume-wrappers and dedicated checkpointer invoker. The last category of GCS components are the pre-existing ones that constitute the operating environment but do not require any special integration effort.

Some of the GCS' components have to communicate with the "external word" (e.g. with the Grid Resource Broker or with checkpoint images repository) and these are positioned on the head-node. On the other hand, the execute- and resume-wrappers as well as the actual checkpointers and the related checkpointers invokers are positioned on execute-nodes. Since only the head-node has public IP address, if one of the components from the execute-node requires the action that involves access to any external services, the action is delegated to the proper components on the head-node. Similarly, when the head-node is going to take the action on the execute-node, the action is delegated to it. In both situations the delegation is performed with the help of properly configured standard ssh, scp and sudo tools.

The functionality of individual components of the GCS is also described in subsequent sections when the control- and data-flow of job submitting, checkpointing and resuming is presented.

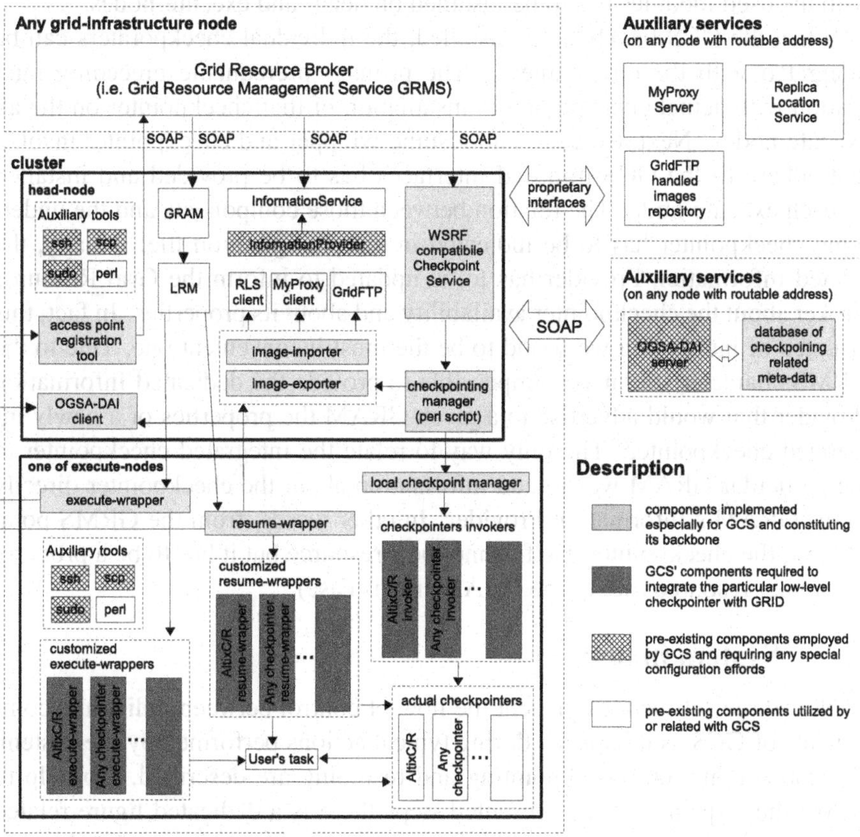

Figure 2. Deployment perspective of the GCS environment

3. Installation and integration issues

The purpose of this section is to highlight the difference between the installation of the GCS' backbone and the integration of a particular checkpointer with the GCS. The backbone is to be installed only once in the cluster. It performs a lot of work that is common for all installed checkpointers, including management of checkpointing-related meta-data and of the checkpointing images. The backbone utilizes the properly configured auxiliary tools like ssh, scp and sudo on a cluster-level range and OGSA-DAI based interface to GRID-level database of checkpointing related meta-data. The backbone requires access to services such as MyProxy Server [13], Replica Location Service and GridFTP handled images repository. The location and other properties of all external services are configured with the help of configuration files. Additionally, since a part of the GCS' backbone is written in perl, this language together with the used modules has to be installed on head- and execute-nodes.

When the GCS backbone is installed, the individual checkpointers can be integrated with the environment. The primary prerequisite preceding integration with actual checkpointer is installation of that checkpointer on the all execute-nodes. Next, execute- and resume-wrapper and checkpointer invoker that adhere to the GCS-imposed interfaces has to be provided and installed on each execute-node. The relation between those components and the underlying checkpointer has to be indicated in the configuration file. Finally, the related Information Provider has to be updated to inform the Grid Resource Broker about the checkpointer availability and about its properties. In fact, this last step of integration we found to be the most inconvenient one. Due to the GRMS characteristic, it was impossible to provide the dedicated Information Provider that would advertise to a given GRAM the properties of a newly integrated checkpointer. The only way to relate the integrated checkpointer to the particular GRAM was to add information about the checkpointer directly to the GRAM's Information Provider. In other words, from the GRMS point of view, the checkpointer itself cannot be a resource but it has to be a property of another resource (i.e. of the GRAM in this case).

4. System in action

Next three subsections present the flow of control between individual components of GCS as it happens during typical actions performed by the system. The job submission, checkpointing and resuming are described. To help to follow the sequence of the presented steps there is a dedicated figure related with each usage scenario. These figures focus on the flow of control and not on any deployment details. The arrows are labeled with numbers that indicate the order in which the control is passed to the pointed components. Additionally, the beneath description is decorated with the numbers enclosed in parentheses. These numbers correspond to the ones from the figures and are meant to assist you in tracking the proceeding steps. Each figure contains one box that is filled with gray color. These gray boxes symbolize the components that are to be provided by the checkpointer integrator in order to integrate a particular checkpointing tool with the GCS environment.

4.1 Submitting the task

The components and relationships involved in task submission are depicted in Figure 3. (1) The GRMS allows the end user to submit the jobs to the Grid with the help of the user provided job descriptor and GRMS' command line interface. The mentioned job descriptor specifies the submitted job as a set of tasks that are to be executed in the Grid environment. Additionally, the job descriptor contains requirements and constraints regarding the computing resource and optionally a workflow definition.

Providing that the user is going to take advantage of the presented GCS, he/she has to modify the related job descriptor (a more advanced GRMS client could do it on the fly, transparently to the end user). The original tasks binaries' name has to be replaced with the name of a special execute-wrapper. This is a general wrapper that has to be installed on each GCS compatible execute-node. The user's original task binary name is to be specified in the job descriptor with the help of environment variables that are passed to the wrapper. If the original task is defined by the executable file pointed out by the URL, then that executable has to be marked in the job descriptor as the input file for the execute-wrapper. Moreover, the requirements regarding the functionality of the checkpointer that is able to deal with the submitted tasks has to be included in the job descriptor. These properties can identify the checkpointer in an unambiguous way or can only specify the desired functionality or the class of the required checkpointer. Finally, the task itself has to be marked as checkpointable.

(2) When GRMS is determining the proper computing resource for such defined tasks, then, among other parameters, it takes into account the specified checkpointer's properties and matches them against the ones provided by the GCS-related Information Services. (2) Once the computing resource is selected, the user's task is passed to the associated GRAM, (3) and further to the underlying LRM. The LRM, according to the local scheduling policy, (4) executes the execute-wrapper on the assigned execute-node. As the execute-node can be equipped with more than one checkpointer, the GRMS passes to the wrapper the lists of the checkpointers that match the user-defined requirements. If the list contains more than one checkpointer, then the wrapper has to decide which one would be assigned to the current task. (5) Next, with the help of the OGSA-DAI mechanism, (6) the wrapper stores in the GRID-

level database the meta-data required later when the checkpoint is taken (see section 5). The most important meta-data includes the information about the assigned checkpointer, the OS-level wrapper's owner, the address of current execute-node (can be a cluster-level, non-routable one) and PID of the application. The involved job and task identifiers are used as keys to the meta-data in the database. (7) After that, the wrapper uses the access point registration tool to register in the GRMS the access point to the WSRF-compatible Checkpoint Service. The access point has the form of the URL address and is used by the GRMS as the destination address for the checkpoint requests. (9) Finally, the wrapper executes the customized execute-wrapper associated with the selected checkpointer. The GCS contract says that the purpose of the customized execute-wrapper is to execute the user's task in a way allowing doing checkpoints later. In case of AltixC/R checkpointer, the provided customized wrapper is simply a bash script which calls the exec command to replace itself with the user's task. Such a solution ensures that the process constituting user task preserves the wrapper's PID, so the earlier stored PID now refers to the user task.

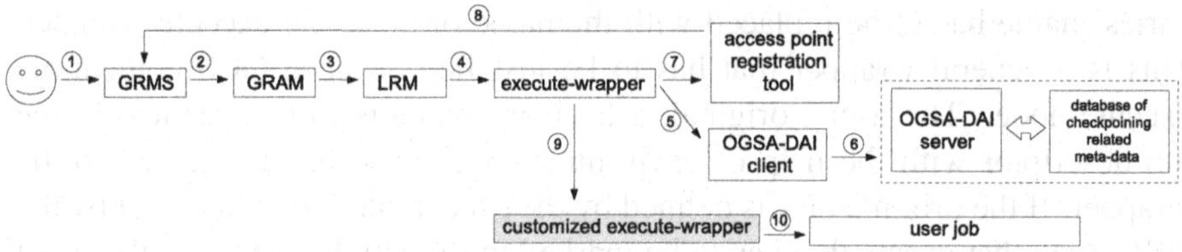

Figure 3. Submission related flow of control.

4.2 Triggering the checkpoint

The flow of control as it happens when the checkpoint is being done is depicted in figure 4. (1) In order to take checkpoint of the task managed by the GRMS, the user issues the suspend task command with the help of GRMS' command line interface. The only parameters the command depends on are the GRMS' job and task identifiers which uniquely specify each task. (2) As each checkpointable task has a registered access point, the GRMS sends to it the checkpoint request together with job and task identifiers. In the GCS environment the access point corresponds to the WSRF compatible Checkpoint Service, which is the interface to the checkpointers installed locally in the cluster. (3) This service is just an interface to the checkpointing manager (4) which through the OGSA-DAI derived interface obtains (5) the meta-data about the task. These meta-data help to determine the checkpoint invoker that is to be used, the address of the execute-node on which the checkpoint invoker is to be called, the PID of the process that is to be checkpointed, and the name of a local-scope task owner. (6) Basing on these data, the properly configured ssh and sudo commands are used to execute the local checkpoint manager. This manager is passed most of the earlier obtained meta-data and resides on the same node as the task that is to be checkpointed. (7) According to parameters passed to the manager the right checkpoint invoker is selected and executed. The aforementioned PID value is propagated to the checkpoint invoker. (8) In case of AltixC/R checkpointer, the checkpoint invoker is just a bash script which with the help of AltxiC/R's chkpnt command does checkpoint of the process indicated by the passed PID. When the checkpoint invoker finishes its work, the local checkpoint manager forces the user task to be terminated (due to GRMS assumptions that task is finished after checkpoint is done) with the help of a standard signal mechanism, and relying on the standard output of the checkpoint invoker (format of that output is defined by GCS) prepares a single tarball which contains all files constituting the checkpoint image. (10) Then, the tarball is moved to the head-node and the original checkpoint image is removed. (11) Now, as the head-node has access to the "external world", the tarball file is stored in an external repository and the location of the file is remembered in RLS.

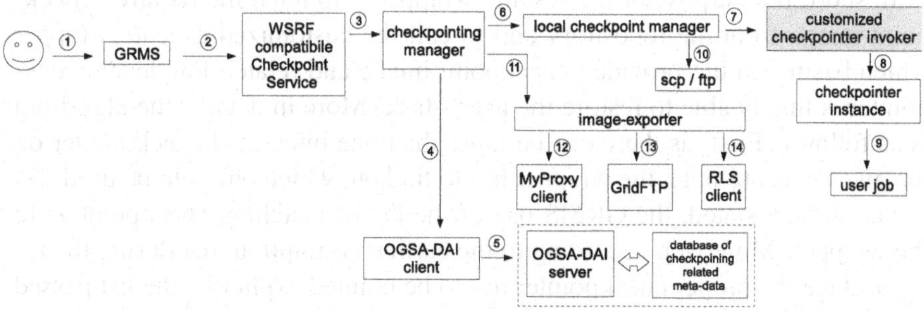

Figure 4. Checkpoint related flow of control.

4.3 Task's resuming

The flow of control associated with the task resuming scenario is depicted in figure 5. The task's resuming scenario is quite similar to the task submitting. Instead of the original task's binaries the user has to execute the GCS provided resume-wrapper. The main difference from the submitting scenario comes down to the fact that the task can be resumed only with exactly the same checkpointer type that was previously used to create the checkpoint image, and that during the resume stage the GRMS does not assign new job and task identifiers but uses the previous ones. In the discussed implementation this information has to be provided by the user in a form of command line arguments. To satisfy the first condition, the job descriptor used with the resume command has to unambiguously specify the required checkpointer. Unfortunately, currently there is no support in the GRMS to do it automatically or transparently. The only way to find out what checkpointer was assigned to the task is to query the GCS' database of checkpointing meta-data. To simplify this task, the GCS provides the command line tool that can be used to inquire the related database about the previously assigned checkpoiner's name.

Providing that the user acquired the required checkpointer's name, he/she has to edit the job descriptor to specify the involved checkpointer's name and to replace the original user task with the resume-wrapper. In fact, to make things a little easier, the GRMS allows to define the tasks executed on submit and resume stage in the same job descriptor. So the same descriptor can define the wrapper executed on first-submit and on the resume scenario adequately. (1) (2) (3) (4) The way the resume-wrapper reaches the final execute-node is the same as in case of the execute-wrapper. Moreover, it still should be possible to do checkpoints of the previously recovered task. Hence, the functionality of the resume- and execute-wrappers partly overlaps. Therefore, to shorten the overall description, the current section covers only the activity essential to resume the task.

In short, the purpose of the resume-wrapper is to fetch the required checkpoint image from the repository and to call the customized execute-wrapper which basing on the provided checkpoint image and related low-level checkpointer is finally able to restore the user's task. More in details, the algorithm is as follows. First, as there can be more than one integrated checkpointer on the given execute-note, the wrapper has to find out which one is to be used. As it was already stated, the GRMS passes the list of matching checkpointers to the wrapper. Moreover, according to the earlier assumption that during the resume stage the proper checkpointer has to be pointed explicitly, the list passed to the wrapper should contain only one item. So, this time, the assignment of the proper checkpointer is trivial. (5) (6) (7) (8) Next, the resume-wrapper asks the image-exporter from the head-node to fetch the checkpoint image from the external repository to the local cluster (9) and later to the given execute-node. (10) After that, the associated customized resume-wrapper is executed with the path to the checkpoint image as a passed parameter. (11) That customized wrapper is in charge of using the underlying low-level checkpointer to resume the user task. In case of AltixC/R checkpointer, the customized wrapper ultimately resumes the user job using the associated resume command. As this command returns control only after the resumed user task finishes execution the customized wrapper is able to remove the checkpoint image that was used to resume the task. Unfortunately, in case of other low-level checkpointers there might not be an opportunity to perform any action after the resumed user task finishes. In such a situation, the additional service that would remove the "utilized" images should be implemented. The mechanism could be based on the GRMS' ability to send events notifications to the registered listeners.

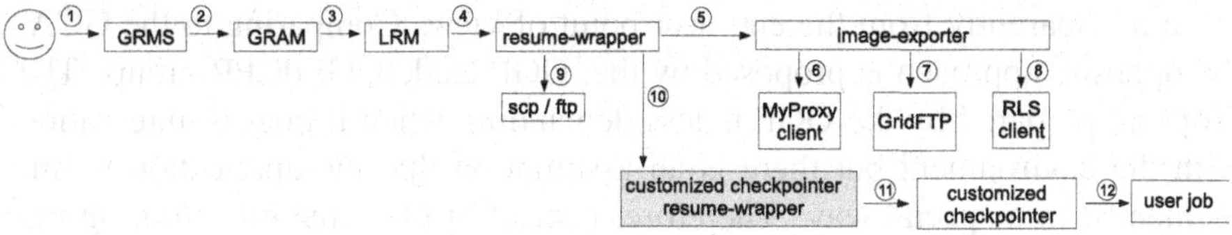

Figure 5. Recovery related control of flow.

5. Pros and Cons

It is hard to compare the GCA specification or GCS implementation with proposals or implementations of other architectures providing similar functionality because there are no alternative initiatives available. Therefore we will try to sum out the pros and cons of the solution presented in this paper in terms of costs introduced by the deployment of the GCA in the "plain" Grid environment and, where possible, to point out the differences in the assumptions with the solutions based only on dedicated application-level checkpointing.

The GCA causes virtually no overhead in terms of latency in processing of the job by the Grid environment. The additional steps required to enable the checkpointing capabilities of the environment are executed during the submission of the job and in most cases are only necessary to prepare the environment or to store additional information about the application. The majority of the additional costs in terms of the CPU cycles, the storage space or the network bandwidth are imposed by the low-level checkpointer and if someone wants to employ checkpointing functionality these costs will occur regardless of the high-level architecture which provides interface the particular checkpointer.

The major drawback of the presented solutions is the increased complexity of the deployment process. The installation of the Grid environment is complex and multi staged process by itself and the modifications introduced by the GCS (or in general by GCA) make the installation even more complex. The need for additional components that have to be installed and configured properly and in some cases modifications of the standard configuration files requires additional knowledge from the administrators. Nevertheless, the GCS has been implemented in a way that separates deployment of "backbone" GCS services from the actions required to integrate given low-level checkpointer with the GCS. In result the actual integration is significantly easer than installation of the whole framework that supports this integration.

The additional checkpointing functionality requires extending job description with fields that were not present in the original version of the grid environment. Even though in the presented GCS implementation the job descriptor has to be adjusted manually, it is possible that more advanced user interfaces or even the Grid Broker itself will take over this function to make the GCA more transparently from the end user point of view. Comparing to the GCA, the opposite approach is proposed by the, OGF leaded, GridCPR group. The proposal prepared by the OGF is less demanding when it goes to integration with the environment but there is an assumption that the application is implemented in a special way. Therefore, instead of one-time effort during the deployment of the computational environment (as it is in the GCA case), the work on making the application checkpointable has to be repeated for each application separately. Moreover, thanks to the experience gained with the proof-of-concept implementations, the GCA seems to be more detailed from the technical point of view while the OGF proposal is more conceptual architecture in which some functionality is enclosed into "black boxes". Next important note is that although the GCA is not a checkpointer itself, it makes it possible to use any of the already-existing checkpointing tools regardless of the way they were implemented. This is a huge advantage in comparison with the solution proposed by the OGF where the application-level checkpointing is the only supported mechanism.

Finally, it cannot be overlooked that the availability of checkpointing functionality in Grids allows the Grid Resource Brokers to perform load balancing by enforcing checkpoint-kill-restart sequence, or achieving a high fault tolerance by periodical checkpoints of the applications.

6. Further Work

Even though the presented GCS implementation is just a proof-of-concept work related with the GCA architecture specification, the obtained end result is the autonomous system which is capable of being deployed within the Grid environment managed by the GRMS Grid Resource Broker. Hence, it is reasonable to consider potential future work extending the current GCS' functionality or removing any noticed shortcomings.

At the moment the most noticeable drawback of the CTS is a lack of any checkpoint images-related garbage collector. When the user job finishes successfully, the images stored in the repository are not useful anymore. Similarly, there is currently no general mechanism that would remove from the execute-node the images used to resume the user task. The service that would delete such outdated images would be easy to implement thanks to the GRMS' events notification mechanism.

At the moment, only the most recent checkpoint image can be used to resume the user task. Therefore, the GCS would be extended with the possibility of images versioning. Moreover, GRMS utilizes the checkpointing functionality as a tool to achieve the load-balancing capability. So, the tests in fault-tolerance oriented environment could also be valuable from the GCS point of view.

7. Conclusions

The presented GCS implementation proves the correctness and feasibility of the crucial GCA architecture assumptions. The obtained product is general and flexible enough to allow integrating the Grid with any checkpointer in a relatively simple way. However, the GCS does not implement the GCA specification precisely. Instead, it has been adapted to be operational within the currently available GRMS and Globus-based Grid environments.

Thanks to the performed work, some shortcomings of the GCA design stage and of the employed Grid middleware have been disclosed. The GCA intention is to perceive the functionality and availability of the checkpointers being integrated independently of the hosting compute resources. In other words, the functionality and availability of a checkpointer should be advertised through the Information Service separately from advertising the related compute resource. However, this functionality will be possible to implement when the related Grid Resource Broker will be capable of somehow associating such an advertising checkpointer with the involved computing resource. Currently the checkpointers have to be considered as integral computing resource features (similarly to such features as the amount of available memory or storage space). Other issues, considered as the GCS internal drawbacks are briefly outlined in section 8 entitled "Future Work".

Additionally, according to our integration experience, we would like to propose an additional feature related to the Grid Resource Broker's functionality. We propose to enhance the job description language with the possibility of including the in-line invocations of external Grid Services which would be resolved to the text treated as an ordinary part of the descriptor. Such functionality would facilitate any potential integration with any other systems. In case of GCS, in-line Grid Services invocations would simplify the resume stage by excusing the end user from the duty of finding out what checkpointer was used during the checkpoint stage. This information would be provided to the Grid Resource Broker by placing in a job descriptor the in-line invocation of a specialized Grid Service. However, the Grid Service's addresses format can be inconvenient to remember for a human being so a correlated mechanism of logical Grid Service's names or aliases would also be helpful.

The final remark is that all the tests of the GCS were performed within the cluster or clusters set up on homogenous nodes with the same version of OS and accompanying tools installed. It can mean that in a more diverse environment the constraints pertaining to the jobs resuming could be tighter.

Acknowledgments

This research work is carried out under the FP6 Network of Excellence Core-GRID funded by the European Commission (Contract IST-2002-004265).

Appendix - list of main terms and abbreviations

This is a reference list of terms and abbreviations used in the paper.

access point URL address to Grid Service that is able to receive and handle a checkpoint request.

AltixC/R Low-level checkpointer dedicated to IA64 and Linux platform.

checkpoint invoker The CTS' component that utilizes a particular low-level checkpointer to take checkpoints of user's tasks.

CS Checkpoint Service is a GCS' component implemented in a form of a Grid Service. It is the component that provides the access point.

CTS Checkpoint Translation Service is one of components of the GCA. From the GCS point of view, it resembles the CS component.

customized execute-wrapper The GCS' component assigned to an individual low-level checkpointer and intended to execute the checkpointable user tasks.

customized resume-wrapper The GCS' component assigned to individual low-level checkpointer and intended to resume the user tasks.

execute-node A cluster's nodes executing the submitted jobs. This node is not required to have a public IP address.

execute-wrapper The general wrapper that is executed in place of the original user task.

GCA Grid Checkpointing Architecture specifies general rules and requirements to integrate low-level checkpointers with the Grid. GCS is a proof-of-concept implementation of GCA.

GCS Grid Checkpointing Service is described in the paper, a proof-of-concept implementation of GCA.

Globus Globus Toolkit is a set of services and tools that constitute the middleware used to develop Grids.

Grid Resource Broker The general name for a component that manages resource allocation in the Grid environment.

Grid Service The Web Service compliant with the WSRF standard.

GridCPR The OGF initiative to define an interface for checkpointable Grid-aware applications.

GridFTP The file transport protocol for Grid installations.

GRMS Grid Resource Management Service is the actual implementation of the Grid Resource Broker.

head-node A cluster's node with the public IP address.

image-exporter The GCS' component installed on the head-node and responsible for storing checkpoint images in the external repository.

image-importer The GCS' component installed on the head-node intended to fetch checkpoint images from the external repository.

Information Provider The component that is able to provide the Information Service with adequate information.

Information Service The component that advertises to the Grid the information provided by Information Providers.

LRM Local Resource Manager is a general name for clusters' managers. Examples of LRM are Torque, PBS and LSF.

MyProxy Part of a Grid ecosystem allowing credentials to be managed and shared.

OGF Open Grid Forum is an international community dealing with Grids dissemination and standardization.

OGSA-DAI The middleware to assist access and integration of data within the Grid.

resume-wrapper The general wrapper that is executed in place of the original user task in order to resume this task.

RLS Replica Location Service is a part of the Globus Toolkit, and was designed to support mapping of logical names of files to their physical localization.

VMM The Virtual Machine Monitor refers to the technology of virtual machines. Example implementations are Xen and WMware.

WSRF Web Services Resource Framework is a framework for modeling and accessing the stateful resources through the Web Services. The WSRF-compliant Web Service is also named the Grid Service.

References

[1] OGF's GridCPR Home Page *https://forge.gridforum.org/sf/projects/gridcpr-wg*

[2] G. Jankowski, J. Kovacs, N. Meyer, R. Januszewski, and R. Mikolajczak, *Towards Checkpointing Grid Architecture* in PPAM2005 Proceedings, Poznan, Poland, Sept. 2005.

[3] G. Jankowski, R. Mikolajczak, R. Januszewski, J. Kovacs, A. Kertesz, and M. Stroinski, *Grid checkpointing architecture integration of low-level checkpointing capabilities with grid*, CoreGRID Network of Excellence (NoE), Tech. Rep. TR-0075, Feb. 2007.

[4] CoreGRID Network of Excellence *http://www.coregrid.org*

[5] Kernel Level Checkpointing for SGI Altix *http://checkpointing.psnc.pl/SGIGrid/*

[6] User Level Checkpointing psncLibCkpt library *http://checkpointing.psnc.pl/Progress/psncLibCkpt/*

[7] GRMS Home Page *http://www.gridge.org/content/view/18/99/*

[8] Gridge Toolkit Home Page: *http://www.gridge.org/*

[9] *http://www.oasis-open.org/committees/tc_home.php?wg_abbrev=wsrf*

[10] Replica Location Service Home Page *http://www.globus.org/toolkit/docs/4.0/data/rls/*

[11] *https://forge.gridforum.org/sf/projects/gridftp-wg*

[12] The OGSA-DAI project *http://www.ogsadai.org.uk/*

[13] MyProxy Home Page *http://www.globus.org/toolkit/docs/4.0/security/myproxy/*

[14] Nathan Stone, Derek Simmel, Thilo Kielmann, *An Architecture for Grid Checkpoint Recovery Services and a GridCPR API*, September 2005

[15] Paul Stodghill, *Use Cases for Grid Checkpoint and Recovery*, September 2005.

[16] Gracjan Jankowski, Radoslaw Januszewski, Rafal Mikolajczak, Jozsef Kovacs, *The Grid Checkpointing Architecture*, Institute on Grid Information, Resource and Workflow Monitoring Services, "CoreGRID White Paper, WHP-0003", May 13 2008.

EXTENDING GWORKFLOWDL: A MULTI-PURPOSE LANGUAGE FOR WORKFLOW ENACTMENT

Simone Pellegrini, Francesco Giacomini
INFN Cnaf
Viale Berti Pichat, 6/2 - 40127 Bologna, Italy
simone.pellegrini@cnaf.infn.it
francesco.giacomini@cnaf.infn.it

Abstract Scientific workflows are becoming increasingly important as a vehicle for enabling science at a large scale. Lately, many *Workflow Management Systems* (WfMSs) have been introduced in order to support the needs of several scientific fields, such as *bioinformatics* and *cheminformatics*. However, no platform is practically capable to address the computational power and storage capacity provided by production Grids needed by complex scientific processes. In this paper, we introduce a *novel* design for a WfMS which has been proposed inside the CoreGRID project. Based on the *micro-kernel* design pattern, we have developed a *lightweight* Petri Net engine where complex functionalities – such as the interaction towards Grid middlewares – are provided at higher-level and described by means of Petri Net-based workflows. As the interaction with resources is described by workflows, it is possible to extend our platform by *programming* it using the *Grid Workflow Description Language* (GWorkflowDL).

Keywords: Grid Workflow, Workflow Enactment, Workflow Description Languages, Language Conversions, Petri Nets, GWorkflowDL, gLite, Sub-Workflows, Web Services

1. Introduction

Workflows are a modern phenomenon which, in the 1920, have been applied to the manufacturing industry for *rationalizing* the organization of work. Less than a decade ago, those concepts have been applied to the *Information Technology* (IT) world. Commonly, workflows are used to describe *business processes*, which consist of the flow or progression of *activities* – each of which represents the work of a *person*, an *internal system*, or the *process of a partner company* – toward some *business goal*. A *Workflow Management Sys-*

tem (WfMS) is a software component that takes as input a formal description of processes and maintains the state of processes executions, thereby delegating activities amongst people and applications. Recently, workflows have also emerged as a paradigm for representing and managing complex distributed *scientific* computation, specially in the fields of *bioinformatics* and *cheminformatics*.

Actually, many of the motivations of scientific workflows are also typical in business workflows. However, according to [1], it is possible to identify scientific workflow specific requirements such as *data* and *computation intensity* and dynamic resource allocation, scheduling and mapping to underlying distributed infrastructure such as Grid computing environments. While in business workflows the attention is indeed mainly placed in defining the *control-flow* (*control-driven*), in the scientific environment the *data-flow* definitely covers the principal role (*data-driven*) of the process design. This aspect also reflects in the workflow description languages and the underlying modeling formalisms. While scientific workflows are mainly based on *Directed Acyclic Graphs* (DAGs) the business workflows are modeled by means of the π-*Calculus* [2] and Activity Diagrams [3] formalisms.

Unfortunately, today, most of scientific WfMSs are not practically able to deal with complex and highly demanding processes. Many of them can address just a small set of computational resources and therefore they are not able to exploit real *production* Grids, which provide the computational power and storage capacity needed by complex scientific processes. Furthermore, a *standard* for workflow description has not been established yet and the variety of existing workflow languages intend to be specific to a platform limiting the *interoperability* of the workflow descriptions.

For these reasons, interoperability is becoming one of the main issues in the next-generation WfMSs and the CoreGRID project is taking large efforts in this direction. Inside the CoreGRID project, the FIRST Fraunhofer research group has proposed a workflow language, called the *Grid Workflow Description Language* (GWorkflowDL) which is based on the *High Level Petri Nets* (HLPNs) formalism [4]. The Petri Nets formalism has been chosen for several reasons [5] [6], and its semantics fits well with the majority of scientific processes. Furthermore, the expressivity of Petri Nets makes interoperability possible by *theorically* allowing the translation of the majority of scientific workflow descriptions – usually expressed in terms of DAGs – into a Petri Net-based description such as GWorkflowDL.

In this paper a *novel* WfMS architecture developed within the CoreGRID project is presented [7]. The characteristic of the system relies on its unique design which is based on the *micro-kernel* design pattern [8] [10] [9]. The purpose is to develop a *lightweight*, *fast* and *reliable* Petri Net-based engine with the ability to perform just few types of operations: *local method* calls, remote *Web Service* and *sub-workflows* invocation [11]. The main idea behind the WfMS is that '*everything is a workflow*' and therefore complex processes – e.g. the execution of a job on a Grid environment – can be modeled by means of a workflow whose *atomic* tasks can be executed by the engine. The GWorkflowDL language has been improved in order to make it more expressive and deal with the *sub-workflows invocation mechanism* which, as we will see in Section 3, covers an important role in the *workflow enactment* process. Unlike other approaches, the presented design guarantees the neutrality towards the underlying mechanisms for task execution, in order not to compromise interoperability with multiple infrastructures and resources. In order to evaluate the capabilities of our design, tests have been done with workflows accessing resources available on the Grid provided by the EGEE project, a large and relatively mature infrastructure.

Section 2 introduces the GWorkflowDL language and the extensions introduced in order to make it more expressive and suitable for the internal representation of sub-workflows in our WfMS. In Section 3 an overview of the system will be presented. In Section 4 the language interoperability problem will be faced by introducing language translators. Section 5 presents how this work will progress in the future.

2. The Grid Workflow Description Language

The power of workflows relies in their *graph-oriented* programming model which is appealing for average users. In these years many formalisms have been considered for workflow modeling (DAGs, UML Activity Diagrams) and today, we see Petri Nets and π-Calculus as the main formalisms respectively for *data-driven* and *control-driven* workflows. Actually, π-Calculus is the formalism on which the *Business Process Execution Language for Web Services* (BPEL4WS) is based. BPEL4WS is a *de facto* standard for business workflows created by merging two workflow languages previously proposed by IBM (WSFL) and Microsoft (XLANG) [12]. On the other side, Petri Net-based workflow languages have not been yet standardized, but projects such as *Yet Another Workflow Language* (YAWL) [13] and the *Grid Workflow Execution Service* (GWES) [14] are demonstrating that Petri Nets can be used either to address the needs of business workflows as well as scientific ones.

The GWorkflowDL has been proposed by the FIRST Fraunhofer research group inside the CoreGRID project. Its main purpose is to define a *standard* for the description of Petri Net-based scientific workflows. It is *formally* based on the HLPN formalism and used in the *Knowledge-based Workflow System for Grid Applications* K-Wf and actually in its core component represented by the GWES. It is an XML-based language for representing Grid workflows which consists of two parts: (*i*) a *generic* part, used to define the structure of

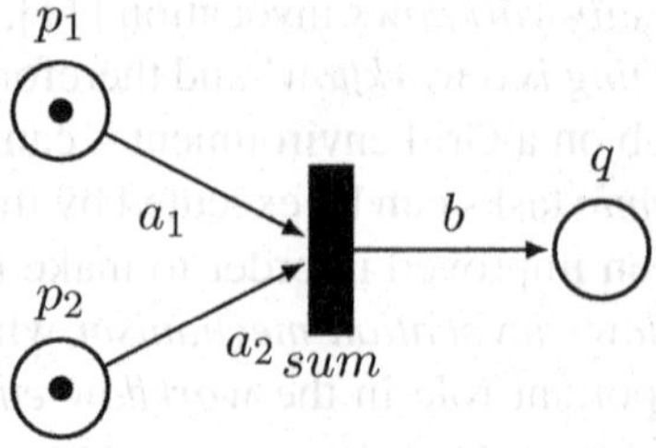

Figure 1. A two-operands sum operation modelled as a HLPN-based workflow

```
<workflow xmlns:op="http://www.gridworkflow.org/gworkflowdl/operation">
  <place ID="p1">
    <token><data><t1 xsd:type="xsd:int">3</t1></data></token>
  </place>
  <place ID="p2">
    <token><data><t2 xsd:type="xsd:int">2</t2></data></token>
  </place>
  <place ID="q" />
  <transition ID="T">
    <inputPlace placeID="p1" edgeExpression="a1"/>
    <inputPlace placeID="p2" edgeExpression="a2"/>
    <outputPlace placeID="q" edgeExpression="b"/>
    <op:operation>
      <op:operationClass name="plus"/>
    </op:operation>
  </transition>
</workflow>
```

Figure 2. GWorkflowDL abstract description of the Petri Net in Figure 1

the workflow, reflecting the data and control flow in the application, and (*ii*) a middleware-specific part (*extensions*) that defines how the workflow should be executed in the context of a specific Grid computing middleware.

Recently [15], the language has been extended in order to represent *platform-independent* operations and therefore to make the workflow descriptions portable upon different WfMSs. Considering the workflow, expressed in HLPN, in figure 1, the *abstract workflow* can be expressed in GWorkflowDL as depicted in figure 2. At the abstract level, the structure of the Petri Net is *fully* described while operations – which are associated with transitions – are not specified. In figure 3, two *concrete, platform-specific*, implementation of the sum operation are provided. The sum operation is mapped (by the WfMS) into: (*i*) the invocation of a Web Service method and (*ii*) the execution of a local script.

```
...
  <op:operationClass name="plus">
    <op:wsOperation wsdl="http://localhost/math?wsdl"
                    operationName="plus" quality="0.6"/>
    <op:pyOperation operation="b = a1 + a2"
                    selected="true" quality="0.3"/>
  </op:operationClass>
...
```

Figure 3. Two *concrete, platform-specific,* implementations of the sum operation.

In order to make the GWorkflowDL language compliant with our purposes and with the formal definition of HLPNs, it has been extended with several features. In the following sections, *three* extensions will be introduced with the main purpose to increase the GWorkflowDL language modeling capabilities and to introduce the mechanisms (e.g. the sub-workflows invocation) used by the WfMS during the workflow *enactment process.*

Sub-workflows

Real workflows have the tendency to become too large and complex, for this reason the *hierarchy* construct has been provided in order to reduce the overall complexity by structuring into sub-workflows. The sub-workflow concept allows for *hierarchical modelling*, i.e. it is possible to decompose complex systems into smaller systems allowing workflow reuse. A sub-workflow (also called *system*) is an aggregate of places, transitions and (possibly) subsystems. A sub-system, as happens with software components, defines an interface which is composed by a set of places, also called *connectors*. These connectors are divided into two categories, the *input connectors* (where tokens may enter into the system) and *output connectors* (where tokens may leave the system). The principle is very similar to the method invocation mechanism provided by common programming languages, where a piece of code can be packed into a method which exposes a signature.

In order to add support for sub-workflows in the GWorkflowDL language, we have introduced the `swOperation` element. For example, consider the workflow in Figure 4, its semantics is to sum the three numbers coming from the input places in_1, in_2, in_3 (which are the input connectors) and returns the result in the output place *out* (which is the output connector). The mapping between incoming/outgoing edges and input/output connectors can be *implicit* or *explicit*. The former uses a *positional semantics*, the N input places of the transition are mapped with the first N ($[0, N]$) places defined in the sub-workflow, while the M output places are mapped with the next M places ($[N+$

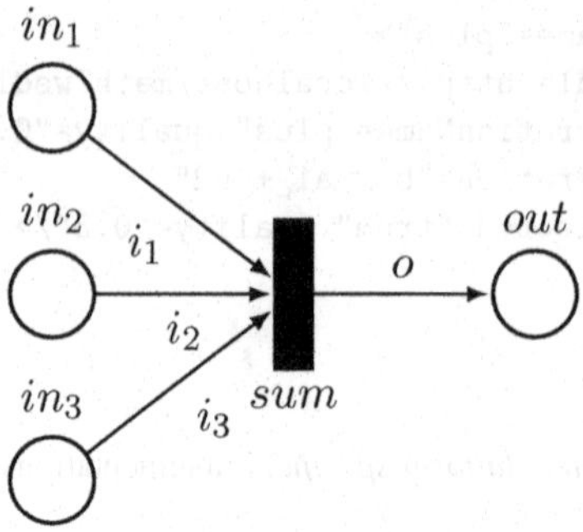

Figure 4. An abstract workflow which sums three *integer* numbers.

```
...
<transition ID="T">
  <inputPlace placeID="p1" edgeExpression="a1"/>
  <inputPlace placeID="p2" edgeExpression="a2"/>
  <outputPlace placeID="q" edgeExpression="b"/>
  <operation>
    <op:operationClass name="plus">
      <op:swOperation wsdl="http://localhost/math?wsdl"
                      operationName="plus" quality="0.6">
        <in name="in1">a1</in>
        <in name="in2">a2</in>
        <in name="in3">0</in>
        <out name="out">q</out>
      </op:swOperation>
    </op:operationClass>
  </operation>
</transition>
...
```

Figure 5. Explicit invocation of the sub-workflow depicted in Figure 4.

1, $N+M$]). The latter one uses the optional `in` and `out` XML elements in order to make the mapping explicit as discussed in [15].

The invocation of such workflow is performed by using the `swOperation`. In the Figure 5 a concrete implementation of the *sum* operation via a sub-workflow is showed. In this case the optional XML elements `in` and `out` are used in order to map incoming edge variables to input connectors and outgoing edges variables to output connectors. The invocation of the sub-workflow is then managed by the engine in a platform specific way.

Place with Type

According to the *Coloured* Petri Nets formalism [16], tokens and also places have a *type* (also called *color*). Currently, the GWorkflowDL language allows to specify type constraints for the tokens but not for the places. Add typing information to the places allows to check, even at *compile-time*, type *safety* of a Petri Net. For this reason, we have introduced an XML attribute – `type` – to the place element schema.

Typing information are also useful in order to check the *compatibility* of a transition operation with the relative incoming and outgoing places. For example consider the workflow in Figure 1 where places $p1$, $p2$ and q are of *integer* type; these constraints make the *signature* of the sum operation clear, i.e. $int\ sum(int,\ int)$. This feature avoids possible type *casting* errors which could raise at runtime and also helps the *mapping* from abstract to concrete workflow process by providing information of the operation signature.

Timed Transitions

In *Timed* Petri Nets, a time duration can be assigned to the transitions; tokens are meant to spend that time as reserved in the input places of the corresponding transitions. The GWorkflowDL language is currently not able to represent timed transitions and we think this feature is useful in order to make workflows deal with several design patterns which involve a delay, such as *polling*. Timed transitions can be supported at language level by introducing an *optional* XML attribute – `delay` – in the `transition` element. The delay is an integer value expressed in seconds.

3. The WfMS Overview

In order to evaluate the proposed language extensions and to demonstrate the capabilities of our design, we have developed a WfMS from the scratch. The project focuses the attention on different aspects of workflow management: (*i*) the *execution* of Petri Net-based workflows, the (*ii*) *mapping* from an abstract to a concrete workflow and the (*iii*) *conversion* between workflow description languages. The enactment of a workflow is performed by the engine which is the core of a WfMS and responsible of executing the workflow *tasks* respecting their dependencies. The second aspect is pursued by a *refinement process* which is based on the sub-workflow invocation mechanism. As stated, abstract workflows simply define the dependencies and the flow of data among macro-activities; the way in which tasks are performed is transparent to users and is managed by the WfMS. In our implementation, these macro-activities are implemented by concrete workflows which use primitives provided by the underlying platform. Interoperability is made possible by means of *transla-*

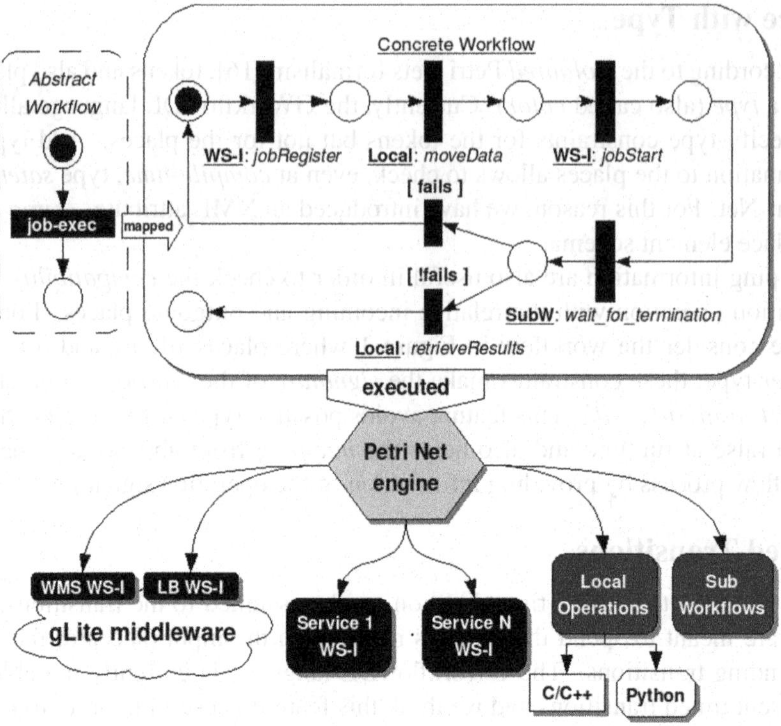

Figure 6. The WfMS architecture overview.

tors. Workflow language conversion will be discussed in more detail in the next section.

Tests have done with workflows accessing resources available on the Grid provided by the EGEE project, a large and relatively mature infrastructure. In particular, the execution of Grid jobs is performed by relying on the gLite *Workload Management System* (WMS) [17] through its Web Service interface (WMProxy). The WMS takes care of the resource management in gLite by finding the best available resources considering a set of users requirements and preferences (such as CPU architecture, OS, current load).

3.1 The Workflow Engine

The engine of a WfMS is the component which has, among others, the responsibility to interact with the underlying resources. Commonly, the support toward a specific resource or a Grid middleware is *hard-coded* into the workflow engine itself making the interaction with new platforms very difficult. Many of the existing WfMSs are designed to address just specific resources or Grid infrastructure and this choice also reflects in the associated workflow language which – instead to be unaware of the implementation details – risks to become too bound to a platform. This kind of design limits both the capabilities of the WfMSs and the *portability* of the workflow descriptions making their reuse impossible.

An alternative approach is to design a *lightweight* engine based on the *micro-kernel* design pattern [8] [10]. The engine is able to execute efficiently Petri Nets where the operations associated with transitions are of few, well defined, types. As depicted in Figure 6, the interaction with arbitrary *Web Services*, the execution of *local methods* and the invocation of *sub-workflows* are the only concrete operations supported by the engine and also provided at GWorkflowDL language level (see previous Section). New functionalities are provided at *higher* level through sub-workflows. This makes the GWorkflowDL, and thus Petri Nets, the main *programming language* of our platform.

The engine internally keeps the HLPN model of a workflow and executes it according to the Petri Nets *semantics*. The implementation of such semantics, and in particular the *non-determinism*, faces with the *imperative paradigm* provided by the mainstream programming languages such as C/C++ and Java. In [11], the engine design details are discussed together with the problems of sub-workflow invocations, non-determinism, parallelism, and transition firing which are practically faced and efficiently solved.

3.2 The Refinement Process

As happens with programming languages, where new functionalities are provided through *libraries*, in our WfMS new functionalities can be provided by defining new workflows which are accessed using the sub-workflow invocation mechanism. The mapping from abstract operations onto a concrete implementation is currently established by the correspondence of the operation name and the sub-workflow name. The overview of the refinement process is depicted in Figure 6 where the execution of a job in a Grid environment is implemented by a sub-workflow able to interact with the EGEE/gLite middleware services. Interaction with a different Grid platform, e.g. UNICORE, can be provided – even at *runtime* – simply by defining a new sub-workflow which describes the job submission and job monitoring processes.

Despite its simplicity, this strategy cannot be considered to be *multi-purpose* as far as a name-to-name mapping could fail in many situations. As stated, the mapping of an abstract operation f onto a concrete workflow implementing f is done by the WfMS using an associative map which binds the f's name into a workflow definition. In those situations, where an operation has several implementations, this strategy cannot be exploited. For the future, in order to improve the refinement process and make it more flexible, we are investigating the possibility to use *ontologies*.

Furthermore, thanks to the adopted design the engine has no information about the state of the workflow. As far as all the macro-operations of a workflow are decomposed into sub-workflows which use *atomic* operations (i.e. a local method or a remote Web Service invocation), it is possible to represent the overall workflow *state* simply by using the Petri Net *marking*. In this way, it is possible to provide a *checkpointing* mechanism able to restore the execution of a workflow, after a system failure, just re-establishing the last marking of the net.

4. Language Translators

One of the main interests of the CoreGRID project is the interoperability among heterogeneous systems. The growing number of WfMSs and workflow languages is making interoperability one of the main issues in the workflow environment. In a WfMS, interoperability can be achieved at different levels of complexity. The simpler one is about the description languages and the possibility to run legacy workflows on different platforms; it can be achieved – under certain circumstances – by means of language *translators*. On the other side, the interoperability among WfMSs is more complex to achieve as far as no recognized standard exists and no platform exposes a clear interface.

In our activity, we have focused on the language conversion problem enabling our WfMS to execute legacy workflows written in the JDL and the SCUFL languages. The *Job Description Language* (JDL) is used in the gLite middleware for job description. It is based on Condor's *Classified Advertisements* (ClassAds) and allows the description of DAG-based workflows which are executed by DAGMan [22]. The *Simple Conceptual Unified Flow Language* (SCUFL) is the underlying language of the Taverna WfMS [23]. Scufl is widely used in bioinformatics and several *primitive* operations are provided at language level in order to interact with *biological-specific* services such as `biomoby` [20].

In this section we introduce two language translators able to convert DAGMan and Taverna workflows into GWorkflowDL descriptions. Our efforts proves the power of Petri Nets in describing workflows. Recent studies have indeed demonstrated that the modeling capabilities of Petri Nets outperform other formalisms in describing workflows [18]. Actually, it is also possible to convert workflows based on several formalisms in terms of Petri Nets making language interoperability possible. We choose GWorkflowDL as description language because it has been proposed inside the CoreGRID project and additionally we think it has the characteristics to become a standard for scientific processes description.

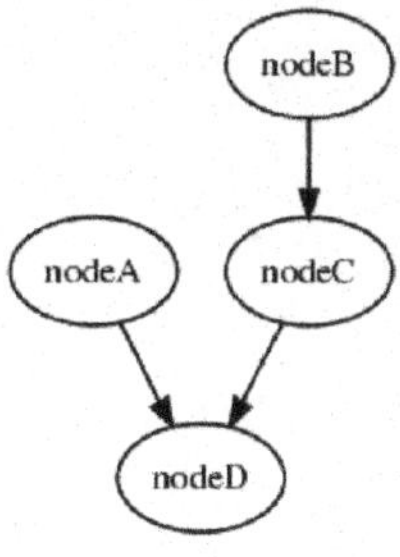

Figure 7. A simple DAG workflow.

4.1 JDL to GWorkflowDL

DAGMan [22] acts as a meta-scheduler for Condor jobs submitting job respecting their inter-dependencies which are expressed as a *Directed Acyclic Graph*. In case of job failure, DAGMan continues until it can no longer make progress. The example of a DAG-based workflow is showed in the Figure 7. While `nodeA` and `nodeB` can be executed concurrently, `nodeC` must wait the termination of `nodeB` and `nodeD` can be executed only when `nodeA` and `nodeC` have been completed. However, DAGMan totally lacks control structures (such as *branches* and *loops*) and a customizable error handling; the default strategy after a node failure is the *re-execution* of the node up to a configurable number of times.

The *Job Description Language* (JDL) is an extension of the Condor's *Classified Advertisements* (ClassAds): a record-like structure composed of a finite number of attributes separated by semi-colons (`;`). It is used in the gLite middleware for describing Grid jobs. A workflow in JDL is defined by a set of *nodes* and a set of *dependencies* which define *precedence relations* between nodes. The conversion of a DAG to a Petri Net is quite *trivial*: a DAG node can be modeled by a Petri Net transition and the flow of data among nodes by using tokens. However, a DAG node represents the execution of a Grid job and that practically means (*i*) the submission of the job description, (*ii*) the transfer of its input files (also called the input sandbox), (*iii*) waiting for the job termination and (*iv*) the retrievement of the results (the output sandbox). As stated in the previous section, the sequence of these operations can be modeled via a workflow and each DAG node can be substituted by a sub-workflow invocation. The Figure 8 depicts the Petri Net-based *concrete* workflow resulting from the conversion of the DAG represented in Figure 7. In the workflow are visible some implementation details (`certificate` and `delegationId`) which are specific to the gLite Grid middleware.

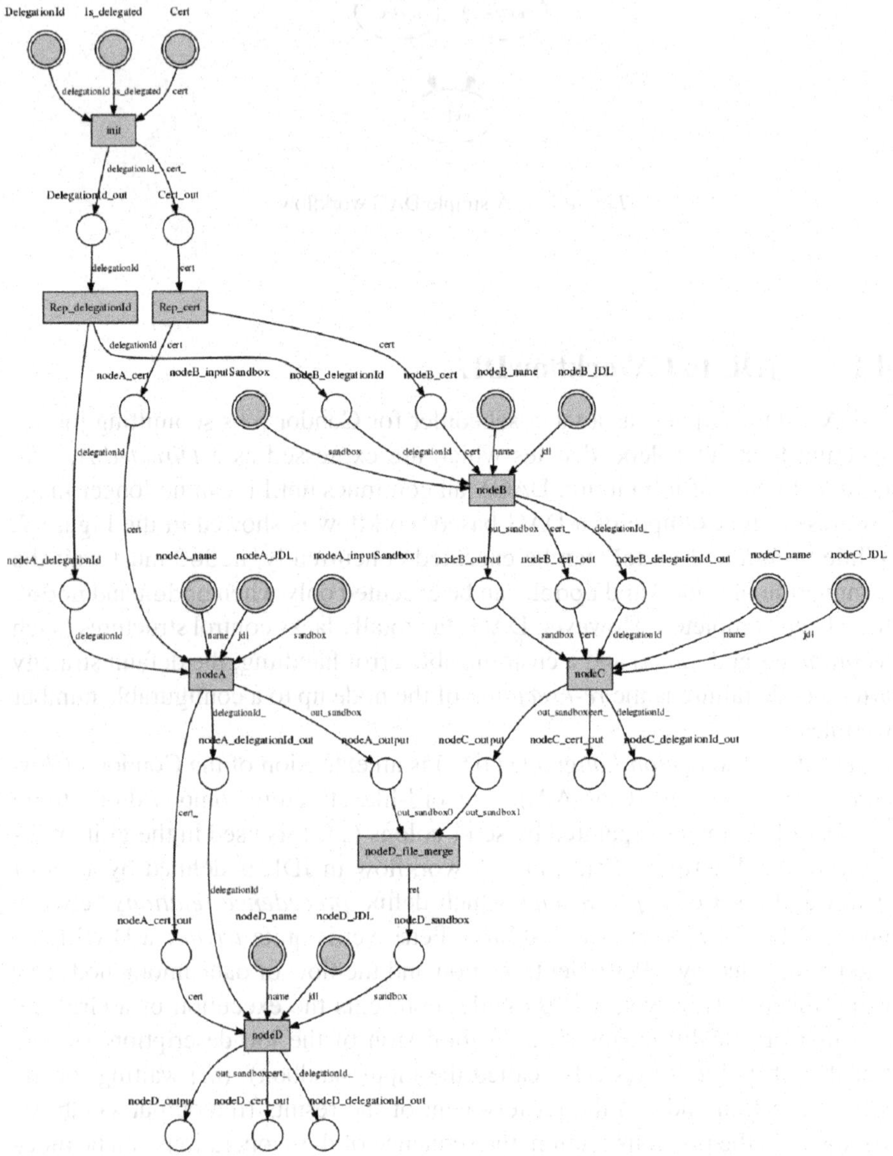

Figure 8. The result of the conversion of the DAG in Figure 7 into a Petri Net-based description.

4.2 Scufl to GWorkflowDL

Scufl is an XML-based language which allows to model DAG-based workflows. As stated, Scufl is the description language used by the Taverna WfMS and in particular by the FreeFluo engine. Unlike JDL, Scufl allows to define several control structures which make the language more expressive. In Scufl several types of nodes exist: *processors*, *sources* and *sinks*. Sources and sinks represent respectively the input and output nodes of the process, the concept of computational node is represented by the processor. A processor can be either (and not limited to) a *local operation*, a *string constant*, a *generic Web Service invocation* or a *sub-workflow execution*. Nodes are connected via edges (or *links*) which define precedence relations and the data-flow.

Additionally, Scufl allows to model the control-flow by using the *coordination* element. Coordination constraints are used to prevent a processor transitioning between states until some constraint condition has been satisfied. An example is depicted in Figure 9 where the execution of processors `tempC` and `tempF` are respectively subordinated to the result of the `Fail_if_True` and `Fail_if_False` processors. Processors can be also decorated by several *properties* which allow to define: the *retry behaviour*, the *alternate* processor and the *iteration* strategy. The iteration strategy is one of the most powerful feature in Taverna, and it defines the implicit iteration over the incoming data sets. The complete Scufl language reference can be found in [21].

As Scufl and GWorkflowDL are XML-based the conversion is made possible by means of an *Extensible Stylesheet Language Transformations* (XSLT). We do not want to go deep into the translation process because this is a work in progress and the converter is still under development. However, we are currently able to translate simple Scufl workflows which interact with arbitrary Web Services as depicted in Figure 9. The workflow shows an example of a *conditional execution* where the input value of the source node `condition` determines the execution of the left branch – when the input value is `false` – or the right one, otherwise. The left branch performs a temperature conversion from Fahrenheit to Celsius using a Web Service, the right one the inverse operation. The result of the conversion is stored into the corresponding sink node, `tempF` or `tempC`.

The Figure 9 shows how the workflow can be converted into a Petri Net-based description which keeps the same semantics. However, the majority of Scufl workflows uses local bindings to the *Java platform* making the conversion process even more difficult.

5. Conclusions and Future Work

This paper presents an overview of the design of a WfMS developed in the context of the CoreGRID project. Interaction with multiple resources and

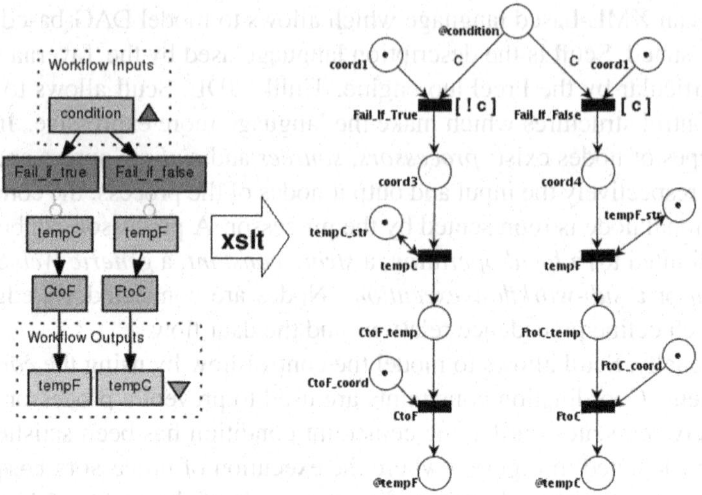

Figure 9. Conversion of a Scufl workflow (on the left) to a GWorkflowDL Petri Net-based workflow (on the right) by means of a XSL Translator

Grid infrastructures is made possible by adopting a novel design based on the micro-kernel design pattern, which makes the platform extensible by using sub-workflows. We have also investigated the language interoperability issues which are made possible by the use, and improvement, of the GWorkflowDL language. The *Turing-complete* semantics of GWorkflowDL makes the conversion from other formalisms (such as DAGs and π-calculus) possible by means of language translators.

The WfMS is nevertheless still under development and further work is needed in order to improve it and make it usable in production environments. As stated, the mapping from abstract to concrete workflow should be improved by using *ontologies* and other features – such as *planning* and *advance reservation* – should be investigated in order to make the system more compliant to the needs of scientific processes.

References

[1] On Scientific Workflow. *TCSC Newsletter, IEEE Technical Committee on Scalable Computing*, 9(1), 2007.

[2] F. Puhlmann1 and M. Weske1. Using the π-Calculus for Formalizing Workflow Patterns. *Lecture Notes in Computer Science*, pages 153-168, 2005.

[3] M. Dumas and A. H. M. ter Hofstede. UML Activity Diagrams as a Workflow Specification Language. *Lecture Notes in Computer Science*, pages 76–90, 2001.

[4] A. Hoheisel and U. Der. An XML-based framework for loosely coupled applications on grid environments. In P. Sloot, editor, *ICCS 2003*, number 2657 in Lecture Notes in Computer Science, pages 245–254. Springer-Verlag, 2003.

[5] M. Alt et al. Using High Level Petri-Nets for Describing and Analysing Hierarchical Grid Workflows. In *Proceedings of the CoreGRID Integration Workshop 2005, Pisa*, 2005.

[6] W. Aalst. Three Good reasons for Using a Petri-net-based Workflow Management System. In *Proceedings of the International Working Conference on Information and Process Integration in Enterprises (IPIC'96)*, pages 179–201, Camebridge, Massachusetts, 1996.

[7] CppWfMS, http://wfms.forge.cnaf.infn.it/

[8] Douglas Schmidt et al.: *Pattern-Oriented Software Architecture*, Siemens AG, pages 171-192, 2000.

[9] S. Pellegrini et al. A Practical Approach to a Workflow Management System. *Proceedings of the CoreGRID Workshop 2007*, Dresden, Germany, 2007

[10] Dragos A. Manolescu: *An extensible Workflow Architecture with Object and Patterns*, TOOLSEE 2001.

[11] S. Pellegrini, F. Giacomini Design of a Petri Net-Based Workflow Engine. In *Proceedings of the 3rd International Workshop on Workflow Management and Applications in Grid Environments (WaGe08)*, Kunming, China, 2008.

[12] T. Andrews et al. Business process execution language for web services version 1.1. Technical report, BEA Systems, IBM, Microsoft, SAP AG and Siebel Systems, 2003.

[13] W. M. P. van der Aalst and A. H. M. ter Hofstede. Yawl: yet another workflow language. *Inf. Syst.*, 30(4):245–275, 2005.

[14] A. Hoheisel. Grid Workflow Execution Service – Dynamic and Interactive Execution and Visualization of Distributed Workflows. In *Proceedings of the Cracow Grid Workshop 2006*, Cracow, Poland, 2007

[15] S. Pellegrini, A. Hoheisel et al. Using GWorkflowDL for Middleware-Independent Modeling and Enactment of Workflows. In *Proceedings of the CoreGRID Integration Workshop 2008, Crete*, 2008.

[16] Kurt Jensen: *An Introduction to the Theoretical Aspects of Colored Petri Nets*, Lecture Notes in Computer Science (Springer), 1994.

[17] P. Andreetto et al. Practical approaches to grid workload and resource management in the egee project. In *Proceedings of the Conference for Computing in High-Energy and Nuclear Physics (CHEP 04)*, Interlaken, Switzerland, 2004.

[18] W. van der Aalst. The application of Petri Nets to workflow management. *The Journal of Circuits, Systems and Computers*, 8(1):21–66, 1998.

[19] W. van der Aalst. Pi calculus versus petri nets: Let us eat humble pie rather than further inflate the pi hype. *unpublished discussion paper*, 2003.

[20] BioMoby, http://biomoby.org/

[21] T. Oinn. XScufl Language Reference.
http://www.ebi.ac.uk/ tmo/mygrid/XScuflSpecification.html, 2004.

[22] Condor DAGMan, http://www.cs.wisc.edu/condor/dagman/

[23] Tom Oinn et al.. Taverna: a tool for the composition and enactment of bioinformatics workflows. *Bioinformatics*, 20(17):3045–3054, June 2004.

[24] A. Hoheisel and M. Alt. Petri Nets. In I.J. Taylor, D. Gannon, E. Deelman, and M.S. Shields, editors, *Workflows for e-Science – Scientific Workflows for Grids*, Springer, 2006.

WORKFLOW MONITORING AND ANALYSIS TOOL FOR ASKALON

Simon Ostermann, Kassian Plankensteiner, Radu Prodan, Thomas Fahringer
University of Innsbruck, AT
simon@dps.uibk.ac.at
kassian@dps.uibk.ac.at
radu@dps.uibk.ac.at
tf@dps.uibk.ac.at

Alexandru Iosup
Delft University of Technology, NL
A.Iosup@tudelft.nl

Abstract Grid computing promises to enable a reliable and easy-to-use computational infrastructure for e-Science. To materialize this promise, Grids need to provide full automation from the experiment design to the final result. Often, this automation relies on the execution of workflows, that is, on jobs comprising many inter-related computing and data transfer tasks. While several Grid workflow execution tools already exist, not much details are known about their executions. Using the ASKALON Grid middleware for workflow execution, a performance evaluation of the executed workflows is done. We introduce a tool which provides online as well as offline interactive graphical visualisation of the performance of workflow executions. Analysis of logged workflow executions on the Austrian Grid with this performance tool facilitates the detection of various performance problems and of resulting improvement possibilities for the ASKALON system.

Keywords: Grid, workflow execution, monitoring, performance, analysis

1. Introduction

ASKALON is a Grid Application Development and Computing Environment. Its purpose is to simplify the development and optimization of applications that can benefit from the power of Grid computing. The ASKALON project crafts a novel environment based on new innovative tools, services, and methodologies to make Grid application development and optimization for real applications an everyday practice. ASKALON is an approach to realize an invisible Grid that can easily be used by scientists [5].

2. Motivation

Workflow execution systems are complex and in most cases are built from multiple services communicating with each other. The overall performance of such a system quickly gets unsatisfying when each of these services adds a little overhead. A fine grained middleware service analysis is required to find these overheads of the system. To get the best possible execution results and speedup values compared to serial or cluster computing, the knowledge and elimination of system bottlenecks is crucial. But the identification process for these bottlenecks cannot be done automatically with state of the art systems as the complexity of Grid executions is too high. The most currently available systems are designed to analyze and visualize the physical resources of a Grid, which are also vital for gaining best possible results. Even with knowledge of the external states no middleware can guarantee or prove that the system works efficiently under all circumstances as external situation can always disturb theoretical plans and calculated behaviors. Feature lists of most state of the art execution engines are impressive but only a detailed analysis can show if they really hold their promises.

The developers of ASKALON were facing similar problems with their workflow execution environment. The performance of the system was in most cases satisfying but the problems in the exceptional runs were hard to identify. There was a need for a detailed analysis of the execution process to identify the different overheads that arise under special circumstances. Only known overheads can be taken into account by the developers optimizations which led to the development of the monitoring tool, called Perftool, that is capable of giving a fine grain overview of workflow executions. The logging mechanism of execution states needed to be extended to collect the relevant information for later analysis.

To analyze the internals of the ASKALON workflow execution, the Perftool was used to identify chronological problems in the execution. This allowed the identification of crucial design flaws and incremental improvement of the overall system by giving the system developers feedback about the weak points of their components. This analysis technique, combined with different execution scenarios, can show if a system can hold the promises it made. Added functionality for creation of execution logs in an open standard format [13] allows comparisons with competitors.

There are several workflow execution systems for the Grid [11] currently available but there is no neutral comparison of the execution efficiency of the different systems. A comparable execution logging format needs to be supported to allow such a comparison. In Section 6 we present an open format supported by ASKALON.

3. Background

Workflow execution is the process of dealing with the runtime jobs in the environments, and handling the fault tolerance and runtime optimization. The *Execution Engine* is a service responsible for distributing the jobs to different Grid resources and builds the main interface between the abstract workflows description in AGWL [9]and their real execution.

ASKALON uses a *Distributed workflow Execution Engine* (DEE) [3]. The executor uses the scheduler and resource manager to decide where jobs will be executed. DEE is the main entry point of the ASKALON services in the case of execution of workflows on the Grid. Different workflow optimizations have been proposed and presented in different publications [4]. DEE is also responsible for collecting the timestamps of the execution and the storage of this information to a database. Detailed analysis of this collected data with the tool presented in this work resulted in the decision of a redesign and new implementation of the execution system.

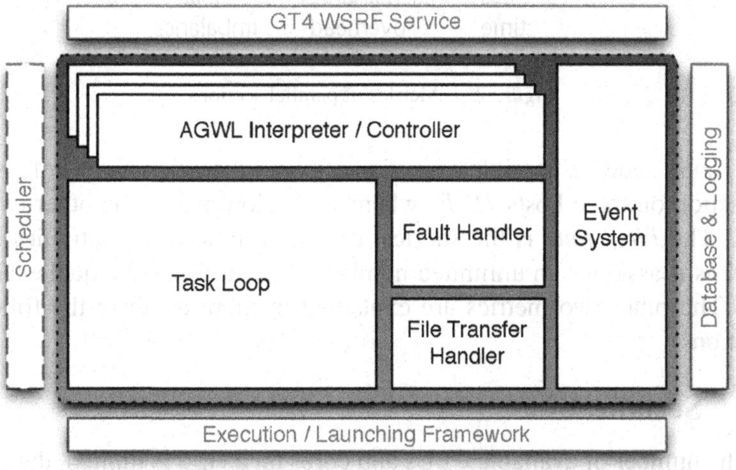

Figure 1. Execution engine 2 architecture

The new execution engine system (EE2) [7] which is currently work in progress, uses an event based approach for best possible scalability. The DEE systems performance was worst when executing massive parallel workflows. The logging to the database was a time-limiting factor and throttled the whole execution process. EE2 avoids such bottlenecks by using separate threads for each tasks with different priorities. This results in a possible delay in the transfer of messages to the database which only delays the realtime monitoring but improves performance in critical regions dramatically. Figure 1 shows the architecture of the new engine where all parts are connected via event queues and work in separate threads.

This design allows to add multiple instances of each component to improve the scalability and add parallelism. Future performance tests will show which components will benefit from additional instances.

4. Methods

For analysis of parallel sections we take the most common metrics into account (see Figure 2). We split up the workflow into parallel sections as defined by the AGWL language and analyze these sections with the defined metric.

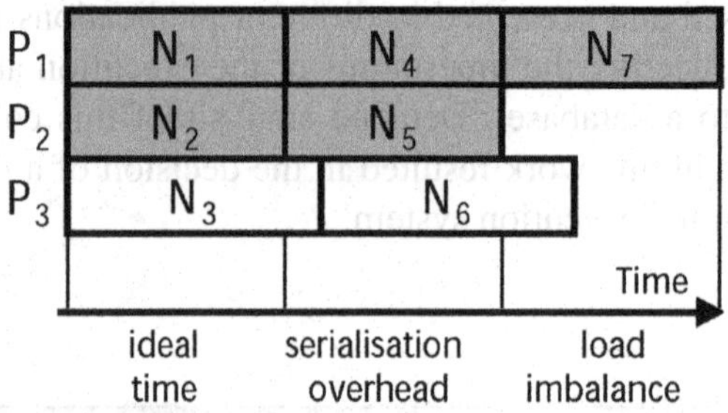

Figure 2. Metrics of parallel sections

The figure shows a possible execution of seven activities N_1-N_7 of one parallel section on three hosts P_1-P_3 where P_3 is slower than the other two machines. The *ideal time* is the shortest execution time of all activities run in parallel as it assumes an unlimited number of resources with equal execution times. The other two metrics are explained in more detail in the following subsections.

4.1 Serialization

As the number of available CPUs and cores on a Grid is limited, the chosen parallelism factor of a workflow execution may be too high. At runtime, this will result in jobs being queued in the clusters local queueing system or in the middleware internal queue as in the case of ASKALON. This lost parallelism can be identified as a serialization overhead. Tasks that could be run in parallel can only be executed sequentially. Identification of such behavior is difficult from execution logs as a delayed start may have resulted from job-submission or other overheads. The defined indicator for serialization for a parallel section is (PS = ParallelSection, Active_n =Timestamp for the activity n when it changed to active, Complete_n = Timestamp for the activity n when its state changed to completed):

$$\max_{\forall n \in PS} \text{Active}_n > \min_{\forall n \in PS} \text{Complete}_n$$

If any job starts after one of the other parallel jobs of a section has finished a serialization occurred in this parallel section. This overhead can easily be removed by adding more free resources to the Grid. This metric is a useful indicator of potential better speedup if the Grid gets extended or more resources become available.

4.2 Imbalance

When executing activities of the same type in a parallel section of a workflow in parallel, the executions on the different resources does not take the exact same time to complete. This may be a result of:

- external load
- different binary files or libraries on different resources
- different speed or architecture of resources
- activities with different amount of computation work

External load typically occurs when someone else uses the fork job-+manager or directly logs into an execution node of a Grid-site and executes applications there. This can only be avoided if the cluster administrator disables such behaviors of the cluster and forces everyone to use a fair job-manager. This case is not controllable from the point of view of the user.

Even different compiler settings or libraries can influence the runtime of an application dramatically. The scheduler service is aware of different host-speeds and can choose the fastest sites for execution as long as free CPUs are available on that resource. If the Grid does not offer enough free CPUs, the execution has a serialization overhead. The scheduler has the job to select hosts which will result in executions with the shortest possible runtime. If the execution tasks themselves have different amount of work the scheduler has a more challenging job distributing them over the free resources. This decision making will require additional information from the prediction service. This service tries to predict the estimated runtime of an application on a given host and takes the input parameters into account. This is a very difficult task for the predictor. Even simple problems like rendering a movie may take different amounts of work per frame and this will not be predictable without having rendered the whole movie once before or developing some own rendering engine. Normally a movie is only rendered once and therefore such precise predictions cannot be done.

These problems result in an imbalance factor of a parallel section execution (B_n = time when the activity n started execution and E_n = completion time of the activity n):

$$\text{Imbalance}_{PS} = \max_{\forall n \in PS} \text{E}_n - \min_{\forall n \in PS} \text{E}_n$$

In case of a serialization overhead a different formula has to be used to approximate which end timestamp is taken as the minimum end-time (so that serialization and imbalance can be distinguished):

$$\text{ImbalanceSer}_{PS} = \max_{\forall n \in PS} E_n - \min_{\forall n \in PS} (E_n | E_n > \max_{\forall n \in PS} B_n)$$

This overhead indicates how long the workflow execution had to wait for the slowest branch of a parallel section. An improvement of the scheduling and prediction services is required to minimize this overhead. Splitting the parallel tasks into smaller pieces may reduce this overhead as well. Serialization of smaller work-portions may result in less imbalance and better resource utilization. But this will increase the amount of job-submission and the overheads produced by these transmissions.

5. Implementation

The performance monitoring tool (Perftool) [10] architecture is shown in Figure 3 and is implemented in Java^{TM}. The database logging part of the enactment engine writes the information into a database on a PostrgreSQL server where a client, developed for direct connection with a database server (fat client), can gather this information to analyze and visualize it. A thin client plus server architecture can be added by encapsulating the *DataConnection* layer in a service running on the database host using RPC if the database is not accessible from the outside.

The logging part is embedded in the execution engine. In case of the DEE, the logging is completely integrated in the engine code. The EE2 decouples the logging into an event listening component which can be plugged into the event-system inside of the Java code and is included there by default.

The architecture includes a well documented API to simplify extensions of the tool for additional data sources. The connection to the external service that

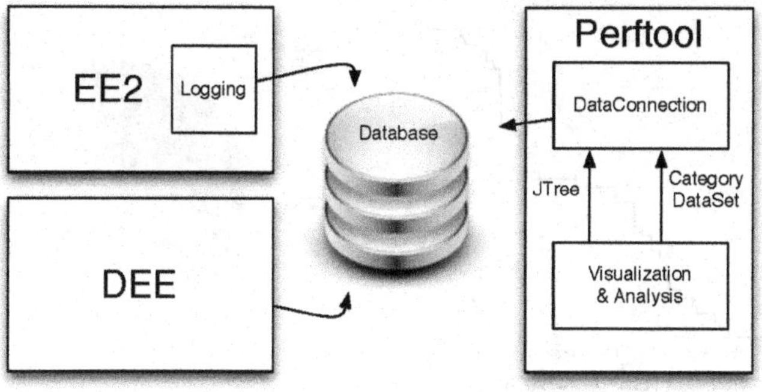

Figure 3. Performance monitoring tool architecture

provides workflow information is not limited to a database and may connect directly to an event-system or similar components

The presented tool for monitoring of workflow execution can be used for a realtime or post mortem analysis. Especially the analysis of past executions is useful to track and improve the development of a complex execution environment like ASKALON. Figure 4 shows a snapshot of the tool showing a finished WIEN2K [1] workflow execution.

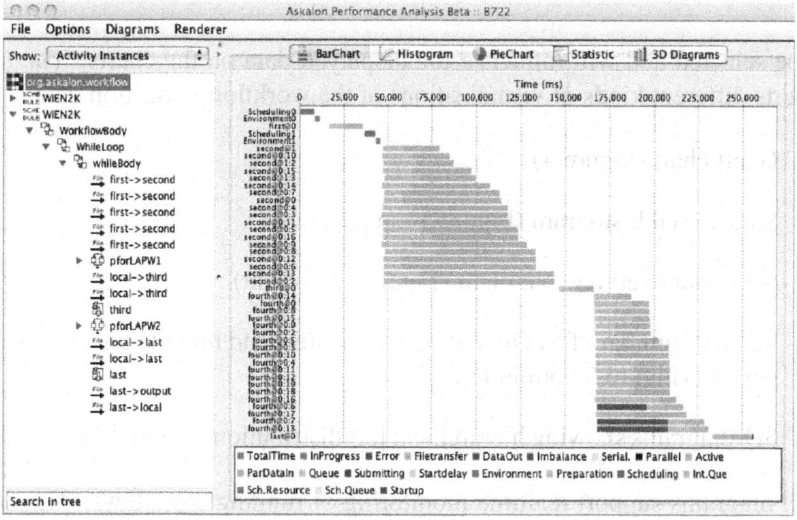

Figure 4. Perftool displaying a WIEN2K workflow run

On the left side, a tree representation of the workflow is shown; the displayed workflow area can be modified. Multiple parts of the workflow (tree)

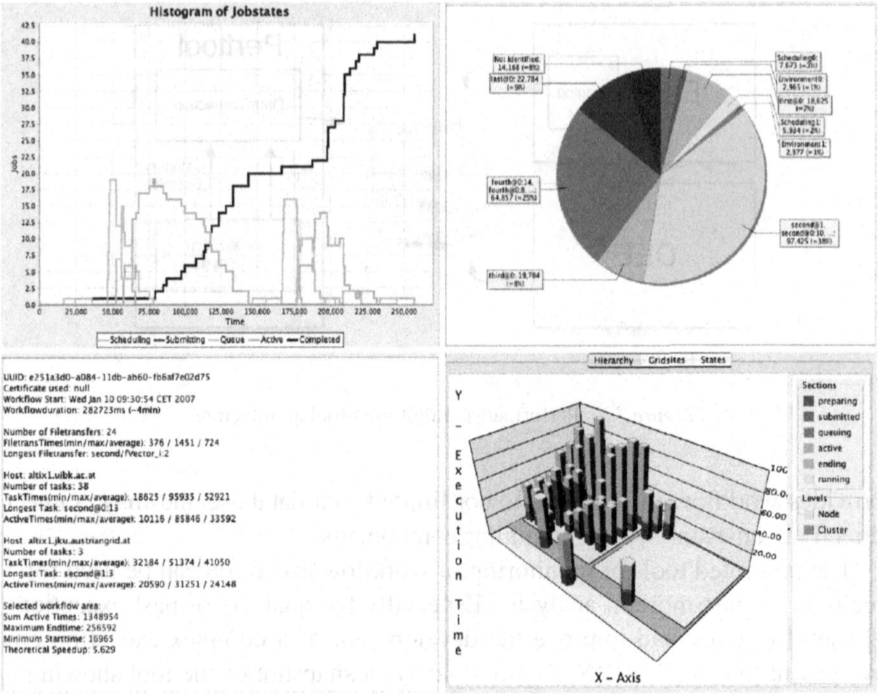

Figure 5. Four possible visualizations of a workflow execution in Perftool

can be selected and will influence the displayed data on the charts. The tool supports different kinds of visualizations of the workflow execution data:

- Gantt chart (Figure 4)
- State based histogram (Figure 5 top left)
- Sectional overview pie-chart (Figure 5 top right)
- Textual summary form including filetransfers and min/max/average times per site (Figure 5 bottom left)
- 3D-diagrams showing hierarchical job-distribution (Figure 5 bottom right)

All diagrams support realtime monitoring of running workflows. The only compromise that has to be taken with the EE2 logging mechanism is the possible delay of database updates as the events that are critical for the execution of the workflow are handled first. Execution of a workflow is still the highest priority of ASKALON and therefore logging is not allowed to reduce the performance of the overall system more than absolutely necessary.

6. Comparability

The architecture presented in this work stores the workflow execution timestamps in a database to allow post mortem analysis, statistical observations or exporting to a file. We have chosen the Grid Workload Format (GWF) from the Grid Workloads Archive [12]. The format is open and has a rich set of supported values where we only deliver the workflow execution related ones as our system does not store monitoring data about the physical resources. The workflow structure can be stored using a DAG-construct by specifying the previous and next tasks for each task of the workflow.

7. Results

The monitoring system described in this work can be used to visualize over 10.000 workflows executed in the past as shown in Table 1 and will be used for realtime monitoring of future executions done with ASKALON. The rather

Engine	*Workflow executions*	*Completed*	*Failed*
DEE	9748	3988 (41%)	5760 (59%)
EE2	1437	991 (69%)	446 (31%)
Sum	11185	4979 (45%)	6206 (55%)

Table 1. Overview of workflow runs done using ASKALON

high amount of failed workflows can be explained by the high amount of workflow executions solely done to find bugs and test the behavior of the environment. These were intended to fail by definition.

The metrics presented in Section 4 are supported by the visualization mode that represents the workflow regions only where parallel regions are combined to a single bar in the chart as shown in Figure 6.

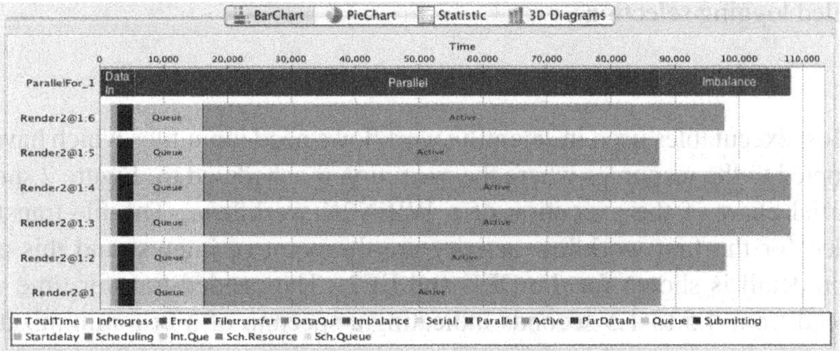

Figure 6. Parallel section view: the first bar in the chart represents a accumulation of all the bars contained in this section

In the next sections we want to present some specific problems that we were able to identify by usage of this novel way of workflow execution monitoring.

7.1 Logging level

An important factor for the achievable performance and the middleware overheads is the logging level setting. In the case of ASKALON and Globus the framework log4j [8] is used. If debug output of the WSRF services is enabled during execution, the times spent on the different stages of execution are affected as well. Table 2 shows the times of the first activity execution in a workflow run with different log levels. The logging messages were printed to an open console for these runs. The first activity needs the longest time as resource information has to be fetched from the resource manager via WSRF-calls. Especially there the massive logging output slows down the execution process as shown in Table 2. First the resources where an activity can possibly be executed on have to be collected. This resource request time is highly dependent on the debugging level. The engine has to decide on which of the possible resources the task will be executed, which is done without invocation of external services and therefore less dependent on the log level. Once the resource for execution is chosen, some initial tasks have to be done. A working directory has to be created and files have to be copied to the resource. The used COG-kit is also very sensible to the logging level and is throttled by a too detailed logging selection.

Engine	*Logging level*	*Resourcerequest*	*Scheduling*	*Start – del.*
EE2	FATAL	$0.8 sec$	3.0sec	$1.5 sec$
EE2	INFO	$0.9 sec$	3.0sec	$1.5 sec$
EE2	DEBUG	$16.7 sec$	4.1sec	$15.0 sec$

Table 2. Execution times affected by logging-levels

7.2 Filetransfers

Most executables used in scientific workflows need input files which have to be copied to the resources where the execution is scheduled to. Figure 7 shows a partial chart of the execution of a WIEN2K workflow. The file-transfers needed for the first workflow activity are the point of interest and this execution detail is shown for the DEE and EE2. The needed transfer time was reduced from 4.5 to 1.5 seconds indicating a speedup of 3 or a minimization of the transfer overhead by 66%. The sequential execution of these five file-transfers from the old DEE is far away from an optimal solution and can be improved by parallelization. The new EE2 system uses parallel file-transfers

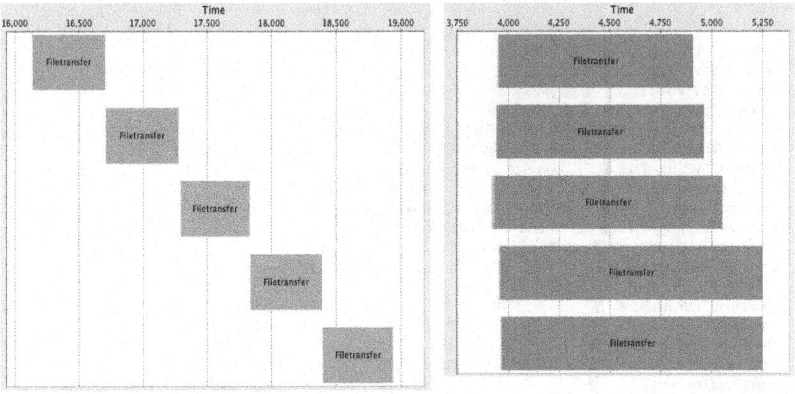

Figure 7. File-transfers for the start of a WIEN2K workflow (*left*) DEE. (*right*) EE2.

and is able to transmit the same files in a shorter overall time. The limiting factor for the parallelism of these file-transfers is the server connection limit and stability. GridFTP is able to maximize the used bandwidth for transfers by using multiple connections per transfer but in cases like ours with multiple small files, multiple logins to the server are needed. Some sites can handle multiple of these connections without any problems, while others give a "`the GridFTP server has gone away`"-error message when opening more than five concurrent connections at a time. Therefore, the newly developed engine has a limit of five parallel file transfers per GridFTP server which should generally be enough to use the available bandwidth and avoid flooding of the server.

7.3 Job submissions

One of the important time-consuming parts of executions on the Grid where ASKALON aims to be faster than other systems is the job-submission. An application cannot be started directly on the Grid. A job-description is sent to the local queueing system of a Grid-site that will start the job if it has free resources. The connection to the queueing system, the job-description transmission, and the systems response takes some time. When trying to start hundreds or thousands of jobs concurrently, as common for workflows with massive parallel sections, the job-submission time may become a critical overhead for the overall execution performance. The jobs have to be submitted in parallel to minimize the time taken for this submission process. The queueing systems of a Grid-site cannot handle unlimited connections simultaneously. In some cases on the Austrian Grid, the system already begins to struggle when more than 5 connections are open for job submission at a time. Analysis of executions with the provided tool helped to identify these limits in parallelism.

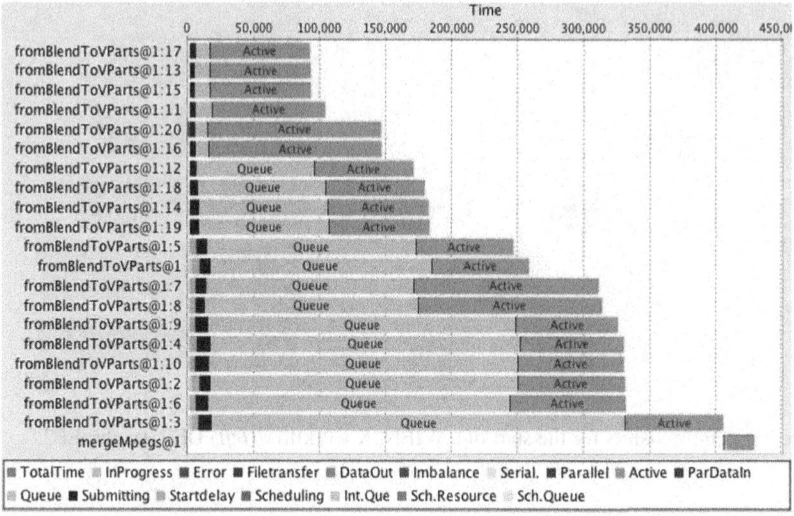

Figure 8. Workflow execution with a job-submission rate that is too high

When submitting jobs to resources it can happen that there are less CPUs/cores available then previously reported because resource information is always from a state that may have changed while the information was forwarded and processed. Figure 8 shows a trace where the number of reported free CPUs was incorrect and the local scheduler was not able to start all jobs as the number of job-submissions was too high.

8. Related Work

There are other systems that can be used for monitoring and analysis of workflow executions on the Grid. The biggest disadvantages of most systems are their quite extensive architecture and complexity. No easily usable solution was found that could be integrated into ASKALON.

SCALEA-G [2] tries to develop a system that provides facilities for conducting performance instrumentation, monitoring and analysis of Grid services. Grid services can be computational resources (e.g. host), networks and applications. Currently, SCALEA-G has been extended to cover also non-functional parameters (e.g., QoS metrics). The system uses a sensor network that can be installed on a Grid and can be used to gather all possible information. The execution monitoring is based on XML-streams and was included in an earlier version of ASKALON but rarely used cause of its complex usage that required sensor networks to be deployed and kept in a running state. It has no built in possibility to analyze past workflows as information is not stored. The system is event based but no logging component is available at this point in time.

The Mercury Monitor [6] is designed to satisfy requirements of Grid performance monitoring: it provides monitoring data represented as metrics via both pull and push access semantics and also supports steering by controls. Mercury supports monitoring of Grid entities such as resources and applications in a generic, extensible and scalable way. Mercury is implemented in a modular way with emphasis on simplicity, efficiency, portability and low intrusiveness on the monitored system. This system is not developed in Java and cannot be easily integrated into ASKALON without the loss off operating system- and library independency. The main concept of Mercury is promising but too complex for workflow execution analysis.

Additional monitoring of the Grid could be done with Mercury or SCALEA-G to store states of the physical resources to extend the analysis by external parameters.

9. Future Work

The current visualization in the Perftool does only take into account workflow specific execution data. To get a better understanding for the execution behavior, additional Grid resource related information could be added to the visualization. Knowledge about external load and availability of free CPUs helps to understand scheduling decisions and possible reasons for load imbalance.

The chosen graphical representation can be improved by features supporting better scalability for big workflows and extended by additional features to visualize the different metrics in a broader spectrum.

In addition to the current data sources using database storage, a direct connection to the event system of the execution engine would be possible.

10. Conclusion

Execution of workflows on the Grid is still a challenging task. An easy to use graphical monitoring tool like the presented Perftool helps to find out if the execution runs as expected and, if not, to find the bottlenecks of an execution system like ASKALON. The integration of this tool and the logging of the workflow execution is a important step for future developments.

The end user of the system does also gain a benefit from using this additional feature as execution monitoring cannot be made easier than by total integration into a system.

The system architecture allows to add additional data-sources by well defined interfaces and therefore other workflow execution frameworks can extend this tool to visualize their workflow executions as well.

Acknowledgements

This work is supported by the European Union through IST-004265 and IST-2002-004265 CoreGrid and partially carried out in the context of Virtual Laboratory for e-Science project (www.vl-e.nl), supported by a BSIK grant from the Dutch Ministry of Education, Culture and Science, and which is part of the ICT innovation program Affairs. This work is co-funded by the European Commission through the EGEE-II project INFSO-RI-031688.

References

[1] P. Blaha, K. Schwarz, and J. Luitz. WIEN2k, a full potential linearized augmented plane wave package for calculating crystal properties. Austria 1999. ISBN 3-9501031-1-2.

[2] Hong-Linh Truong and Thomas Fahringer. SCALEA-G: A Unified Monitoring and Performance Analysis System for the Grid. *Scientific Programming*, 12(4):225–237, 2004.

[3] Rubing Duan, Radu Prodan, and Thomas Fahringer. Dee: A distributed fault tolerant workflow enactment engine for Grid computing. In *HPCC*, volume 3726 of *LNCS*, pages 704–716. Springer-Verlag, 2005.

[4] Rubing Duan, Radu Prodan, and Thomas Fahringer. Run-time Optimization for Grid Workflow Applications. In *Proceedings of 7th IEEE/ACM International Conference on Grid Computing (Grid'06)*, Barcelona, Spain, 2006. IEEE Computer Society Press.

[5] T. Fahringer, A. Jugravu, S. Pllana, R. Prodan, C. S. Jr., and H. L. Truong. ASKALON: a tool set for cluster and Grid computing. *CP&E*, 17(2-4):143–169, 2005.

[6] Norbert Podhorszki, Zoltán Balaton, and Gabor Gombás. Monitoring Message-Passing Parallel Applications in the Grid with GRM and Mercury Monitor. In *European Across Grids Conference*, pages 179–181, 2004.

[7] Kassian Plankensteiner. EE2: A scalable execution engine for scientific Grid workflows. U.Innsbruck, Master Thesis, 2008.

[8] Apache log4j. Website. accessed on 2/2008, `http://logging.apache.org/log4j/`.

[9] Thomas Fahringer, Jun Qin and Stefan Hainzer Specification of Grid Workflow Applications with AGWL: An Abstract Grid Workflow Language In *Proceedings of IEEE International Symposium on Cluster Computing and the Grid 2005*.

[10] Simon Ostermann. Performance analysis of workflows in ASKALON. U.Innsbruck, Master Thesis, 2008.

[11] Jia Yu and Rajkumar Buyya. A taxonomy of scientific workflow systems for Grid computing. *ACM SIGMOD Rec.*, 34(3):44–49, 2005.

[12] The Grid Workloads Archive. Website. accessed on 03/2008, `http://gwa.ewi.tudelft.nl/pmwiki/`.

[13] A.Iosup, H. Li, C. Dumitrescu, L. Wolters, D.H.J.Epema The Grid Workload Format. `http://gwa.ewi.tudelft.nl/TheGridWorkloadFormat_v001.pdf`.

USING THE GLITE MIDDLEWARE TO IMPLEMENT A SECURE INTENSIVE CARE GRID SYSTEM

Jesus Luna*, Marios D. Dikaiakos, Harald Gjermundrod
Department of Computer Science. University of Cyprus. PO Box 1678. Nicosia, Cyprus
jluna@cs.ucy.ac.cy
mdd@cs.ucy.ac.cy
harald@cs.ucy.ac.cy

Michail Flouris†, Manolis Marazakis, Angelos Bilas‡
Institute of Computer Science (ICS). Foundation for Research and Technology - Hellas (FORTH) PO Box 1385. GR-71110. Heraklion, Greece.
flouris@ics.forth.gr
maraz@ics.forth.gr
bilas@ics.forth.gr

Abstract Storage capabilities in novel "Health Grids" are quite suitable for the requirements of systems like ICGrid, which captures, stores and manages data and metadata from Intensive Care Units. However, this paradigm depends on widely distributed storage sites, therefore requiring new security mechanisms, able to avoid potential leaks to cope with modification and destruction of stored data under the presence of external or internal attacks. Particular emphasis must be put on the patient's personal data, the protection of which is required by legislations in many countries of the European Union and the world in general.

In a previous paper we performed a security analysis of ICGrid, from the point of view of metadata and data, where we found the need to protect the data-at-rest from untrusted Storage Elements (SE). That research also proposed a privacy protocol to protect a patients' private metadata and data.

This paper is the follow-up of our previous research, proposing an architecture based on gLite middleware's components, to deploy the contributed privacy protocol. As a proof of concept we show how to implement a Mandatory Access

*This work was carried out for the CoreGRID IST project n°004265, funded by the European Commission.
†Also with the Dept. of Computer Science, University of Toronto, Toronto, Ontario M5S 3G4, Canada.
‡Also with the Dept. of Computer Science, University of Crete, P.O. Box 2208, Heraklion, GR 71409, Greece.

Control model for the metadata stored into the AMGA service. To protect the data itself, this paper presents our first experimental results on the performance that can be achieved with a prototyped "cryptographic" Storage Resource Manager -CryptoSRM- service. Obtained results show that encrypting and decrypting at the CryptoSRM, instead of doing these at the SE or even at the Grid client, not only improve overall security, but also exhibit a higher performance that can be further improved with the aid of specialized hardware accelerators.

Keywords: Cryptography, gLite, Intensive Care Grid, privacy, security.

1. Introduction

Modern eHealth systems require advanced computing and storage capabilities, leading to the adoption of technologies like the Grid and giving birth to novel *Health Grid* systems. In particular, Intensive Care Medicine uses this paradigm when facing a high flow of data coming from Intensive Care Unit's (ICU) inpatients. These data needs to be stored, so for example data-mining techniques could be used afterwards to find helpful correlations for the practitioners facing similar problems. Unfortunately, moving an ICU patient's data from the *traditionally isolated* hospital's computing facilities to Data Grids via public networks (i.e. the Internet) makes it imperative to establish an integral and standardized security solution, harmonized with current eHealth Legislations, and able to avoid common attacks on the data and metadata being managed.

In our previous research related with the security analysis of Grid Storage Systems [19] we concluded that current technological mechanisms were not providing comprehensive privacy solutions and worst of all, several security gaps at the Storage Elements were found to be open. In an effort to cover these security gaps, the second part of our research [20] contributed with a *low-level* protocol for providing privacy to current Intensive Care Grid systems from a data-centric point of view, but taking into account the legal framework and keeping compliance with *high-level* mechanisms (i.e. the Electronic Health Card [22]). The contributed protocol proposed the use of a cryptographic mechanism, co-located with the the Storage Resource Manager (SRM [24]), to enhance a patient's data confidentiality. A second mechanism based on data-fragmentation was also proposed by our research to benefit data's assurance and overall performance. The latter mechanism has been investigated in [18].

Due to performance concerns, this paper presents an architecture for implementing the cryptographic mechanisms of the proposed privacy protocol, using components from the gLite middleware [7], and applying it to the ICGrid [15] system's data. As a proof of concept we present our first results on "the cost of security", that is, a performance comparison among a commonly used security approach (data encryption and decryption at the Grid client) and the proposed privacy protocol (data encryption and decryption at a central *cryptoSRM*). Also this paper contributes with a proposal for protecting ICGrid's metadata via a Mandatory Access Control model in AMGA [26], to enforce different levels of authorization to the patient's personal information, thus fulfilling current eHealth Legislations.

The rest of this paper is organized as follows: Section 2 reviews the basic terminology related with the ICGrid system, along with the privacy issues that appear in the eHealth context. Section 3 describes a gLite-based middleware architecture required to implement the proposed privacy protocol for ICGrid. Our first experimental results on the cryptographic performance achieved by our proposal are shown in Section 4. Section 5 briefly presents the State of the Art related with our research. Finally, Section 6 presents our conclusions and future work.

2. The ICGrid system

In this Section we present the required data and security background of the ICGrid system studied in this paper.

2.1 Data and metadata architecture

Although a number of dedicated and commercially available information systems have been proposed for use in Intensive Care Units (ICUs) [13], which support real-time data acquisition, data validation and storage, analysis of data, reporting and charting of the findings, none of these systems was appropriate in our application context. Another important issue with ICU is the need for data storage: an estimate of the amount of data that would be generated daily is given in the following scenario. Suppose that each sensor is acquiring data for storage and processing at a rate of 50 bytes per second (it is stored as text) and that there are 100 hospitals with 10 beds each, where each bed has 100 sensors. Assuming that each bed is used for 2 hours per day, the data collected amounts to 33.5275 GB per day. But this number only represents the data from the sensors. Additional information includes metadata, images, etc. Because Grids represented a promising venue for addressing the challenges described above, the Intensive Care Grid (ICGrid) system [15] has been prototyped over the EGEE infrastructure (Enabling Grids for E-sciencE [1]). ICGrid is based on a hybrid architecture that combines a heterogeneous set of monitors that sense the inpatients and three Grid-enabled software tools that support the storage, processing and information sharing tasks.

The diagram of Figure 1 represents a Virtual Organization of the ICGrid system, which depicts the acquisition and annotation of parameters of an in-patient at an ICU Site (bottom left) and the transfer of data replicas to two *Storage Elements (SEs)*. The transfer comprises the actual sensor data, denoted as *Data*, and the information which is provided by physicians during the annotation phase, denoted as *Metadata*. We utilize the notion of a *Clinically Interesting Episode (CIE)* to refer to the captured sensor data along with the metadata that is added by the physician to annotate all the events of interest.

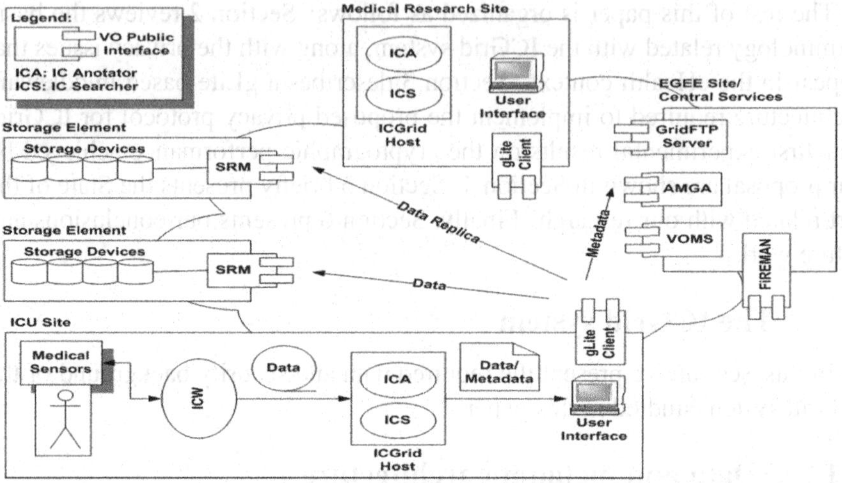

Figure 1. Architecture of an ICGrid's Virtual Organization.

When ICGrid's Data and Metadata are transferred to Storage Elements and Metadata servers (currently a gLite Metadata Catalogue -AMGA- service [26]) respectively, a set of messages are exchanged among the different entities. In particular we should highlight that file catalog services are being provided by FiReMAN (File Replication MAnager [12]) and, authorization mechanisms rely on the X.509 credentials issued by the Virtual Organization Membership Service (VOMS [9]).

2.2 Security and privacy issues

The deployment of production-level Health Grids, such as the ICGrid, should provide assurances of the patient's data, in particular when referring to personal information, which is currently the subject of increasing concerns in most legislations in the European Union [23]. Unfortunately, when personal data is being transferred from the Hospital to the Grid new vulnerabilities may appear: on the wire, at-rest, within the metadata servers, etc. A major concern in Health Grids is the adequate confidentiality of the individual records being managed electronically, which are usually stored as metadata. In the European Union, the patient's personal data is protected through the concept of *consent*, which can be interpreted as the freely given decision of the patient -or authorized party- to proceed with the processing of his personal data. Taking into consideration the legal framework and as a first step in proposing a privacy mechanism for the ICGrid, a previous paper [20] performed a security analysis of ICGrid's data and metadata by applying a framework previously extended and used in Grid storage services [19]. The results of the analysis have shown the need to protect the system from *untrusted Storage Elements*, which have full control over the stored information, thus allowing its leak, destruction of change due to successful external or even internal attacks. It is also worth highlighting that the mentioned analysis took into consideration the use of commonly deployed security mechanisms, namely the Grid Security Infrastructure [29] and the novel Electronic Health Card [22].

Based on the ICGrid's security analysis, the research presented in [20] also introduced a privacy protocol able to provide a well differentiated protection to the patient's data and metadata. The contributed protocol proposed the use of the gLite middleware [7] not only to provide data confidentiality, but also integrity, high availability and a privacy mechanism for the metadata, keeping compliance with the legal and technological aspects widely discussed in [10].

3. Secure ICGrid: protecting Metadata and Data

In this section we will present the main components of an architecture proposed to provide security to the ICGrid system introduced in Section 2. The specific goal of our proposal is to avoid data and metadata attacks (leakage, change or destruction) while at-rest into the untrusted Storage Elements. It is worth noticing that performance issues related with the cryptographic mechanism have been carefully considered in our design (more about this in Section 4). Because our previous security analysis [20] found that ICGrid's metadata and data require different security policies, the enforcement mechanisms presented in this section implement a differentiated approach for metadata (Section 3.2) and data (Section 3.3).

3.1 Architecture

Based on ICGrid's current architecture (figure 1), our proposal contributes with the following *Privacy Services*, co-located with the Central Services (scoped at the Virtual Organization level) and interacting directly with the GridFTP Server [14] and AMGA:

- CryptoSRM: This component is a modified Storage Resource Manager that apart from implementing the interface defined in [24], uses a cryptographic engine for encrypting and decrypting staged data stored in its local cache.
- Hydra Key Store: Implements a secure repository for the encryption keys [3]. The repository itself uses a fragmentation algorithm [25] for

providing confidentiality and high-availability to the cryptographic material.

- Secure Log: A secure logging service may help to back-trace potential abuses (even those performed by Grid administrators colluded with attackers).

3.2 Metadata Security

AMGA stores metadata in a hierarchical structure that resembles a Unix File System, and also its native authorization model is based on Access Control Lists [5] with POSIX-like permissions per-entry and directory (*r*=read, *w*=write and *x*=change into directory) and, an additional "admin flag" allowing users in a group to administer the ACLs of an entry. Using the latter mechanism, we have defined an authorization model for ICGrid's metadata based on the Bell-LaPadula Model's Mandatory Access Control (MAC) rules [11]:

1 The *Simple Security Property* states that a subject at a given security level may not read an object at a higher security level (no read-up).

2 The **-Property* (read star-property) states that a subject at a given security level must not write to any object at a lower security level (no write-down) and, may only append new data to any object at a higher security level.

Bell-Lapadula's Model applied to ICGrid's metadata (implemented over AMGA) can be seen in figure 2. The proposed MAC model is able to provide a basic level of confidentiality to the patient's private metadata, while at the same time "protecting" him from accidentally disclosing this information to the lower-security levels. In this example we have defined three different players (Patient -owner-, Paramedics -group- and the Intentive Care Unit Receptionist -others-) and also, three levels of authorization (Public, Semi-Private and Private). With the proposed AMGA's permissions on directories and entries it is possible to achieve the following Mandatory Access Control:

- Public Metadata: both Patient and Paramedics can read the entries, but only the ICU Receptionist can read and write them (i.e. schedule a new appointment with the physician).

- Semi-Private Metadata: the Paramedics can read and write entries (i.e. emergency information), the ICU Receptionist can only append new ones (the Paramedics group requires the admin flag to set read-only permissions to these newly created entries) and, the Patient is only able to read this metadata.

- Private Metadata: This is the most confidential level of the metadata, therefore only the Patient has full control over it (administrative permissions are implicit since he is the owner of his directories), while Paramedics and ICU Receptionists only can append new entries (the Patient must manage permissions of these newly created entries).

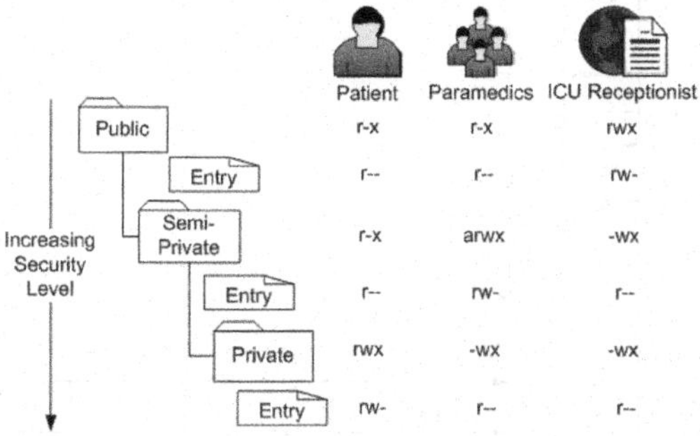

Figure 2. Mandatory Access Control model for ICGrid's Metadata.

Enforcing the *-Property's append-only mode conveys an administrative overhead for both, Patients and Paramedics, which must manage permissions for entries being created by lower-security subjects. Also it is worth to notice that native AMGA's authorization mechanism can not prevent a malicious System Administrator from accessing the metadata of all the stored patients. To cope with these issues, our future work considers the use of cryptographic techniques to provide greater confidentiality and even a consent-like mechanism (based on electronic signatures) to AMGA's metadata. This research will be briefly introduced in Section 6.

3.3 Data Security

Using the Privacy Services discussed in Section 3.1 it is possible to improve overall security and privacy using cryptography. Figure 3 shows how the different Privacy Services interact with the Central Services when an IC Annotator (ICA) stores data into the ICGrid system. In this figure we use the file naming notation from [16], when referring to the data being managed by the Grid: *(i)* Logical File Name -LFN- (a human readable identifier for a file), *(ii)* Global Unique Identifer -GUID- (a logical identifier which guarantees its uniqueness by construction) and, *(iii)* Site URL -SURL- (specifies a physical instance of a file replica, which is accepted by the Storage Element's SRM interface).

The core of our proposal is the CryptoSRM, which is responsible for symmetrically encrypting the staged data, previously transferred via a *secure channel* by the ICA's GridFTP client. Afterwards the encryption key is securely stored in the Hydra service and the encrypted data moved to the untrusted Storage Element. It is obvious that attackers colluded with the latter will be unable to recover the original clear-text. A second scenario (Figure 4) considers an IC

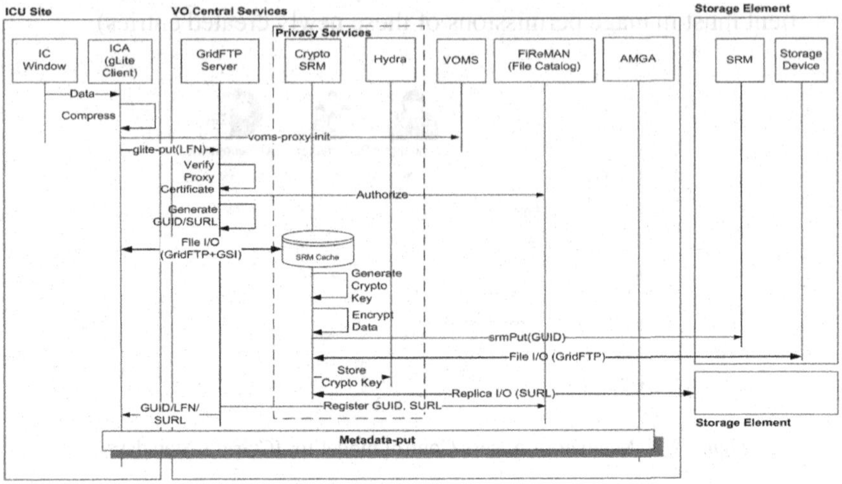

Figure 3. Secure ICGrid: transferring data.

Searcher (ICS) retrieving data from the ICGrid: in this case the encrypted data is transferred from the Storage Element, decrypted at the CryptoSRM (the appropriate key is obtained from Hydra) and conveyed through a secure channel to the ICS' GridFTP client. *Notice that the encryption key is never disclosed to the ICS, therefore avoiding its leak by potential attackers (i.e. reading the DRAM like in [6]).* A more comprehensive analysis of the performance issues related with our proposal is presented in the next section.

4. Experimental Results

We have setup the following testbed to measure the expected performance to be achieved with the protocol proposed in Section 3.3:

- Grid client (GC): this CentOS4-based node has been configured as a "gLite User Interface". It is an IBM xSeries 335, with two Intel Xeon HT processors @ 2.8GHz and 2GB of RAM.
- Storage Element (SE): To simulate the basic functionalities of the proposed CryptoSRM, we have used for the tests a "DPM_mysql Storage Element" running over Scientific Linux version 3.09. The SE uses a Dell PowerEdge1400, with two Intel Pentium III processors @ 800MHz and 784MB of RAM.

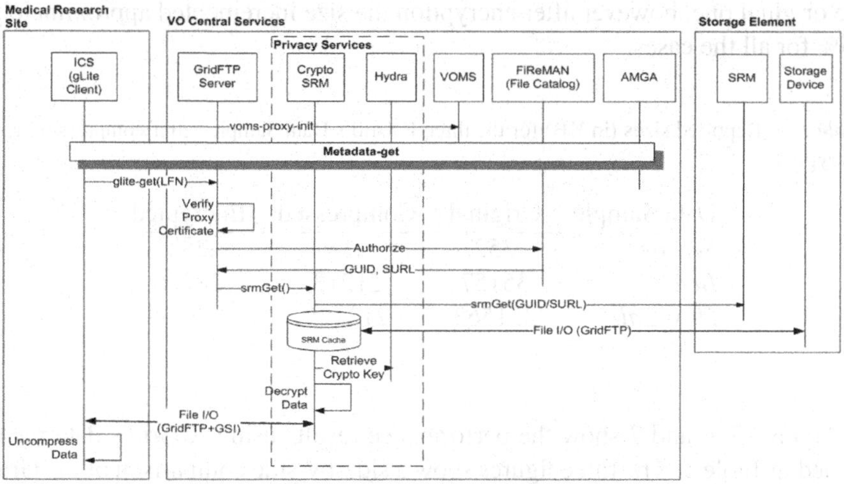

Figure 4. Secure ICGrid: retrieving data.

For the Data, random samples corresponding to one day of ICGrid's operation were generated for *(i)* a sensor (approx. 352 Kb), *(ii)* a bed (approx. 35157 Kb) and, *(iii)* a Hospital (approx. 351563 Kb). The *gzip* utility is used with its default parameters for compression, while for encryption the *aes-128-cbc* algorithm from the OpenSSL library (version 0.9.8g) was used. For comparison purposes we have measured the protocol's performance as the User's time (reported by the Unix *time* command) consumed by each phase of the following scenarios:

1 Grid client Encryption: This approach performs encryption/decryption at the Grid client and is commonly used by existing solutions (see Section 5). The steps taking place are: data compression, encryption and transfer to the SE via clear-text FTP. The inverse sequence is used to retrieve it from the SE.

2 CryptoSRM Encryption: This scenario simulates the basic steps proposed by our protocol: data compress, transfer via a GSIFTP encrypted channel to the CryptoSRM and finally, encryption at this entity. The inverse sequence of steps is used to retrieve stored data from the simulated CryptoSRM.

Each test was repeated 50 times to isolate potential overhead being caused by other processes concurrently running at the server. Table 1 shows how the size of the three data samples changed after the compression and encryption processes. It is worth to notice that the compressed data's size is about 60% of the original one, however after encryption the size incremented approximately 35% for all the cases.

Table 1. Reported sizes (in KB) for the three ICGrid's Data Samples after compression and encryption

Data Sample	Original	Compressed	Encrypted
Sensor	352	213	288
Bed	35157	21213	28726
Hospital	351563	212125	287258

Figures 5, 6 and 7 show the performance results using ICGrid's data mentioned in Table 1. The three figures show a side-by-side comparison of the Grid client encryption (the Sensor, Bed and Hospital graphs), versus the CryptoSRM encryption (the Sensor-Sec, Bed-Sec and Hospital-Sec graphs). Aggregated values for the tested scenarios are given by the *TOTAL UP* and *TOTAL DOWN* bars. Figure 5 shows the only case in which uploading and downloading Data

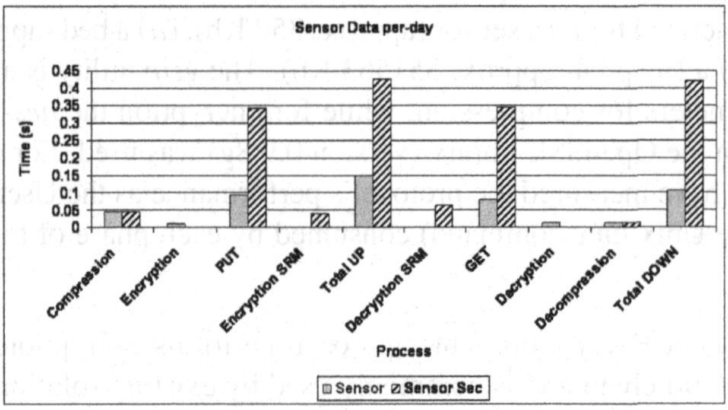

Figure 5. Processing a day of ICGrid's Sensor-data with the proposed privacy protocol.

through a secure GSI channel (the PUT and GET Sensor_Sec graphs), took more time than its equivalent via a clear-text FTP channel. This could be related to the GSI-transfer protocol itself, which for small data sizes requires more processing time (i.e. for encryption or padding). On the other hand for bigger data sizes, the performance achieved when uploading the Bed and Hospital Data (figures 6 and 7) is slightly less with the proposed privacy protocol (between 3%-4%) than with the Grid client encryption. This is because the data's size being uploaded to the SE is *smaller* in clear-text than when encrypted (around 30% according to Table 1), this latter fact helped to masquerade the overhead caused by the SE encryption mechanism (which provided

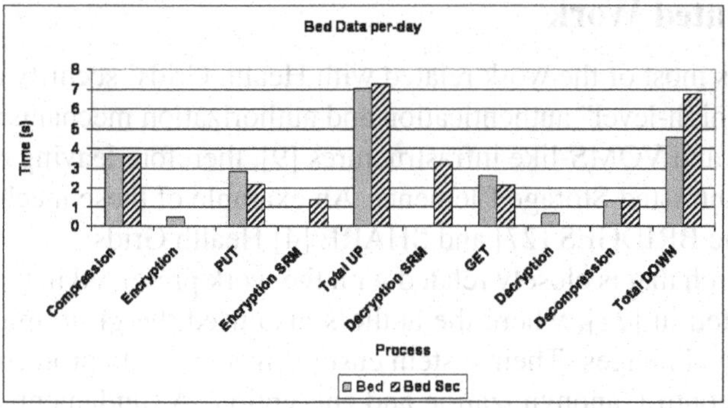

Figure 6. Processing a day of ICGrid's Bed-data with the proposed privacy protocol.

approx. 20% of the TOTAL UP time). When downloading Data the overall performance of the proposed protocol was about 39%-47% less than that of the Grid client encryption, however we have found that most of this overhead is due to the decryption operation taking place at the SE (which spent around 45% of the TOTAL DOWN time). This behavior was predicted, as the used SE is more biased towards storage than processing (this can be easily seen by comparing its hardware configuration with that of the Grid client). Despite this configuration, the experimental results have shown the viability of using the proposed CryptoSRM and it can be foreseen that if both, the SE and the Grid client, would have at-least the same hardware configuration, then for the Hospital's Data our proposal would improve with about 17% for the TOTAL UP time, and approximately with 11% for the TOTAL DOWN time of the Grid client-based encryption approach.

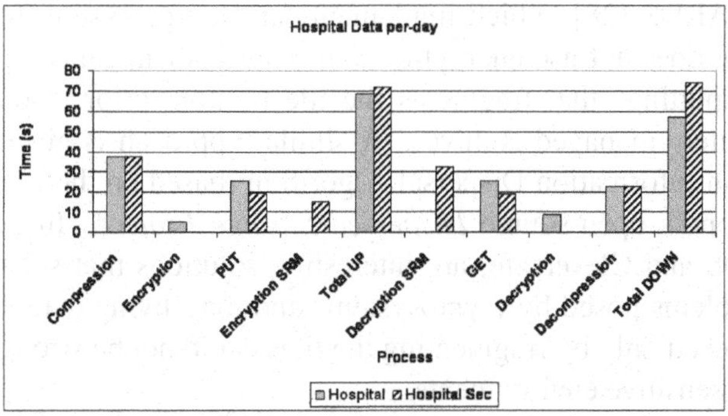

Figure 7. Processing a day of ICGrid's Hospital-data with the proposed privacy protocol.

5. Related Work

Nowadays most of the work related with Health Grids' security and privacy focuses on "high-level" authentication and authorization mechanisms that rely on Grid-IDs and VOMS-like infrastructures [9], therefore leaving data vulnerable in the untrusted Storage Elements. An example of these mechanisms can be seen in the BRIDGES [27] and SHARE [4] Health Grids.

The research that is closely related with the work presented in this paper has been presented in [21], where the authors also used the gLite middleware to protect medical images. Their system ensures medical data protection through data access control, anonymization and encryption. A fundamental difference with our approach is the use of encryption at the Grid client, which requires retrieving the encryption key from a Hydra Keystore for decrypting the image. With our research it has been shown that such approach does not only introduce uncertainties about the key's confidentiality (it may be compromised at the Grid client), but also has a performance lower than our "centralized" proposal (using the CryptoSRM).

There are other state of the art distributed storage systems that, even though they have not been specifically designed for the Health Grid, they have focused on low-level data protection by implementing encryption mechanisms at the "Grid's edges" (therefore disclosing the encryption key to the untrusted SEs and Grid Clients). For example in OceanStore [17], stored data are protected with redundancy and cryptographic mechanisms. An interesting feature in OceanStore is the ability to perform server-side operations directly on the encrypted data, this increases system's performance without sacrificing security. On the other hand it is worth to mention the Farsite system [8], which provides security and high availability by storing encrypted replicas of each file on multiple machines.

A second group of related systems do not rely on cryptography, but in a "data fragmentation" scheme for data protection. In the first place let us mention POTSHARDS [28], which implements an storage system for long-time archiving that does not use encryption, but a mechanism called "probably secure secret splitting" that fragments the file to store prior to distributing it across separately-managed archives. A similar approach is given by Cleversafe [2] via an Information Dispersal Algorithm (based on the Reed-Solomon algorithm) for its open-source *Dispersed Storage Project*. In general both, POTSHARDS and Cleversafe, are interesting solutions that solves the management problems posed by cryptosystems and long-living data, however the security achieved only by fragmenting the files could not be strong enough for some highly-sensitive environments.

6. Conclusions

In this paper we have presented a follow-up to our research on data-level security for Health Grids. After analyzing in a previous work the security requirements of the proposed scenario, we found the need to protect Metadata and Data from untrusted Storage Elements and Grid Clients that could compromise sensitive material (i.e. cryptographic keys). The second part of this research proposed a privacy protocol to protect the patient's personal information (metadata) along with his data, using two basic mechanisms: encryption and fragmentation. This paper has proposed building the cryptographic mechanism using components from the gLite middleware, in particular the Hydra Keystore a Storage Resource Manager with encryption facilities (the CryptoSRM).

About the Metadata, this paper proposed the implementation of an Mandatory Access Control model via AMGA's access control lists. This model was inspired in the Bell-Lapadula's model and the Electronic Health Card, currently being deployed in the European Union. Despite its simplicity, the proposed approach enforces different levels of authorization for a patient's personal data, in compliance with the eHealth Legislations studied in our previous work. However, we still have a lot of work to do in Metadata confidentiality, because currently AMGA is not able to offer protection from malicious administrators with direct access to its database.

Management of Health Grid's Data has taken a different approach in our proposal, so as a proof of concept to justify –from a performance point of view– the use of a "centralized" encryption mechanism (the CryptoSRM), in this paper we have simulated the former with a SE able to encrypt Data coming from an ICGrid client. Data's transfer operations (upload and download) resulted in most of the protocol's overhead, therefore suggesting us to keep transferred Data as small as possible. Taking into account that the encrypted Data is greater in size than its clear-text counterpart, we highly recommend not performing encryption at the "edges" of the Grid (i.e. Grid client, Storage Element). Notice that this argument is fully compatible with our previous security analysis, which established that Storage Elements are untrusted, thus encryption keys should not be delivered neither to them or even to the Grid Clients. Despite the hardware configuration being used to simulate the CryptoSRM in our experiments, it was possible to conclude its viability for the proposed privacy protocol. We can foresee that an important improvement in overall security and performance can be achieved, if the CryptoSRM uses a hardware-based cryptographic-accelerator, future work should prove this point.

Even though we have shown that for ICGrid using the proposed CryptoSRM is feasible, we believe that a more general solution (i.e. for demanding HEP applications) may be willing to "sacrifize" security by moving the cryptographic mechanism to the Storage Elements, thus benefiting performance and scalability. To cope with untrusted Storage Elements under such assumption, the next part of our ongoing research will also focus on the fragmentation mechanism proposed in [20], which benefits Data's availability and bandwidth use. We are planning to build analytical models, as those used in [18], to show the relationship between Data's assurance, Data's fragments and incurred overhead. A prototype using Cleversafe's API (Section 5) will be also developed for our test. Also as Future Work we are planning to study, along with AMGA's creators, the repercussions of using encryption at different levels of the Metadata.

Acknowledgments

The authors would like to thank EGEE-II (contract number INFSO-RI-031688) and Asterios Katsifodimos (University of Cyprus) for his technological support to perform the tests presented in this paper.

References

[1] Enabling Grids for E-SciencE project. http://www.eu-egee.org/.

[2] Cleversafe. http://www.cleversafe.com, 2007.

[3] Encrypted Storage and Hydra. https://twiki.cern.ch/twiki/bin/view/EGEE/DMEDS, September 2007.

[4] SHARE: Technology and Security Roadmap. http://wiki.healthgrid.org/index.php/Share_Roadmap_I, February 2007.

[5] Amga: Users, groups and acls. http://project-arda-dev.web.cern.ch/project-arda-dev/metadata/groups_and_acls.html, 2008.

[6] Disk encryption easily cracked. http://www.networkworld.com/news/2008/022108-disk-encryption-cracked.html, 2008.

[7] glite: Lightweight middleware for grid computing. http://www.glite.org/, 2008.

[8] Atul Adya, William J. Bolosky, Miguel Castro, Gerald Cermak, Ronnie Chaiken, John R. Douceur, Jon Howell, Jacob R. Lorch, Marvin Theimer, and Roger Wattenhofer. Farsite: Federated, available, and reliable storage for an incompletely trusted environment. In *OSDI*, 2002.

[9] R. Alfieri, R. Cecchini, V. Ciaschini, L. dellÕAgnello and?A. Frohner, A. Gianoli, K. Lorentey, and F. Spataro. VOMS, an Authorization System for Virtual Organizations. In *First European Across Grids Conference*, February 2003.

[10] European Health Management Association. Legally eHealth - Deliverable 2. http://www.ehma.org/_fileupload/Downloads/Legally_eHealth-Del_02-Data_Protection-v08(revised_after_submission).pdf, January 2006. Processing Medical data: data protection, confidentiallity and security.

[11] D. Elliot Bell and Leonard J. LaPadula. Secure computer systems: A mathematical model, volume ii. *Journal of Computer Security*, 4(2/3):229–263, 1996.

[12] JRA1 Data Management Cluster. EGEE: FiReMAN Catalog User Guide. https://edms.cern.ch/document/570780, 2005.

[13] B.M. Dawant et al. Knowledge-based systems for intelligent patient monitoring and management in critical care environments. In Joseph D. Bronzino, editor, *Biomedical Engineering Handbook*. CRC Press Ltd, 2000.

[14] Open Grid Forum. GridFTP: Protocol Extensions to FTP for the Grid. http://www.ggf.org/documents/GWD-R/GFD-R.020.pdf, April 2003.

[15] K. Gjermundrod, M. Dikaiakos, D. Zeinalipour-Yazti, G. Panayi, and Th. Kyprianou. Icgrid: Enabling intensive care medical research on the egee grid. In *From Genes to Personalized HealthCare: Grid Solutons for the Life Sciences. Proceedings of HealthGrid 2007*, pages 248–257. IOS Press, 2007.

[16] JRA1. EGEE gLite User's Guide. https://edms.cern.ch/document/570643/, March 2005.

[17] John Kubiatowicz, David Bindel, Yan Chen, Steven E. Czerwinski, Patrick R. Eaton, Dennis Geels, Ramakrishna Gummadi, Sean C. Rhea, Hakim Weatherspoon, Westley Weimer, Chris Wells, and Ben Y. Zhao. Oceanstore: An architecture for global-scale persistent storage. In *ASPLOS*, pages 190–201, 2000.

[18] J. Luna et al. Providing security to the desktop data grid. Submitted to the 2nd. Workshop on Desktop Grids and Volunteer Computing Systems (PCGrid 2008).

[19] J. Luna et al. An analysis of security services in grid storage systems. In *CoreGRID Workshop on Grid Middleware 2007*, June 2007.

[20] Jesus Luna, Michail Flouris, Manolis Marazakis, Angelos Bilas, Marios Dikaiakos, Harald Gjermundrod, and Theodoros Kyprianou. A data-centric security analysis of icgrid. In *Proceedings of the CoreGRID Integrated Research in Grid Computing*, pages 165–176, 2008.

[21] Johan Montagnat, Ákos Frohner, Daniel Jouvenot, Christophe Pera, Peter Kunszt, Birger Koblitz, Nuno Santos, Charles Loomis, Romain Texier, Diane Lingrand, Patrick Guio, Ricardo Brito Da Rocha, Antonio Sobreira de Almeida, and Zoltan Farkas. A secure grid medical data manager interfaced to the glite middleware. *J. Grid Comput.*, 6(1):45–59, 2008.

[22] Federal Ministry of Health. The Electronic Health Card. http://www.die-gesundheitskarte.de/download/dokumente/broschuere_elektronische_gesundheitskarte_engl.pdf, October 2006. Public Relations Section. Berlin, Germany.

[23] European Parliament. Directive 95/46/EC of the European Parliament and of the Council of 24 October 1995 on the protection of individuals with regard to the processing of personal data and on the free movement of such data. Official Journal of the European Communities of 23 November 1995 No L. 281 p. 31., October 1995.

[24] T. Perelmutov et al. SRM Interface Specification v2.2. Technical Report, FNAL, USA, 2002.

[25] Michael O. Rabin. Efficient dispersal of information for security, load balancing, and fault tolerance. *J. ACM*, 36(2):335–348, 1989.

[26] N. Santos and B. Koblitz. Distributed Metadata with the AMGA Metadata Catalog. In *Workshop on Next-Generation Distributed Data Management HPDC-15*, June 2006.

[27] Richard O. Sinnott, Micha Bayer, A. J. Stell, and Jos Koetsier. Grid infrastructures for secure access to and use of bioinformatics data: Experiences from the bridges project. In *ARES*, pages 950–957, 2006.

[28] Mark W. Storer, Kevin M. Greenan, Ethan L. Miller, and Kaladhar Voruganti. Secure, archival storage with potshards. In *FAST'07: Proceedings of the 5th conference on USENIX Conference on File and Storage Technologies*, pages 11–11, Berkeley, CA, USA, 2007. USENIX Association.

[29] Von Welch. Globus toolkit version 4 grid security infrastructure: A standards perspective. http://www.globus.org/toolkit/docs/4.0/security/GT4-GSI-Overview.pdf, 2005. The Globus Security Team.

GRID-BASED WORKFLOW MANAGEMENT FOR AUTOMATIC PERFORMANCE ANALYSIS OF MASSIVELY PARALLEL APPLICATIONS

Daniel Becker*, Morris Riedel, Achim Streit, Felix Wolf†
Forschungszentrum Jülich, Institute for Advanced Simulation
52425 Jülich, Germany
{d.becker, m.riedel, a.streit, f.wolf}@fz-juelich.de

Abstract

Many Grid infrastructures have begun to offer services to end-users during the past several years with an increasing number of complex scientific applications and software tools that require seamless access to different Grid resources via Grid middleware during one workflow. End-users of the rather HPC-driven DEISA Grid infrastructure take not only advantage of Grid workflow management capabilities for massively parallel applications to solve critical problems of high complexity (e.g. protein folding, global weather prediction), but also leverage software tools to achieve satisfactory application performance on contemporary massively parallel machines (e.g., IBM Blue Gene/P). In this context, event tracing is one technique widely used by software tools with a broad spectrum of applications ranging from performance analysis, performance prediction and modeling to debugging. In particular, automatic performance analysis has emerged as an powerful and robust instrument to make the optimization of parallel applications both more effective and more efficient. The approach of automatic performance analysis implies multiple steps that can perfectly leverage the workflow capabilities in Grids. In this paper, we present how this approach is implemented by using the workflow management capabilities of the UNICORE Grid middleware, which is deployed on DEISA, and thus, demonstrate by using a Grid application that the approach taken is feasible.

Keywords:

Middleware, workflow management, performance analysis, HPC applications.

---

*Also with RWTH Aachen University, Department of Computer Science, 52056 Aachen, Germany
†Also with RWTH Aachen University, Department of Computer Science, 52056 Aachen, Germany

1. Introduction

Grid infrastructures offer services to end-users with an increasing number of complex scientific applications and software tools. Due to the increased complexity of contemporary High-Performance Computing (HPC) systems, software tools that are used to tune parallel applications are important. Using these rather complicated software tools can be significant simplified by Grid middleware providing multi-step workflow capabilities. While a wide variety of Grid middleware systems exist (gLite [17], Globus Toolkits [14]) today, only a few systems incorporate massive workflow support, and are also driven by HPC needs.

One of those systems is UNICORE, which is deployed on DEISA [3]. This HPC-driven DEISA Grid infrastructure offers not only Grid workflow management capabilities for massively parallel applications to solve critical problems of high complexity (e.g. protein folding, global weather prediction), but also software tools to achieve satisfactory application performance on contemporary massively parallel machines (e.g., IBM Blue Gene/P).

In the area of HPC, event tracing is a popular technique for software tools with a broad spectrum of applications ranging from performance analysis, performance prediction and modeling to debugging. Event traces are helpful in understanding the performance behavior of message-passing applications since they allow in-depth analysis of communication and synchronization patterns. Graphical trace browsers, such as VAMPIR [20] and Paraver [16], allow the fine-grained investigation of parallel performance behavior and provide statistical summaries. By contrast, automatic trace analysis scans event traces of parallel applications for wait states that occur when processes fail to reach synchronization points in a timely manner, e.g., as a result of an unevenly distributed workload.

The automatic performance analysis approach is a powerful and robust instrument to make the optimization of parallel applications both more effective and more efficient. For instance, SCALASCA, which has been specifically designed for large-scale systems, searches event traces of parallel programs for patterns of inefficient behavior, classifies detected instances by category, and quantifies the associated performance penalty [7]. This allows developers to study the performance of their applications on a higher level of abstraction, while requiring significantly less time and expertise than a manual analysis [23].

SCALASCA's analysis approach implies multiple steps that can perfectly leverage the workflow capabilities in Grids. In this paper, we present how this approach is implemented by using the UNICORE workflow management capabilities that are deployed on DEISA and thus demonstrate by using a Grid application that the approach taken is feasible. While we automize SCALASCA's performance analysis workflow, we show that Grid workflow capabilities in general, and UNICOREs workflow engine in particular, efficiently support the performance analysis process of HPC-driven Grid applications.

The outline of this paper is as follows: After describing the basics of Grid middleware components in Section 2, we review the automatic trace analysis approaches in Section 3 including a brief description of the event tracing technique. In Section 4, we evaluate the feasibility of the approach taken using the state-of-the-art massively parallel machines deployed on the DEISA Grid and show how automatic performance analysis is augmented by UNICORE's workflow capabilities. Finally, after reviewing the related work in Section 5, we summarize our results and give an outlook on future work in Section 6.

2. Grid Middleware

Today, large-scale scientific research often relies on the shared use of a Grid with computational or storage related resources. One of the fundamental ideas of modern Grids is to facilitate the routine interaction of scientists and their workflow-based applications with advanced problem solving tools such as Grid middleware systems. Many of these systems have been evolved in the past, typically influenced by the nature of their deployments. To provide an example, the gLite middleware [17] deployed in the EGEE infrastructure [4] was specifically optimized to handle large data-sets, while the UNICORE middleware [11] deployed in the DEISA infrastructure [3] is rather designed to satisfy the requirements in HPC environments.

Since our approach of supporting the performance analysis of massively parallel applications with Grid-based workflow capabilities relies on a HPC environments, we used key concepts of the HPC-driven Grid middleware UNICORE. Other Grid middleware systems (i.e. Globus Toolkits [14]) may also provide similar capabilities, but the inherently provided workflow functionalities of UNICORE are also fundamental to our approach and thus we choose UNICORE.

The UNICORE Grid middleware has been developed since the late 1990s to support distributed computing applications in Grids in general, and massively parallel HPC applications in particular. The vertically integrated design provides components on each tier of its layered architecture as shown in Figure 1. The UNICORE 5 architecture [22] mainly consists of proprietary components and protocols, while the more recently developed UNICORE 6 architecture is based on open standards such as the Web services resource framework (WS-RF) [5] and thus relies on the concept of Service-Oriented Architectures (SOAs).

In more detail, UNICORE 6 conforms to the Open Grid Services Architecture (OGSA) of the Open Grid Forum (OGF) and several projects such as the OMII-

Europe project [6] augmented it with open standards during the last couple of month. The loosely coupled Web services connection technology provides a perfect base to meet the common use case within Grid that conform to OGSA thus allowing dynamic interaction dispersed in conceptual, institutional, and geographical space. The approach presented in this paper takes advantage of this service-oriented concept by using key characteristics of the UNICORE Grid middleware. These characteristics are basic job submission and data management functionalities using the UNICORE Atomic Services (UAS) [21], and the workflow capabilities of the UNICORE workflow engine and service orchestrator.

The UAS consists of a set of core services such as the TargetSystemService (TSS) that represents a computational resource (e.g. supercomputers or clusters) in the Grid. While the TargetSystemFactory (TSF) can be used to create an end-user specific instance of a TSS, the TSS itself is able to execute jobs defined in the Job Submission and Description Language (JSDL) [12]. Each submitted job is represented as another resource aligned with the TSS and can be controlled with the Job Management Service (JMS). Finally, different flavors of the FileTransferServices (FTS) can be used for data transfer.

While the UAS and its services (i.e. TSS, JMS, FTS, etc.) operate on the service level, they are supported by a strong execution backend named as the enhanced Network Job Supervisor (XNJS), which uses the Incarnation Database (IDB) to map abstract job descriptions to system-specific definitions. In terms of security, the UAS are protected via the UNICORE Gateway [18], which does authentication. This means it checks whether the certificate of an end-user has been signed by a trusted Certificate Authority (CA), that its still valid, and not revoked. For authorization the NJS, relies on the UNICORE User DataBase (UUDB) service and checks policies based on Extensible Access Control Markup Language (XACML) [19]. The roles and general attributes of end-users as well as their group and project membership are encoded using Security Assertion Markup Language (SAML) [13] assertions.

Typically, scientists use the UNICORE middleware to reduce their management overheads in usual scientific workflows to a minimum or to automize parts of their workflow. Without Grid middleware, the workflows of scientists often start with the manual creation of a Secure Shell (SSH) connection to a remote system such as a supercomputer via username and password or keys configured before. The trend towards service-oriented Grids allows for more flexibility and orchestration of services and thus makes it easier to enable end-users with multi-step workflow capabilities. While there are many workflow-related tools in Grids (e.g. TAVERNA [8], ASKALON [2], TRIANA [10]), we shortly describe the functionalities of UNICORE that are later intensively used to verify our approach.

To satisfy scalability requirements, the overall workflow capabilities of UNICORE are developed using a two layer architecture. The Workflow Engine is based on the Shark open-source XPDL engine. In addition, plug-ins allow for domain-specific workflow language support. The Workflow engine is responsible to take Directed Acyclic Graph (DAG)-based workflow descriptions and map them to specific steps.

The Service Orchestrator on the other hand, is responsible for the job submission and monitoring of workflow steps. While the execution site can be chosen manually, the orchestrator also supports brokering based on pluggable strategies. In addition, it supports callback functions to the workflow engine.

Finally, all the above described services can be seamlessly accessed using the graphical UNICORE Rich Client based on Eclipse. End-users are able to create DAGs of different services that typically invoke different applications including necessary data staging elements. In addition, the Tracing Service of UNICORE allows for monitoring of each execution step of a UNICORE workflow, which can be easily followed in the client.

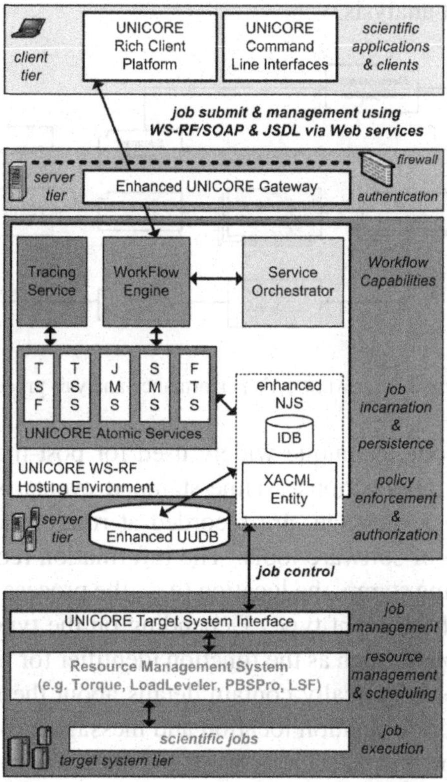

Figure 1. UNICORE's layered architecture with workflow functionalities.

3. Automatic Performance Analysis

In this section, we illustrate the automatic performance analysis workflow including instrumentation, measurement, analysis, and result visualization used to optimize parallel applications running on thousands of processes. After a general description of the event tracing technique and a brief description of the graphical trace browser VAMPIR [20], we especially focus on the SCALASCA tool set [7] and its workflow requirements.

Often, parallel applications which are free of computational errors need to be optimized. This requires the information which component of the program is responsible for what kind of inefficient behavior. Performance analysis is the process of identifying those parts, exploring the reasons for their unsatisfactory performance, and quantifying their overall influence. To do this, performance data are mapped onto program entities. A developer can now investigate application's runtime behavior using software tools. Thus, the developer is enabled to understand the performance behavior of his application. The process of gathering performance data is called performance measurement and forms the basis for subsequent analysis.

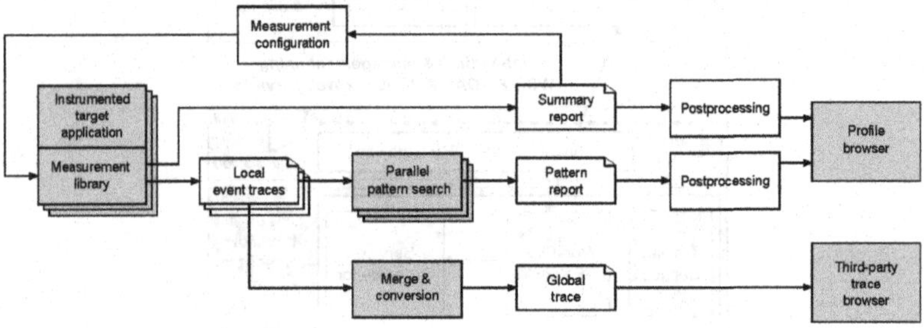

Figure 2. SCALASCA's performance analysis process.

Event tracing is one technique widely used for post-mortem performance analysis of parallel applications. Time-stamped events, such as entering a function or sending a message, are recorded at runtime and analyzed afterwards with the help of software tools. The information recorded for an event includes at least a time stamp, the location (e.g., the process or node) where the event happened and the event type. Depending on the type, additional information may be supplied, such as the function identifier for function call events. Message event records typically contain details about the message they refer to (e.g., the source or destination location and message tag).

Graphical trace browsers, such as VAMPIR, allow the fine-grained, manual investigation of parallel performance behavior using a zoomable time-line display and provide statistical summaries of communication behavior. However, in view of the large amounts of data generated on contemporary parallel machines, the depth and coverage of the visual analysis offered by a browser is limited as soon as it targets more complex patterns not included in the statistics generated by such tools.

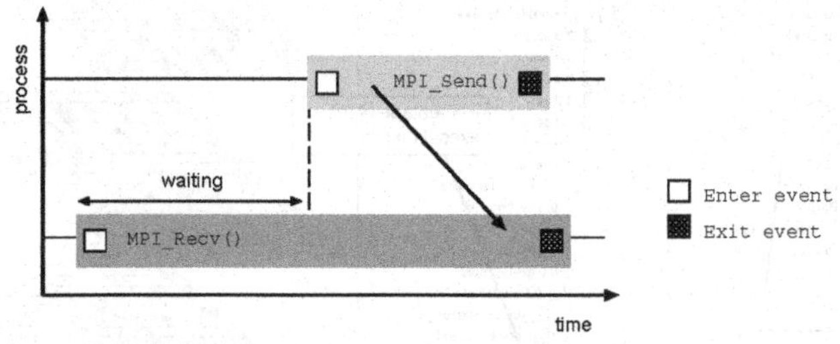

Figure 3. Late Sender pattern.

By contrast, the basic principle of the SCALASCA project is the summarization of events, that is, the transformation of an event stream into a compact representation of execution behavior, aggregating metric values associated with individual events across the entire execution. On a more technical level, the trace analyzer of the SCALASCA tool set automatically searches event traces for patterns of inefficient behavior, classifies detected instances by category, and quantifies the associated performance penalty [15]. To do this efficiently at larger scales, the traces are analyzed in parallel by replaying the original communication using the same hardware configuration and the same number of CPUs as have been used to execute the target application itself.

As an example of inefficient communication, we consider the point-to-point pattern *Late Sender* (Figure 3). Here, a receive operation is entered by one process before the corresponding send operation has been started by the other. The time lost waiting due to this situation is the time difference between the enter events of the two MPI function instances that precede the corresponding send and receive events.

The current version of SCALASCA can be used for MPI programs written in C/C++ and Fortran. Figure 2 shows the basic analysis workflow supported by SCALASCA. Before any performance data can be collected, the target application must be *instrumented*, that is, it must be modified to record performance-relevant events whenever they occur. On some systems including Blue Gene, this can be done completely automatically using compiler support; on other systems a mix of manual and automatic instrumentation mechanisms is offered.

When running the instrumented code on the parallel machine first a summary report (aka profile) with aggregate performance metrics for individual function call paths is generated and subsequently event traces are generated to

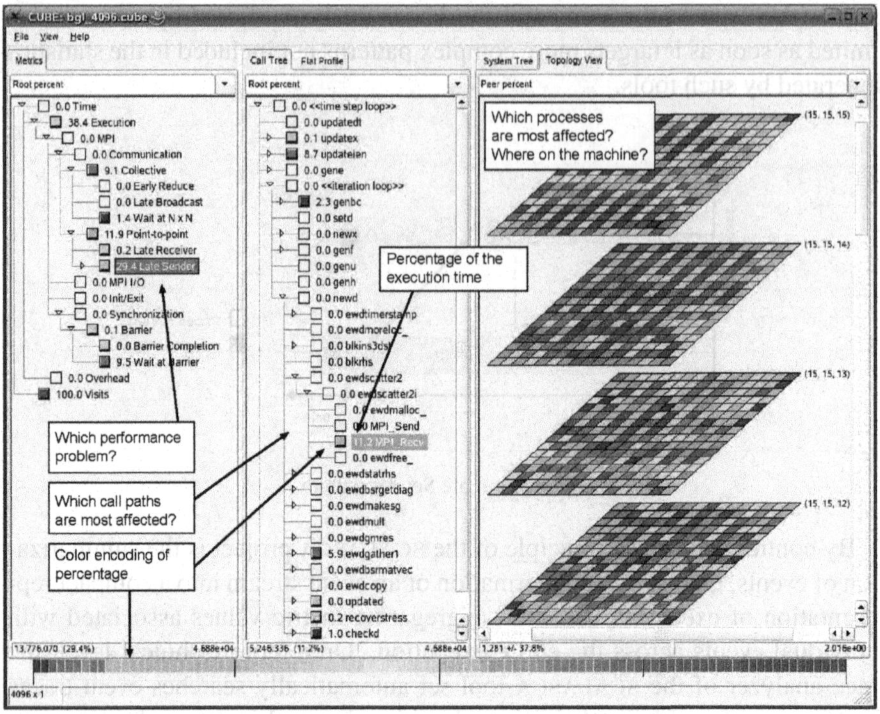

Figure 4. Exemplary trace analysis report: The tree in the left panel displays pattern of inefficient performance behavior arranged in a specialization hierarchy. The numbers left of the pattern names indicate the total execution time penalty in percent. In addition, the color of the little square provides a visual clue of the percentage to quickly guide the user to the most severe performance problems. The middle tree shows the distribution of the selected pattern across the call tree. Finally, the right tree shows the distribution of the selected pattern at the selected call path across the hierarchy of machines, nodes, and processes.

record individual runtime events. The former is useful to obtain an overview of the performance behavior and also to optimize the instrumentation for later trace generation. Since traces tend to become very large, this step is crucial before starting event tracing. When tracing is enabled, each process generates a trace file containing records for all its process-local events.

After performance measurement, SCALASCA loads these trace files into main memory and analyzes them in parallel using as many CPUs as have been used for the target application itself. During the analysis, SCALASCA searches for characteristic patterns indicating wait states and related performance properties, classifies detected instances by category and quantifies their significance for every function-call path and system resource involved. The result is a pattern-analysis report similar in structure to the summary report but enriched with higher-level performance metrics.

After performance analysis, both the summary report as well as the pattern report can be interactively explored in a graphical profile browser (Figure 4) after a postprocessing phase. As an alternative to the automatic search, the event traces can be converted and investigated using third-party trace browsers such as Paraver [16] or VAMPIR [20], taking advantage of their powerful timeline visualizations and rich statistical functionality.

4. Experimental Results

In this section, we present the experimental results of our approach of supporting the performance analysis of massively parallel applications with Grid-based workflow capabilities. Automizing SCALASCA's performance analysis workflow, we show that Grid middleware components efficiently support SCALASCA's pattern search. Finally, we point out that the management overhead is reduced to a minimum and explain the basic performance analysis results detected by the automatic perform.

For our measurements, we used a second generation IBM Blue Gene system, the Blue Gene/P (JUGENE) installed at Research Centre Jülich. The massively parallel JUGENE system is a 16 racks system including 32 nodecards with 32 compute nodes each. While each compute node has a 4-way SMP processor, each core is a 32-bit PowerPC processor core running at 850 MHz. The network architecture of the Blue Gene/P is very similar to that of the L model. That is, the network exhibits a three-dimensional torus, a global tree, and a 10 Gigabit Ethernet network. Ranked as no. 2 in the current Top500 list [9], JUGENE is one of the most powerful high-performance computing systems in the world and especially designed to run massively parallel application.

To evaluate UNICORE's workflow capabilities, we analyzed the performance of the ASC SMG2000 benchmark, a parallel semi-coarsening multigrid solver that uses a complex communication pattern and performs a large number of non-nearest-neighbor point-to-point communication operations. Applying a weak scaling strategy, a fixed $64 \times 64 \times 32$ problem size per process with five solver iterations was configured. In our measurements, we used 512 processes per program run as a prove of concept, while typically a production run uses significant more processors.

Figure 5 shows a snapshot of the UNICORE Rich Client Platform. On the left side of the GUI, we can see the Grid browser showing the actually available services of the infrastructures as well as the status of certain activities. On the right side, we see the runtime summarization of the entire performance analysis workflow. In more detail, both the profiling phase and postprocessing phase (see Figure 2) of the SMG2000 benchmark parallel application is shown. While profiling is enabled, the execution of the pre-compiled and automatically instrumented executable generates a runtime summary. This runtime

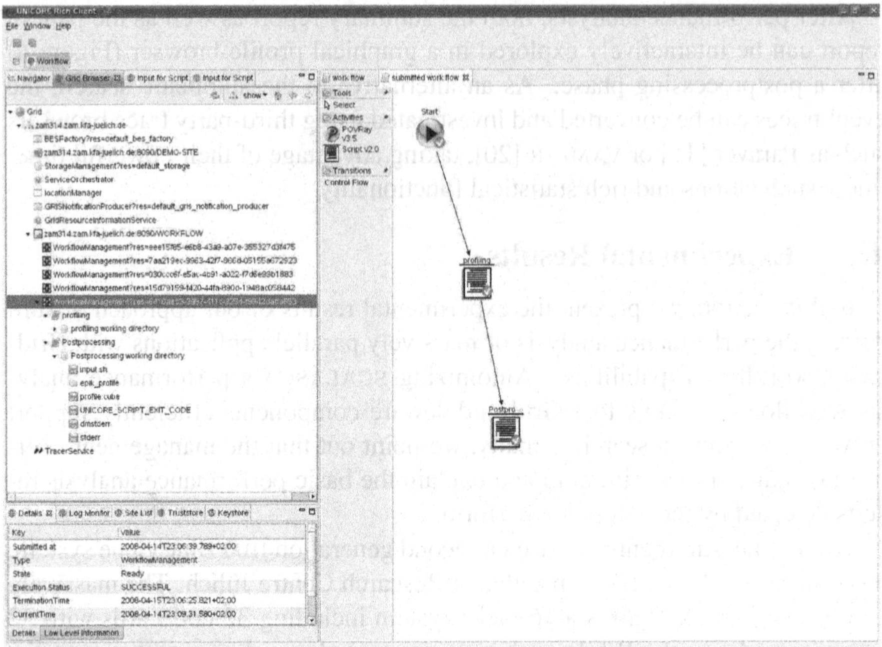

Figure 5. Using UNICORE's workflow capabilities for profiling a parallel application.

summary is subsequently postprocessed via certain preconfigured mappings to be displayed properly to the end-user as shown in Figure 6.

The strength of this runtime summarization is that it avoids storing the events in trace buffers and files, since many execution performance metrics can be most efficiently calculated by accumulating statistics during measurement, avoiding the cost of storing them with events for later analysis. For example, the point-to-point communication time can be immediately determined and finally displayed as shown in Figure 6. Here, the runtime summary report shows a large point-to-point communication fraction distributed across the call tree and the system hierarchy. Obviously, the point-to-point communication time clearly dominated the overall communication behavior making it the most promising target for further analysis efforts. That is, we configured the measurement system to record especially those execution phases related to point-to-point communication and adjusted the buffer sizes, manually.

The UNICORE Rich Client Platform snapshot in Figure 7 shows again the Grid browser with the actually available services of the infrastructures as well as the status of the submitted tracing workflow. This tracing workflow consists of a tracing, trace analysis, and postprocessing phase. During the tracing phase, the measurement system generates process-local event traces maintained in an appropriate measurement archive (`epik_tracing`). The subsequent trace anal-

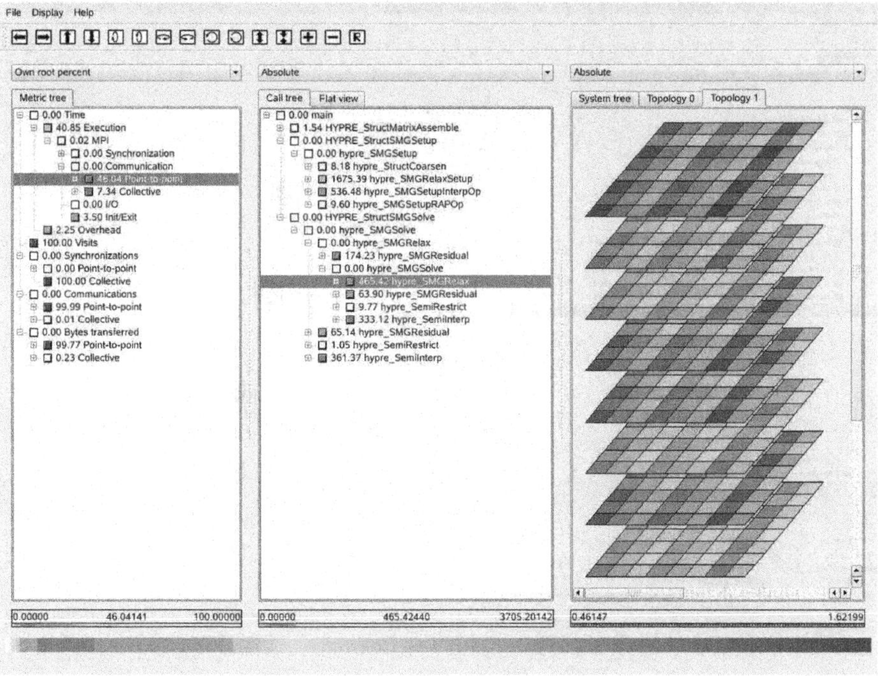

Figure 6. Runtime summary report: Large point-to-point communication fraction distributed across the call tree and the system hierarchy.

ysis starts the parallel trace analyzer, which automatically search those event traces for patterns of inefficient performance behavior. The trace analyzer generates a trace analysis report which is finally postprocessed via certain preconfigured mappings to be displayed properly to the end-user as shown in Figure 8.

SCALASCA searches event traces of parallel programs for patterns of inefficient behavior (e.g., wait states), classifies detected instances by category, and quantifies the associated performance penalty. Often, reasons for such wait states can be found in the scheduling of communication operations or in the distribution of work among the processes involved. Figure 8 shows the trace analysis report similar in structure to the summary report but enriched with higher-level performance metrics. The report indicates that the large point-to-point communication time manifests itself in a Late Sender situation distributed across the call tree and the system hierarchy. Hence, the point-to-point communication would be a prommissing target for performance optimization.

Finally, typical Grid applications execute their workflow steps on different systems, while in our approach all steps (i.e. measurements) are taken on the JUGENE system. This is due to the fact that we analyze the performance for one dedicated scientific HPC application on a distinct parallel machine. How-

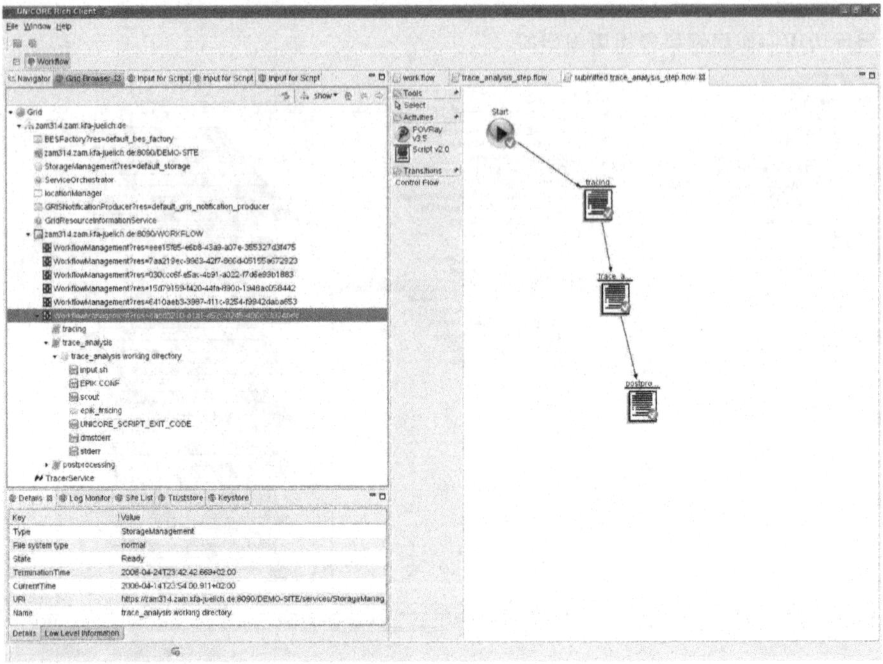

Figure 7. Using UNICORE's workflow capabilities for tracing a parallel application.

ever, using the same workflow on another system is easy to accomplish by just choose another site within the UNICORE Rich Client Platform. Of course, the workflow capabilities cover not only multi-step workflows, but also multi-site workflows that are not substantial to accomplish the performance analysis in this context.

5. Related Work

There is a wide variety of related work in the field. First and foremost, Taverna [8] enables the interoperation between databases and tools by providing a toolkit for composing, executing and managing workflow applications. It's specifically designed to access local and remote resources as well as analysis tools. In comparison to our worfklow approach, this tool is not seamlessly integrated in a Grid middleware.

Another well-known workflow tool named as ASKALON [5]. The fundamental goal of ASKALON is to provide simple, efficient, and effective application development for the Grid. In focusses on workflows as well as parameter studies. It also allows for measurement, analysis and optimization of performance, but also this tool is not closely aligned with HPC environments or any HPC-driven Grid middleware.

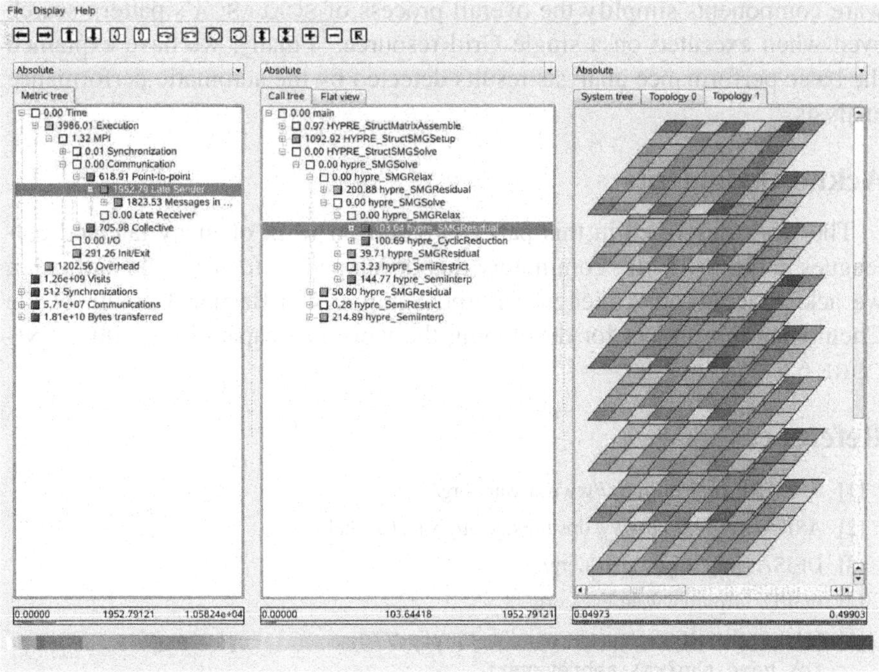

Figure 8. Trace analysis report: Large point-to-point waiting time manifests itself in a Late Sender situation distributed across the call tree and the system hierarchy.

Also, Triana [10] is a problem solving environment especially designed as a Grid workflow tool. Developed by Cardiff University, Triana basically abstracts the core capabilities needed for service-based computing such as P2P, Web services, or Grid Computing. While this approach is rather more oriented to HPC in a way, we also find that the direct support for a Grid middleware was missing.

Finally, also the A-Ware project [1] develops several workflow capabilities specifically designed for service invocation of any kind. Compared to our approach, this work is rather high-level and thus not directly usable for HPC-based environments.

6. Conclusion

In this paper, we have shown that the approach of supporting the performance analysis of parallel HPC applications can be significantly supported by workflow capabilities within Grids. We have mapped the SCALASCA's automatic performance analysis approach of massively parallel applications to UNICORE'S workflow management capabilities. More precisely, by automizing SCALASCA's performance analysis workflow, we have shown that Grid middleware components simplify the overall process of SCALASCA's pattern search even when executed on a single Grid resource. Finally, we have explained the basic performance analysis results detected by the automatic performance analysis.

Acknowledgments

The work described in this paper is based on work of many talented colleagues in the UNICORE community that developed UNICORE 6. In particular, we acknowledge our colleagues Bernd Schuller and Bastian Demuth of the Chemomentum project for developing the workflow capabilities within UNICORE 6.

References

[1] A-WARE Project. http://www.a-ware.org/.

[2] ASKALON. http://www.dps.uibk.ac.at/projects/askalon/.

[3] DEISA. http://www.deisa.org/.

[4] EGEE. http://www.eu-egee.org/.

[5] OASIS - WSRF Technical Committee. `http://www.oasis-open.org/committees/tc\_home.php?wg\_abbrev=wsrf`.

[6] OMII - Europe. http://omii-europe.org/.

[7] Scalasca. `www.scalasca.org`.

[8] TAVERNA. http://taverna.sourceforge.net/.

[9] Top500 project. `www.top500.org/`.

[10] TRIANA grid workflow. http://www.grid.org.il.

[11] UNICORE grid middleware. http://www.unicore.eu.

[12] A. Anjomshoaa, M. Drescher, D. Fellows, S. McGougha, D. Pulsipher, and A. Savva. *Job Submission Description Language (JSDL) - Specification Version 1.0*. Open Grid Forum Proposed Recommendation, 2006.

[13] S. Cantor, J. Kemp, R. Philpott, and E. Maler. *Assertions and Protocols for the OASIS Security Assertion Markup Language*. OASIS Standard, 2005. http://docs.oasis-open.org/security/saml/v2.0/.

[14] I. Foster. Globus Toolkit version 4: Software for Service-Oriented Science. In *Proceedings of IFIP International Conference on Network and Parallel Computing, LNCS 3779*, pages 213–223. Springer-Verlag, 2005.

[15] M. Geimer, F. Wolf, B. J. N. Wylie, and B. Mohr. Scalable parallel trace-based performance analysis. In *Proc. 13th European PVM/MPI Conference*, Bonn, Germany, September 2006. Springer.

[16] J. Labarta, S. Girona, V .Pillet, T. Cortes, and L. Gregoris. DiP : A parallel program development environment. In *Proc. of the 2th International Euro-Par Conference*, Lyon, France, August 1996. Springer.

[17] E. Laure et al. Programming The Grid with gLite. In *Computational Methods in Science and Technology*, pages 33–46. Scientific Publishers OWN, 2006.

[18] R. Menday. The Web Services Architecture and the UNICORE Gateway. In *Proceedings of the International Conference on Internet and Web Applications and Services (ICIW) 2006, Guadeloupe, French Caribbean*, 2006.

[19] T. Moses et al. *eXtensible Access Control Markup Language*. OASIS Standard, 2005.

[20] W. Nagel, M. Weber, H.-C. Hoppe, and K. Solchenbach. VAMPIR: Visualization and analysis of MPI resources. *Supercomputer*, 12(1):69–80, 1996.

[21] M. Riedel and D. Mallmann. Standardization Processes of the UNICORE Grid System. In *Proceedings of 1st Austrian Grid Symposium 2005, Schloss Hagenberg, Austria*, pages 191–203. Austrian Computer Society, 2005.

[22] A. Streit, D. Erwin, Th. Lippert, D. Mallmann, R. Menday, M. Rambadt, M. Riedel, M. Romberg, B. Schuller, and Ph. Wieder. UNICORE - From Project Results to Production Grids. In L. Grandinetti, editor, *Grid Computing: The New Frontiers of High Performance Processing, Advances in Parallel Computing 14*, pages 357–376. Elsevier, 2005.

[23] F. Wolf. *Automatic Performance Analysis on Parallel Computers with SMP Nodes*. PhD thesis, RWTH Aachen, Forschungszentrum Jülich, February 2003. ISBN 3-00-010003-2.

FAULT DETECTION, PREVENTION AND RECOVERY TECHNIQUES IN CURRENT GRID WORKFLOW SYSTEMS

Kassian Plankensteiner, Radu Prodan, Thomas Fahringer
Institute for Computer Science
University of Innsbruck, Austria
kassian.plankensteiner@dps.uibk.ac.at
radu@dps.uibk.ac.at
tf@dps.uibk.ac.at

Attila Kertész, Péter Kacsuk
MTA SZTAKI Computer and Automation Research Institute
Budapest, Hungary
attila.kertesz@sztaki.hu
kacsuk@sztaki.hu

Abstract The workflow paradigm is a highly successful paradigm for the creation of Grid applications. Despite the popularity of the workflow approach, the systems that support the execution of workflow applications in Grid environments are still not able to deliver the quality, robustness and reliability that their users require and demand. To understand the current state-of-the-art and the reasons behind the shortcomings, we sent out a detailed questionnaire to developers of many of the major Grid workflow systems. This paper shows the outcome of the questionnaire evaluation, reveals future directions and helps to guide research towards the identified open issues in adoption of fault tolerance techniques.

Keywords: Fault tolerance, scientific workflow, survey, reliability, fault detection, fault prevention, fault recovery.

1. Introduction

Up to now, most of the existing Grid workflow systems still cannot deliver the quality, robustness, and reliability that is needed for widespread acceptance as tools to be used on a day-to-day basis by scientists from a multitude of scientific fields. The scientists typically want to use the Grid to compute solutions for complex problems, potentially utilizing thousands of resources for workflows that can run for several hours, days, or even weeks. With a system that has a low tolerance for faults, the users will regularly be confronted with a situation that makes them lose days or even weeks of valuable computation time because the system could not recover from a fault that happened before the successful completion of their workflow applications. This is, of course, intolerable for anyone trying to effectively use the Grid, and makes scientists accept a slower solution that only uses their own computing resources that offer a higher reliability and controllability. Due to the heterogeneous and distributed nature of Grid systems, faults inevitably happen. This problem can only be overcome by highly fault tolerant systems.

This paper reports on the current state-of-the-art in fault tolerance techniques for Grid workflow systems. We show which faults can be detected, prevented and recovered by which current Grid workflow system, the areas where the current systems are planned to improve, and which areas are still in need of more research efforts.

We assume that a scientific workflow is modelled as a directed graph of tasks interconnected through control flow and data flow dependencies. Data flow dependencies are typically instantiated by file transfers.

2. Questionnaire

To build a general and objective vision of state-of-the-art fault tolerance support in Grid workflow management systems, we sent out a detailed questionnaire to the developers of many of the major Grid workflow management systems.

On the first page, we asked for general information such as contact data and history on fault tolerance. We divided the target questions into two main categories: fault detection on one hand and fault recovery and prevention on the other. In both categories we defined several layers where detection as well as recovery and prevention can exist.

2.1 Fault detection

Figure 1 shows the identified faults at hardware, operating system, middleware, task, workflow, and user-level. At the lowest hardware-level, machine crashes and network connectivity errors can happen. At the level of operating

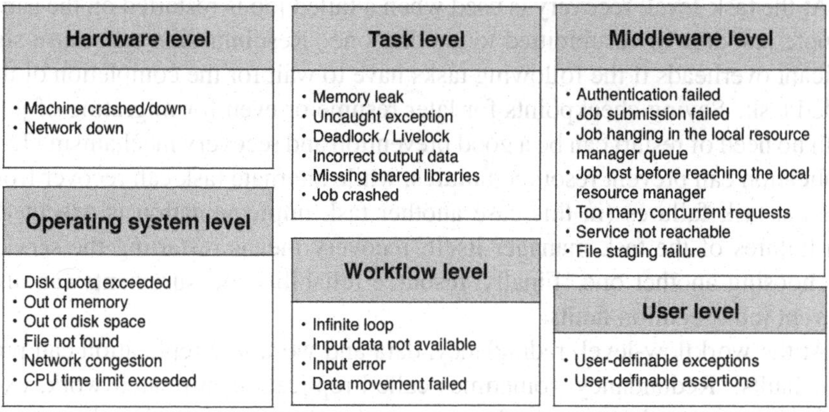

Figure 1. Identified faults and their levels of abstraction

system, tasks may run out of memory or disk space, or exceed CPU time limits or disk quota. Other faults like network congestion or file non-existence can also happen. One level higher at the middleware, we could find non-responding services, probably caused by too many concurrent requests. Authentication, file staging or job submission failures can happen, and submitted jobs could hang in local queues, or even be lost before reaching the local resource manager. At the level of tasks, job-related faults like deadlocks, livelocks, memory leaks, uncaught exceptions, missing shared libraries, or job crashes can happen, and even incorrect output results could be produced. At workflow-level, failures can occur in data movement or infinite loops. Incorrect or unavailable input data could also produce faults. Finally, at the highest user-level, user-defined exceptions and assertions can cause errors. Beside all these attributes, the developers had the opportunity to add new ones, like incorrect job description format at the middleware-level.

We created two tables with questions about the above-mentioned attributes. The first one asks for answers whether the system can detect and cope with these faults (prevent or recover). The second one is used to name the service or component the system uses to detect the listed faults.

2.2 Fault recovery and prevention

In the fault prevention and recovery tables, we distinguished among three abstraction levels: task, workflow, and user-level. The questionnaire also contained two tables for this section: the first is used to tell whether the listed mechanism is supported or not and the second is for naming the service that handles the faults.

At the task-level, recovery is used when a failed job is restarted on the same remote resource or resubmitted to another one. Resubmission can cause significant overheads if the following tasks have to wait for the completion of the failed task. Saving checkpoints for later resume or even for migrating of jobs with no need of restart can be a good prevention and recovery mechanism. Task replication can prevent resource failures, while alternate task can recover from internal task failures (in this case another task implementation is executed). On failures of the task manager itself, recovery means restarting the service or choosing another one. Finally, resource reliability measurements can also prevent job execution faults.

At the workflow-level, redundancy, data and workflow replication can prevent faults. Redundancy, sometimes called replication in related work, executes the same task concurrently on several resources, assuming that one of the tasks will finish without a failure. It can introduce an overhead by occupying more resources than necessary, but guarantees failure-free execution as long as at least one task does not fail. Checkpointing techniques that save the intermediate state of an executing workflow can also be used for both prevention and recovery. Light-weight checkpointing saves only the current location of the intermediate data, but not the data itself. It is fast, but restarting can only work as long as the intermediate data is available at its original location. Heavy-weight checkpointing copies all the intermediate data to a place where it can be safely kept as long as it is needed. In case of a service failure, a management service redundancy technique chooses another equivalent service or restarts the faulty service to resume operation. The transaction and rollback mechanisms can be used for the same reason. Should the workflow manager itself crash, restarting the service or choosing another manager means a high-level recovery option. Finally, the task manager reliability measurements can prevent choosing managers that are known to be unreliable.

At the highest user-level, user-defined exceptions can be taken into account to validate a proper execution.

The questionnaire also contained two tables for this section: the first is used to tell whether the listed mechanism is supported or not and the second is for naming the service that handles the faults.

3. Workflow systems

In this section we review the workflow systems whose developers responded to our questionnaire.

ASKALON 1. The goal of ASKALON [1] is to simplify the development and execution of applications that can harness the power of Grid computing. The system is developed at the University of Innsbruck, Austria, and is centred around a set of high-level services, including a scheduler for optimised

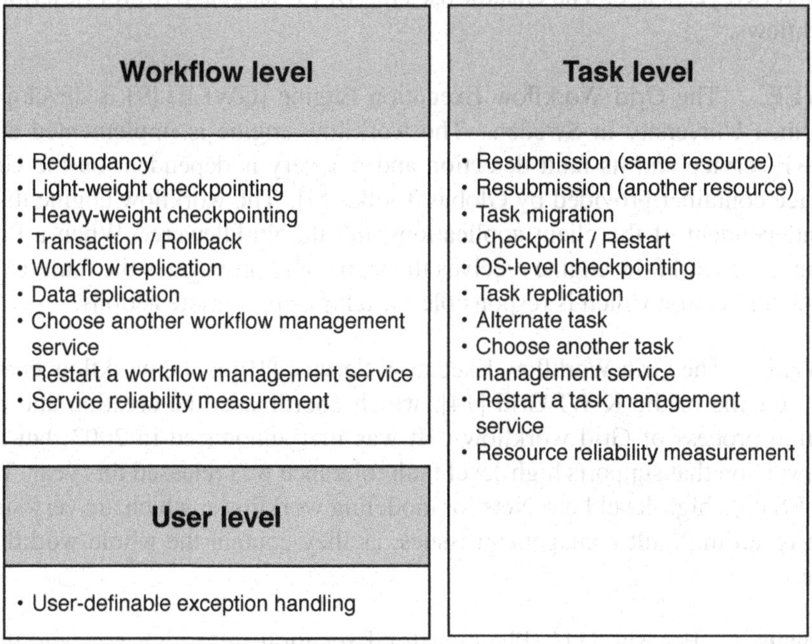

Figure 2. Identified recovery and prevention techniques and their levels of abstraction

mapping of workflows onto the Grid, an enactment engine for application execution, a resource manager covering both computers and application components, and a performance prediction service. ASKALON 1 is developed to run on top of the Globus Toolkit [4].

Chemomentum. The Chemomentum project [5] takes up and enhances state-of-the-art Grid technologies and applies them to real-world challenges in computational chemistry and related application areas. The Chemomentum system is currently under development and will add a two-layer workflow engine on top of the UNICORE 6 [6] Web service-based middleware released in 2007. The top layer, called process engine, deals with the high-level workflow concepts, while the lower layer, called service orchestrator, deals directly with lower-level concepts such as running jobs and moving files.

Escogitare. One of the main targets of the Escogitare project [7] is to enable agriculture scientists, located in several CRA institutes spread all over Italy, conduct bioinformatics and geoinformatics experiments using a workflow management system that is able to select data and instruments installed in several laboratories in a transparent and secure way. The project has been started two years ago. The enactor uses the BPEL language [8] for describing workflows.

GWEE. The Grid Workflow Execution Engine (GWEE) [9] is developed at Umea University in Sweden. The workflow engine is implemented as a WSRF service and its fault detection and recovery is dependent on the Grid service container provided by Globus Toolkit [4]. The workflow engine itself is independent of the client applications and the middleware. When a fault occurs, the workflow engine receives the signal and propagates the fault to the client application which is responsible for taking appropriate actions.

GWES. The Grid Workflow Execution Service [10] is the workflow enactment engine of the K-Wf Grid [14], which coordinates the creation and execution process of Grid workflows. It was first announced in 2003, but the new version that supports high-level fault tolerance was released this year. The GWES uses high-level Petri Nets for modeling workflows, which are very suitable regarding fault management issues, as they contain the whole workflow state.

Pegasus. Pegasus [11] (Planning for Execution in Grids) is a workflow mapping engine first released in 2001. It bridges the scientific domain and the execution environment by automatically mapping high-level workflow descriptions onto distributed infrastructures. Pegasus is built upon Condor DAGman [12], which it uses to execute its workflows on Grid infrastructures.

P-GRADE. The P-GRADE Grid Portal [3] is a Web-based service rich environment for the development, execution, and monitoring of workflows and workflow-based parameter studies on various Grid platforms, which is available since four years. Its workflow manager is based on DAGMan [12], and during the development of the new version advanced fault tolerant features will be taken into account.

ProActive. ProActive [13] is a middleware for parallel, distributed, and multi-threaded computing. ProActive is mainly addressed as a skeleton framework, but generally fits the definitions of a workflow system for the questionnaire. Many of the fault tolerance issues are handled by the lower-level middleware, in this case ProActive. The corresponding components of the architecture are the following: the ProActive executor is the unit of logic that executes the program on the computation resources, the ProActive enactor schedules tasks according to the application's semantics, and the ProActive core provides relations with other services.

Triana. Triana [15] is an open source problem solving environment developed at Cardiff University. Already used by scientists for a range of tasks such as signal, text, and image processing, Triana includes a large library of pre-written analysis tools and the ability for users to easily integrate their own tools. Triana exists since five years. Support for fault tolerance is generally user driven and interactive in Triana with little automated systems. For example, faults will generally cause workflow execution to halt, display a warning or dialog, and allow the user to modify the workflow before continuing the execution.

UNICORE 5. UNICORE (Uniform Interface to Computing Resources) [6] offers a ready-to-run Grid system including client and server software. UNICORE makes distributed computing and data resources available in a seamless and secure way in intranets and the Internet. UNICORE 5 also provides a graphical frontend that can be used to construct and execute workflows on Grids running the UNICORE 5 middleware.

4. Evaluation

In this section we summarise and discuss the results of the questionnaire evaluation. Figure 3 summarizes which of the systems can detect (first entry), prevent (second entry), and recover (third entry) from the identified faults explained in Section 2. It also shows which systems have already planned support (○) for detection, prevention, or recovery in an upcoming version.

Figure 4 shows what fault recovery techniques are currently in use by which of the surveyed workflow management systems, and which techniques are planned for the upcoming versions. A bullet (•) denotes support for the technique in the current version of the system, while a circle (○) denotes that the feature is planned for integration.

Figure 5 shows the percentage of the faults in each of the categories that are detected by a Grid workflow system on average. We can see that hardware-level faults (machine crashed or down, network down) can generally be detected by current workflow systems. When it comes to the other categories, the situation is quite different. At the operating system-level, only 37% of the faults (disk quota exceeded, out of memory, out of disk space, file not found, network congestion, CPU time limit

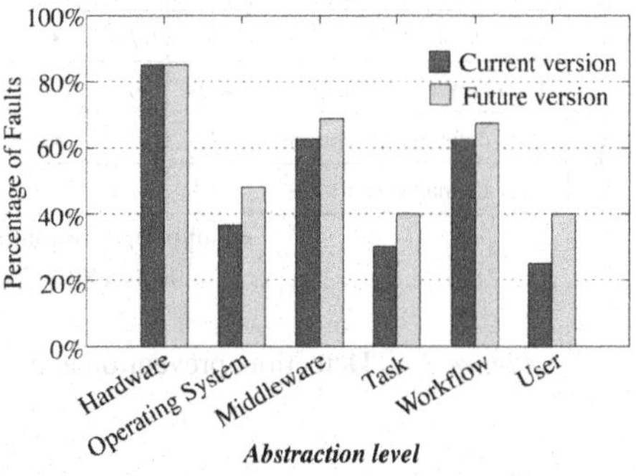

Figure 5. Average fault detection

Abstraction level		ASKALON 1	Chemomentum	Escogitare	GWEE	GWES	Pegasus	P-GRADE	ProActive	Triana	UNICORE 5
HW	Machine crashed/down	●/-/●	●/-/○	●/●/○	-/-/-	●/-/●	●/-/●	●/-/●	●/○/●	●/○/○	●/-/-
	Network down	●/-/●	●/-/○	●/●/○	-/-/-	●/-/●	●/-/●	●/-/●	●/○/●	●/○/○	●/-/-
Operating system	Disk quota exceeded	●/-/-	-/-/-	-/-/-	-/-/-	-/-/-	-/-/○	●/-/●	●/○/○	○/○/○	●/-/-
	Out of memory	-/-/-	-/-/-	-/-/-	-/-/-	-/-/-	-/-/-	●/-/●	●/○/○	○/○/○	●/-/-
	Out of disk space	●/-/●	-/-/-	-/-/-	-/-/-	-/-/-	-/-/○	●/-/●	●/○/○	○/○/○	●/-/-
	File not found	●/-/-	-/-/-	-/-/-	-/-/-	●/-/●	●/-/●	●/●/●	●/○/○	●/○/○	●/-/-
	Network congestion	-/-/-	-/-/-	-/-/-	-/-/-	-/-/-	-/-/-	-/-/-	○/-/○	○/○/○	●/-/-
	CPU time limit exceeded	-/-/-	-/-/-	-/-/-	-/-/-	-/-/-	●/-/-	-/-/-	○/-/○	○/○/○	●/-/-
Middleware	Authentication failed	●/-/-	●/-/-	○/-/-	●/-/●	●/-/●	●/-/-	●/-/●	●/○/●	●/○/○	●/-/-
	Job submission failed	●/-/●	●/-/●	-/-/-	●/-/●	●/-/●	●/-/●	●/-/●	●/○/●	●/○/○	●/-/-
	Job hanging in the local resource manager queue	-/-/-	-/-/-	-/-/-	-/-/-	-/-/-	-/-/-	●/-/●	○/○/○	●/○/○	●/-/-
	Job lost before reaching the local resource manager	-/-/-	-/-/-	-/-/-	-/-/-	-/-/-	-/-/-	●/-/●	○/○/○	●/○/○	●/-/●
	Too many concurrent requests	-/-/-	-/-/-	-/-/-	-/-/-	-/-/-	-/-/-	-/-/-	○/○/○	●/○/○	●/●/-
	Service not reachable	●/-/-	●/-/●	●/-/○	-/-/-	●/-/●	-/-/-	●/-/●	●/○/○	●/○/○	●/○/●
	File staging failure	●/-/-	●/-/-	-/-/-	●/-/●	●/-/-	●/-/●	●/-/●	●/○/○	●/○/○	●/○/○
Task	Memory leak	-/-/-	-/-/-	-/-/-	-/-/-	-/-/-	-/-/-	-/-/-	○/○/○	○/○/○	●/-/-
	Uncaught exception	-/-/-	-/-/-	-/-/-	-/-/-	-/-/-	-/-/-	-/-/-	●/○/○	●/○/○	●/-/-
	Deadlock / Livelock	-/-/-	-/-/-	-/-/-	-/-/-	-/-/-	-/-/-	-/-/-	○/○/○	○/○/○	●/-/-
	Incorrect output data	-/-/-	-/-/-	-/-/-	-/-/-	●/-/-	-/-/-	-/-/-	●/●/○	●/○/○	●/-/-
	Missing shared libraries	-/-/-	-/-/-	-/-/-	-/-/-	-/-/-	-/-/-	-/-/●	○/○/○	●/○/○	●/-/-
	Job crashed	-/-/-	●/-/-	-/-/-	●/-/●	●/-/●	●/-/-	●/-/●	○/○/○	●/○/○	●/-/○
Workflow	Infinite loop	-/-/-	-/-/-	●/-/-	-/-/-	●/-/-	-/-/-	-/-/-	○/○/○	○/○/○	-/-/-
	Input data not available	●/-/-	●/-/-	●/-/-	-/-/-	●/-/-	●/-/-	●/●/●	●/○/○	●/○/○	●/-/-
	Input error	-/-/-	-/-/-	●/-/-	-/-/-	●/-/-	-/-/-	-/-/-	●/○/○	●/○/○	●/-/-
	Data movement failed	●/-/●	●/-/-	-/-/-	●/-/●	●/-/-	●/-/●	●/-/●	●/○/○	●/○/○	●/-/-
User	User-definable exceptions	○/-/-	-/-/-	●/-/○	-/-/-	●/-/●	-/-/-	-/-/-	●/○/○	○/○/○	●/-/-
	User-definable assertions	○/-/-	-/-/-	-/-/-	-/-/-	●/-/●	-/-/-	-/-/-	○/○/○	○/○/○	●/-/-

●=supported; ○=planned; -=not supported
detection/prevention/recovery

Figure 3. Detection, prevention and recovery support for the identified faults.

exceeded) are currently detected on average. Fault detection at middleware-level (authentication failed, job submission failed, job hanging in the queue of the local resource manager, job lost before reaching the local resource man-

Abstraction level		ASKALON 1	Chemomentum	Escogitare	GWEE	GWES	Pegasus	P-GRADE	ProActive	Triana	UNICORE 5
Workflow	Redundancy	•	-	o	-	•	•	•	o	o	-
	Light-weight checkpointing	o	•	-	•	•	•	•	-	•	-
	Heavy-weight checkpointing	o	•	-	•	•	-	-	-	o	-
	Transaction/Rollback mechanism	-	-	o	•	-	-	-	•	o	-
	Workflow replication	-	-	-	-	•	-	-	-	o	-
	Data replication	-	-	o	-	•	-	-	-	o	-
	Choose another workflow management service	-	•	-	-	•	-	-	-	•	-
	Restart a workflow management service	-	-	-	•	-	-	•	o	•	-
	Task management service reliability measurement	o	•	-	-	-	-	-	-	o	•
Task	Resubmission (same resource)	•	•	o	-	•	•	•	•	•	•
	Resubmission (another resource)	•	•	o	-	•	•	•	•	•	o
	Task migration	-	-	-	-	-	o	-	-	o	-
	Checkpoint / Restart mechanism	o	-	-	-	-	•	-	•	o	-
	Checkpoint / Restart at the OS-level	-	-	-	-	-	-	•	-	o	-
	Task replication	-	-	-	-	-	o	-	o	o	-
	Alternate task	-	-	-	-	-	o	-	-	•	-
	Choose another task management service	-	-	-	-	-	-	•	-	•	-
	Restart a task management service	-	-	-	-	-	-	o	o	•	-
	Resource reliability measurement	-	-	-	-	•	-	o	-	o	•
User	User-defined exception handling	-	-	o	-	•	-	-	•	o	-

•=supported; o=planned

Figure 4. Fault tolerance techniques

ager, too many concurrent requests, service not reachable/not responding, file staging failure) is more common, an average of 62.8% of these faults being detected. Almost the same percentage of faults (62.5%) are detected at the workflow-level (infinite loop, input data not available, input error, data movement failed). The worst fault detection support can be observed at the task-level (memory leak, uncaught exception, deadlock/livelock, incorrect output data, missing shared libraries, job crashed) and user-level (user-definable exceptions, user-definable assertions), where only 30% (task-level), respectively 25% (user-level) of the faults are detected.

More insight into the reasons for such a poor support on the task-level faults can be seen in the left part of Figure 6. This figure shows for every task-level fault the percentage of the systems that are able to detect it. We can observe that only one from the ten systems studied is able to detect a memory leak that happens inside an executed task. Deadlocks/livelocks are also only detected by one of the studied systems. While uncaught exceptions (e.g. numerical exceptions) and incorrect output data are detected by three systems, missing shared libraries are only detected by two. Detection of a crashed job seems to be a problem that most of the systems are able to solve, seven out of ten systems implementing this functionality.

The right part of Figure 6 shows the percentage of the faults of every category that is prevented by a Grid workflow system on average. We can see that fault prevention is virtually non-existent in the current versions of the studied workflow systems, which is what we expected. We believe that the reason for this is that Grid workflow management systems are usually built on top of some fundamental Grid middleware such as Globus, gLite, or UNICORE, which do not expose the needed low-level functionality to prevent such faults.

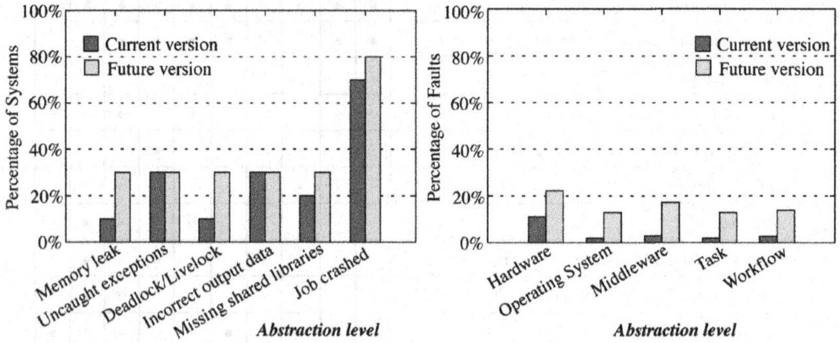

Figure 6. Percentage of systems that can detect the various task level faults (left) and Average fault prevention (right)

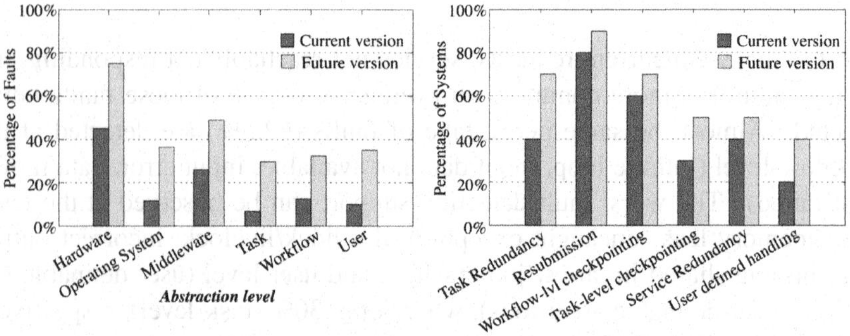

Figure 7. Average fault recovery (left) and Percentage of systems that implement at least one fault tolerance technique of the specified category (right)

The left part of Figure 7 shows the percentage of the faults of every category that a Grid workflow system can recover from, on average. While the average

Grid workflow systems can recover from 45% of the hardware-level faults and 26% of the middleware-level faults, they can only recover from 11.6% of the operating system-level faults, 12.5% of the workflow-level faults, and 6.7% of the task-level faults. Taking a closer look at the task-level faults reveals that only four out of ten systems can recover from a job crash. Generally, it can be concluded that current systems can recover from far fewer faults than they can detect, especially at the middleware and workflow-levels.

The right part of Figure 7 shows the percentage of systems that implement at least one of the fault tolerance techniques in each of the categories: task redundancy (workflow-level and task-level), resubmission (task-level to the same or to another resource), workflow-level checkpointing (light-weight and heavy-weight checkpointing/restart techniques), task-level checkpointing (task-level checkpointing/restart and operating system-level checkpointing/restart techniques), management service redundancy (workflow-level: choose another workflow management service, restart a workflow management service; task-level: choose another task management service, restart a task management service) and user-defined exception handling.

As expected, the techniques that are the easiest to implement are used by most of the systems. Resubmission techniques are used by 80% of the systems; redundancy techniques are used by 40% systems and are planned for implementation in another 30% of the systems in a future version. While 60% of the systems use workflow-level checkpointing techniques, only 30% of the systems are using task-level checkpointing. This shows that it is still hard to implement task-level checkpointing in a satisfactory way, in particular due to portability limitations. While only 40% of the systems use management service redundancy techniques, this might be due to the fact that not all of them use a design that enables them to use redundant instances of management services. Surprisingly, only 20% of the systems enable users to define their own exception handling behavior.

Based on our analysis, we identify the following areas that are in most need of continuing research, so that future systems can easily incorporate the fault tolerance techniques they need for widespread adoption: user-definable assertions and exception handling techniques, fault prevention techniques, task-level checkpointing techniques and extension of fault detection support passing through the middleware-border to lower-levels.

5. Conclusions

In this paper we showed that there definitely exist an effort in the community to make current workflow management systems fault tolerant. We conducted a questionnaire and presented the results in the form of several diagrams that revealed the generally supported features and the open issues. As a final conclusion, the community cannot be satisfied with current achievements. Though fault detection mechanisms are widely used, current middleware limitations definitely draw a border that the available systems cannot cross. New mechanisms should be developed to extend detection to lower-levels, such as hardware and job execution faults. The prevention and recovery features are even weaker. Many of the detected faults are not handled with recovery, and only little support is given to the users. Since Grid development is moving towards creating self-aware solutions, these techniques need to appear in workflow enactors too. We believe the current situation revealed in this paper helps researchers to focus on unsupported requirements. In this way, future planning and work can be carried out more efficiently by paying more attention to user needs and system endurance.

Acknowledgments

This work is co-funded by the European Commission through the FP6 network of excellence CoreGRID (contract IST-2002-004265) and EGEE-II (contract INFSO-RI-031688) projects.

References

[1] T. Fahringer et. al., ASKALON: A Development and Grid Computing Environment for Scientific Workflows, Scientific Workflows for Grids, Chapter Frameworks and Tools: Workflow Generation, Refinement and Execution, Springer Verlag, 2007.

[2] J. Yu and R. Buyya, A Taxonomy of Workflow Management Systems for Grid Computing, Journal of Grid Computing, Volume 3, Numbers 3-4, Pages: 171-200, Springer Science+Business Media B.V., Sept. 2005.

[3] P. Kacsuk, G. Sipos, Multi-Grid, Multi-User Workflows in the P-GRADE Grid Portal, Journal of Grid Computing, Feb 2006, pp. 1-18.

[4] I. Foster C. Kesselman, The Globus project: A status report, Heterogeneous Computing Workshop, IEEE Computer Society Press, 1998, pp. 4-18.

[5] B. Schuller et. al., Chemomentum - UNICORE 6 based infrastructure for complex applications in science and technology, 3rd UNICORE Summit 2007, Rennes, France

[6] A. Streit et. al., UNICORE - From Project Results to Production Grids, Grid Computing: The New Frontiers of High Performance Processing, Advances in Parallel Computing 14, Elsevier, 2005, pages 357-376

[7] D. Laforenza et. al., Biological Experiments on the Grid: A Novel Workflow Management Platform, pp. 489-494, 20th IEEE Int. Symp. on Computer-Based Medical Systems, 2007

[8] http://www.activebpel.org

[9] E. Elmroth, F. Hernandez and J. Tordsson. A light-weight Grid workflow execution service enabling client and middleware independence. Proceedings of the Grid Applications and Middleware Workshop 2007, Springer.

[10] A. Hoheisel and M. Alt: Petri Nets. In: Workflows for eScience, Springer, 2006

[11] N. Mandal et. al., Integrating Existing Scientific Workflow Systems: The Kepler/Pegasus Example, 2nd Workshop on Workflows in Support of Large-Scale Science, Monterrey, CA, June 2007

[12] D. Thain, T. Tannenbaum, and M. Livny, Distributed Computing in Practice: The Condor Experience, Concurrency and Computation: Practice and Experience, 2005, pp. 323-356.

[13] F. Baude et. al., A Hybrid Message Logging-CIC Protocol for Constrained Checkpointability, Proceedings of EuroPar 2005, September 2005, Lisbon, Portugal

[14] M. Bubak, et al., K-WfGrid Consortium: K-Wf Grid - Knowledge based Workflow system for Grid Applications, Proceedings of the Cracow Grid Workshop 2004, Academic Computer Centre CYFRONET AGH, Poland, 2005.

[15] I. Taylor et. al., The Triana Workflow Environment: Architecture and Applications, In Workflows for e-Science, p. 320-339. Springer, New York, Secaucus, NJ, USA, 2007.

TOWARDS SELF-ADAPTABLE MONITORING FRAMEWORK FOR SELF-HEALING

Javier Alonso, Jordi Torres
Technical University of Catalonia
Barcelona Supercomputing Center
Barcelona, Spain.
alonso@ac.upc.edu, torres@ac.upc.edu

Rean Griffith, Gail Kaiser
Department of Computer Science,
Columbia University,
New York, NY, USA
rg2023@columbia.edu, kaiser@cs.columbia.edu

Luis Moura Silva
University of Coimbra
CISUC, Portugal
luis@dei.uc.pt

Abstract Traditionally, monitoring solutions are based on collecting a reduced set of external metrics about the system such as performance, memory consumption or response time. However, these tools are limited to detecting and diagnosing failures or errors in complex systems like application servers and grid services. New applications have embedded monitoring logic merged with business logic to better monitor and trace applications. This approach creates dependence between the "real" code and the monitoring code though, reducing the monitoring approach flexibility. Furthermore, both approaches (external or embedded monitoring) are not adaptable; they cannot change monitoring process level or precision at runtime. In this paper, we present a fine-grain monitoring framework architecture based on aspect-oriented technology. Aspect Oriented Programming offers the possibility to inject monitoring code dynamically, and even activate or deactivate monitoring code at runtime, allowing the collecting of metrics at the appropriate granularity (i.e. application level or method calls level).

Keywords: Monitoring System, Aspect-Oriented Programming, Self-monitoring, Self-healing

1. Introduction

The benefits of including effective monitoring systems which allow us to collect complex systems' real internal state have been recognized in engineering disciplines because they help increasing availability and obtaining more robust systems. For example, the real time monitoring of bridges or buildings [2] or the health monitoring systems integrated in the aircrafts [3]. In fact, the need for including these internal and external monitoring systems is considered fundamental in order to achieve the Autonomic computing goals [1]. The autonomic computing systems are based on an autonomic manager which has to *monitor* the state of the system and performs the self-* tasks in agreement. Monitoring systems have to collect enough data from the monitored system to allow the human administrator or the system itself to detect or even predict failures and avoid them via recovery or preventive techniques. The merge between the monitoring system (with the capability to detect and/or predict failures) and the recovery/preventive techniques is called self-healing.

However, traditionally, the monitoring tools have been focused on collecting a reduced set of external data from the system like performance, memory consumption and response time. As an example, we find several commercial and free solutions like Ganglia [5] or Nagios[6]. Both these systems allow detecting failures in our systems when the failure happens. The detection is based on rules defined by the human System Administrators following their experience. The effectiveness of these solutions is limited. These tools detect failures but they cannot predict them or even determinate where the error is.

In the last years, the new applications have introduced tracing code with the objective to help the System Administrator to determinate where the error is when the failure happens. However, this approach only offers a post-mortem analysis of the root-cause failure. Moreover, these solutions aren't portable to other applications because they're developed ad-hoc and they require a re-engineering work in order to adapt applications to obtaining tracing features. For all of this, it is needed to include monitoring systems which can collect external and internal data from complex systems at runtime to detect and even predict failures as well as to be able to integrate itself in the system without re-engineering the application or obtain the source code. It is also necessary that these monitoring systems are adaptable and flexible to allow activation or monitoring level change (from application to method level or vice versa) at runtime. This adaptability and flexibility of the framework allows to obtain a fine-grain monitoring level, achieving a more effective coverage in front of the potential anomalies of failures.

In this paper we present AOP-monitoring framework based on Aspect Oriented Programming (AOP) [4] technology to achieve our below described objectives. AOP-Monitoring framework, which is presented in detail in section

3, uses AOP to wave monitoring code (we will call them, sensors) within the system code during compile or load time without the need to know how the monitored system source code is, but besides, the AOP-monitoring framework can activate or deactivate these sensors, as well as it is possible to modify the sensors' behavior, all of this at runtime. These features offer an adaptable, flexible and portable monitoring system with an acceptable overhead.

The rest of the paper follows as section 2 presents Aspect Oriented programming and solutions based on this technology in the area of and present the Aspect-Oriented programming paradigm. Section 3 presents our proposal architecture. Section 3.1 presents our approach's overhead and section 4 concludes this paper and presents the next to-do steps.

2. Aspect Oriented Programming

In this section we present the Aspect Oriented Programming technology. Furthermore, we present a brief set of solutions based on AOP in the self-healing and monitoring research area.

2.1 Aspect Oriented Programming

It is out of scope of this paper to present the Aspect Oriented programming technology in detail, though necessary to introduce a brief description of the technology to make clearer the solution presented in this paper. AOP attempts to aid programmers in the separation of concerns, specifically cross-cutting concerns offering a new level of modularization.

Aspects is the name of the main concept of the AOP technology. The Aspects are composed by two elements: *Advices* and *Join Points*. The Advices are the code that is executed when the aspect is invoked: the Advice has access to the class, methods and/or fields of the module which the advice invokes. The Join point is the definition to indicate when the advice will be invoked. We can see the Join point like a trigger: when the condition is true the Advice is invoked.

For this technology's implementation, we have chosen AspectJ [7] because it is a well-known widely used and mature technology developed by the eclipse IDE [8]. In addition, this technology offers a simple and powerful definition of Aspects like Java class, so the learning curve is quite quick for experienced Java developers.

2.2 AOP Self-healing and Self-monitoring solutions

The use of Aspect Oriented programming in the self-healing area is not a new approach. There are several papers where authors present different self-healing architectures based on AOP power to introduce self-healing techniques, like a cross-cutting concern inside the business logic from applications

[9–11]. All of these papers present different recovery systems based on an Aspect Oriented paradigm. However, they don't take into account the monitoring process to determine the exact correct moment to apply the recovery actions.

On the other hand, the use of Aspect Oriented programming in the area of self-monitoring is hardly an explored solution. Currently, the most mature solution in this area could be Glassbox [12]. This monitoring framework is based only on our application's performance monitoring using AspectJ. Although Glassbox is an static powerful monitoring framework and even exploits the power of Aspect Oriented programming to allow a fine-grain monitoring level, Glassbox doesn't offer the possibility to change the monitoring level at real time.

Also, we can find some works in the area of operating systems like TOSKANA [16]. TOSKANA provides before, after and around advice for kernel functions and supports the definition of pointcuts as well as the implementation of aspects.

3. Fine-grain Monitoring Framework Architecture

In this section we present the fine-grain monitoring framework architecture called AOP-Monitoring framework. We have designed an architecture based on a modification of a health monitoring architecture defined in [13]. Figure 1 shows a simplification of the architecture of our framework. AOP-Monitoring Framework is composed by two main modules: *Sensors* and the *Monitor Manager*. The sensors are entrusted to collect data from the system. They are Aspects, which are injected in the code via AspectJ tools. There is one sensor for every data or event that we want to monitor. We can define sensors at different monitoring levels. For example; when a method is called, when a constructor is invoked, before one object is initialized, when a class' field is assigned or even when an exception handler is executed. When the sensor collects enough data (defined by the Monitor manager), this data is sent to the Monitor Manager to be analyzed and to take decisions about the system.

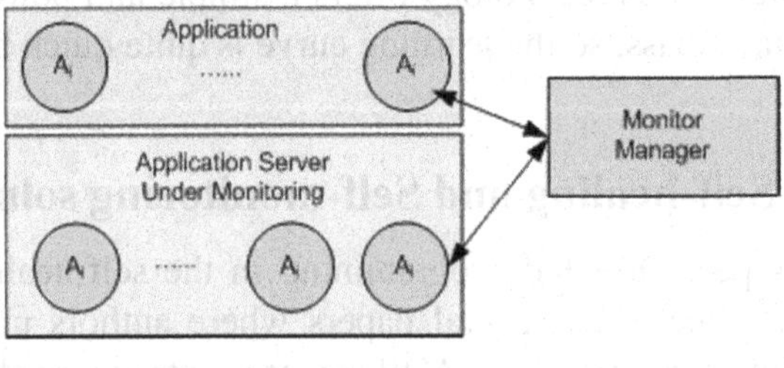

Figure 1. Basic Architecture of AOP Monitoring Framework

The Monitor Manager has the responsibility to recollect all the data from all the active sensors and determine the policy to follow. The monitor manager allows failure prediction by using data mining or forecasting methods using the sensor collected data. If the prediction methods need more data from the system or a low level monitoring, the Monitor Manager can activate new sensors and deactivate others to obtain these data to accurately determine if there will be a failure or an error. Furthermore, the Monitor Manager can change the sensors' behavior, i.e. It is possible to redefine the sensor's elapse time in between collecting data. This offers a great flexibility and adaptability and reduces the overhead when the system behavior seems correct and allows to expand the monitoring level according to the situation when it is needed.

In figure 2, we present a detail of a sensor architecture. We have two components to build a sensor. We have the real sensor (an advice defined using AspectJ) and a Sensor Manager Proxy. The Sensor Manager Proxy has the task to communicate with the Monitor Manager. The Sensor Manager Proxy can activate or deactivate the sensor, it can also change the time between monitoring tasks and has to send the data to the Monitor Manager, as well as receive new orders from the Monitor Manager to then act accordingly.

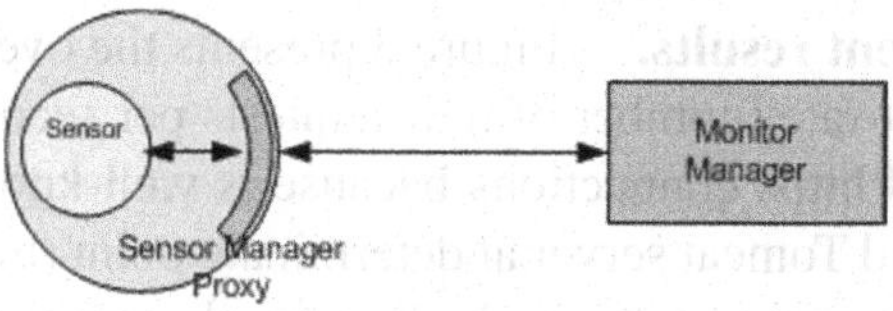

Figure 2. Detailed Architecture of a Sensor

3.1 AOP-Monitoring Framework Overhead

This monitoring framework is still under development. Currently, we have a first version of the framework without data mining or forecasting methods. Moreover, we have developed two sensors at the moment. These sensors monitor the memory consumption and the CPU status. The capability to activate or deactivate a sensor is developed and the possibility to change the time between monitoring tasks is developed too. However, it is needed continue the development to demonstrate the effectiveness of our solution to detect early failures or error and demonstrate the coverage of our solution according to the type of error or failure.

However, an important point has to be evaluated before to continue developing the solution: the overhead of this approach. If the overhead is too high using this simple version of the framework, the approach would be useless for our main goals. We have evaluated the overhead of this solution running a very simplistic web application over a Tomcat Server 5.5.20 [14]. We have injected our two sensors in every method call in the core of Tomcat Server. We have weaved the sensors within Bootstrap, Catalina and Commons-daemon jar files. Before every method call in every Tomcat Thread the sensors collect data from the server every 5 seconds and send data to the Monitor Manager, via Monitor Manager Proxy, every 15 seconds.

3.1.1 Experiment environment. The client workload for the experiments was generated using a workload generator and web performance measurement tool called Httperf [15]. The configuration parameters of the benchmarking tool used for the experiments presented in this paper were set to create a realistic workload. We consider that a simple workload requesting static web content is enough to demonstrate the overhead of our approach, because we are monitoring the Tomcat Server, not the application over it. We have configured Httperf setting the client timeout value to 10 seconds. Tomcat runs on a 4-way Intel XEON 1.4 GHz with 2 GB RAM. We have also a 2-way Intel XEON 2.4 GHz with 2 GB RAM running the workload generator. Two machines run the 2.6.8.1 Linux kernel with Sun JVM 1.4.2, which are connected through a 1 Gbps Ethernet interface.

3.1.2 Experiment results. Figure 3 presents the overhead obtained using different request rate (number of new requests per second). To obtain this curve we have used https connections because is well-know that this type of connections overload Tomcat server at determinate point (in this case when the rate is around 25 new requests/second). We can observe that deviation performance is evident when the curve achieves the maximum value (around 25 new clients per second). In the rest of the curve we can observe that the results are quite the same.

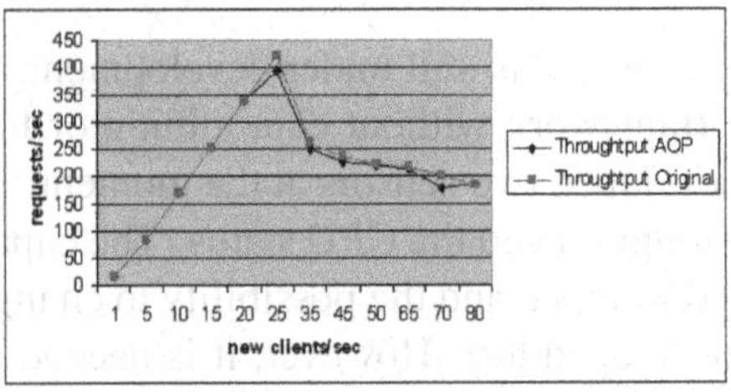

Figure 3. Throughput obtained from Tomcat with and without AOP-Monitoring Framework

If we observe the table 1, we can observe that the overhead introduced in the maximum point is around 6%. On the other hand, we can observe that the response time increase around the 16%, 12 ms. This value has to be improved, however we can observe that the value increased (12ms) is quite imperceptible in the web applications.

Table 1. Detailed results when the request rate is 25 requests/sec

Environment	*Avg. Throughput*	*Avg. Respon. Time*	*Overhead*
Tomcat Original	422 req/sec	84,2 ms	6,2%
Tomcat + AOP Framework	395,7 req/sec	98,4 ms	16%(12ms)

We can conclude that our solution has promising future because the overhead is reduced when we monitor every call method every 5 seconds, and with an heavy workload in this scenario. However, we have to continue working to avoid introducing an important overhead, which could provoke that the solution will be useless for our objectives.

4. Conclusion and Future work

In this paper, we have presented a work in progress fine-grain monitoring framework. The architecture presented is focused on offering a flexible and adaptable fine-grain monitoring framework, which can collect a big set of internal and external metrics to predict offer early detection for potential failures or errors. The architecture presented allows to activate or deactivate sensors and change the behavior of sensors at runtime, changing the level of monitoring when it is needed to obtain more fine-grain data from the system. These capabilities have to offer a better coverage of errors and failures than the traditional external monitoring systems.

In our opinion, our approach could offer a great failure coverage thanks of the possibility to change the level of monitoring. This feature could be very useful in conjunction with self-healing techniques. For example, if we will merge self-healing techniques like [10]or [11]with a mature solution of our approach we could achieve a powerful self-healing system because, we could apply the recovery action in the correct moment improving the benefits of these self-healing solutions.

However, this framework is under development yet. Next steps is to develop new sensors to obtain more data from the server like sensors to handle potential exceptions at server and application levels. After that, it is needed to develop new experiments to demonstrate the effectiveness of our approach to offer early detection failures and measure the coverage of the framework according to the failures or errors. Of course, the overhead has to be evaluated again when the systems will be mature to measure better the overhead introduced for AOP-Monitoring framework as well as how many overhead introduce or reduce the fact of activate or deactivate or change the behavior of sensors.

Last step will be the introduction of machine learning algorithms or forecasting methods, which can predict failures in advance using the metrics obtained from the server. It is important this point to define the policies applied by the Monitor Manager, activating or deactivating sensors according to the needed of forecasting or machine learning methods.

Acknowledgments

This research work is supported by the FP6 Network of Excellence CoreGRID funded by the European Commission (Contract IST-2002-004265), the Ministry of Science and Technology of Spain under contract TIN2007-60625 and The Programming Systems Laboratory which is funded in part by NSF grants CNS-0717544, CNS-0627473, CNS-0426623 and EIA-0202063, NIH grant 1U54CA121852-01A1, and Consolidated Edison Company of New York.

References

[1] Jeffrey O. Kephart and David M. Chess. The vision of Autonomic Computing. In *Computer*,v.36 n.1, p.41-50, January 2003.

[2] H. Sohn et at. A review of Structural Health monitoring literature: 1996-2001. *Los Alamos National Laboratory Report*, LA-13976-MS, 2003.

[3] R. Muldoon, J. Gill, L. Brock. Integrated Mechanical Diagnostic (IMD) Health and Usage Monitoring Systems (HUMS): An Open System Implementation Case Study. *Proc. 18th IEEE Digital Avionics System Conference*, pp. 9.B.4.1-8, Oct. 1999.

[4] G. Kiczales at al. Aspect Oriented Programming. *Lecture Notes in Computer Science*, Vol. 1241, pp.220-242, Springer 1997.

[5] [web-site at April 2008] *http://ganglia.info/*

[6] [web-site at April 2008] *http://www.nagios.org/*

[7] G. Kiczales at al. An Overview of AspectJ. *Proc. European Conference for Object-Oriented Programming(ECOOP 2001).* Lecture notes in Computer Science, Vol. 2072, pp. 626-657, 2001.

[8] [web-site at April 2008] *http://www.eclipse.org/aspectj*

[9] Stelios Sidiroglou, Oren Laadan, Angelos D. Keromytis, and Jason Nieh. Using Rescue Points to Navigate Software Recovery (Short Paper). In *Proceedings of the IEEE Symposium on Security and Privacy*, May 2007.

[10] R. Griffith and G. Kaiser. Adding self-healing capabilities to the common language runtime. *Technical report*, Columbia University, 2005.

[11] L. Baresi, S. Guinea and L. Pasquale. Self-healing BPEL Processes with Dynamo an dthe JBoss Rule Engine. *Int. workshop on Engineering of software services for pervasive environments*, pp. 11-20, 2007.

[12] [web-site at April 2008] *http://www.glassbox.com/glassbox/Home.html*

[13] Alexander Lau and Rudolph E. Seviora. Design Patterns for Software Health Monitoring. *Proceedings of the Tenth International Conference Engineering of Complex Computer Systems (ICECCS)*,IEEE, 2005, pp. 467-476.

[14] The Apache Jakarta Tomcat 5 Servlet/JSP Container. *http://tomcat.apache.org/*[web-site at April 2008]

[15] D. Mosberger and T. Jin. httperf: A Tool for Measuring Web Server Performance. *Workshop on Internet Server Performance*, pp.59-67. WI-USA. June 98.

[16] Michael Engel , Bernd Freisleben. Supporting autonomic computing functionality via dynamic operating system kernel aspects. *Proceedings of the 4th international conference on Aspect-oriented software development*, p.51-62, March 14-18, 2005, Chicago, Illinois

PERFORMANCE MONITORING OF GRID SUPERSCALAR: SUMMING UP

Wlodzimierz Funika, Piotr Machner
Inst. Computer Science, AGH, al. Mickiewicza 30, 30-059 Kraków, Poland
funika@agh.edu.pl
machner@student.agh.edu.pl

Marian Bubak
Inst. Computer Science, AGH, al. Mickiewicza 30, 30-059 Kraków, Poland
Academic Computer Centre – CYFRONET, Nawojki 11, 30-950 Kraków, Poland
bubak@agh.edu.pl

Rosa M. Badia, Raül Sirvent
Univ. Politècnica de Catalunya, C/ Jordi Girona, 1-3, E-08034 Barcelona, Spain
rosab@ac.upc.edu
rsirvent@ac.upc.edu

Abstract

This paper summarizes a series of papers on the integration of the OCM-G monitoring system into the GRID superscalar environment (GS). In this paper we present all the work done to achieve this goal. We briefly discuss the changes to OCM-G and the G-PM tool that were more thoroughly described in the previous papers. We show the monitoring solutions provided for GRID superscalar application developers and how they can influence their work. Both the main advantages and areas that need further research are presented. Based on all this, we come up with final general conclusions.

Keywords: grid computing, grid programming models, monitoring tools, performance analysis, visualization

1. Introduction

Creating distributed systems or applications is a complex task. One comes across problems that just don't exist when writing applications dedicated for a single machine or encounters problems similar to that on single machines but much harder. Such issues can involve the need for synchronization, communication between different parts of the system, maintaining security when exchanging data and so on. These problems manifest themselves especially in Grid environments because such environments are by nature heterogeneous and in most cases undergo constant changes as to system configuration and operation decisions. Because of this, it is especially useful to be able to monitor distributed applications where there exist more reasons for potential bottlenecks or performance, scalability, or security issues.

One of the challenging environments where solving performance issues can be supported by monitoring tools is the GRID superscalar (GS) [1] which was created in order to facilitate the task of creating Grid applications and make it almost as easy as creating a sequential program. The environment (built upon the Globus Toolkit [3]) allows the user to create a master process that invokes so called Grid-enabled functions which, in turn, are executed as worker processes on other machines. Owing to this approach, the programmer can write the master in a manner similar to writing an application for a single machine. Most of the burden of parallelizing the workload is put on the GS framework.

For monitoring GRID superscalar we decided to adapt the OCM-G monitoring system [5], which had already proved to be helpful when used for Grid interactive applications [4]. Its main advantages are the ability to gather data on-line during application lifetime, an extendible set of flexible monitoring services, which can be combined into a needed monitoring request, and low monitoring overhead. It also provides a clearly defined interface allowing other tools to access this data and visualize it: this feature enables to smoothly move from one distributed programming platform to another platform while preserving tool(s) functionality the user got accustomed to.

One of such tools is the G-PM tool [6] for Grid-oriented performance analysis. It enables to evaluate performance with standard and user-defined metrics and to visualize it in a number of ways, for example on multicurve, piechart, histogram and bargraph diagrams. The user can choose from a number of metrics and visualization modes. G-PM itself was created with MPI applications in mind, so a big part of our work was moving from message-passing monitoring functionality to the GS programming paradigm.

In this paper we are present this effort, along with other tasks that allowed to adapt OCM-G and G-PM to the requirements of GRID superscalar. This paper sums up the research whose particular issues were presented in a series of articles [7–10]. We show to what extent we have managed to fulfill our goals (being able to fully monitor a GS application). The biggest difficulties and challenges along with the details on which ones we've managed to overcome and how are also described. Finally, we come up with a general assessment explaining how the monitoring environment can be useful, what capabilities it provides for a GS application developer but also which areas still need improvement.

This paper is organized as follows: in Section 2 we address the concept of adapting OCM-G to the monitoring of GS, while Section 3 describes the research carried out to enable GS monitoring. Individual tasks are presented from a developer's point of view and without going into deeper details (for more information please see our previous papers [7–10]). Section 4 shows the value of this work - the monitoring capabilities of the environment. This is also a short description of how it can be useful and what the main advantages of the final solution are. In Section 5 we are briefly discussing the overhead induced by monitoring. Section 6 presents the challenges that we have not solved yet and possible ideas on how the work done should evolve in the future. Section 7 summarizes the environment as a whole, giving some final conclusions.

2. Issues of the Monitoring of GS Applications with OCM-G

In the paper we outline an adaptation of the ideas underlying the solutions for the monitoring of Grid applications with the OCM-G to different constraints defined by GS–based application features. Below, we describe the architecture and implementation of a monitoring system for GS applications.

The architecture of the GS-oriented application monitoring system is presented in Fig. 1. Between the GS application and GS run-time, we insert an additional event triggering wrapper. The wrapper transparently passes calls from an application to GS run-time, and sends all required monitoring data (the name of a GS method, and call parameters) to the OCM-G.

Our system also supports the monitoring of other user events, e.g. it can send all kinds of messages (integers or floating numbers, character strings) to the monitoring application. This is done using so called *probes*, functions that trigger events. A tool which is connected to OCM-G can enable/disable probes and activate/deactivate the event triggering.

We made the assumptions as follows: The OCM-G enables to gather all information needed by a GUI tool or by an automatic one. In particular, the system can monitor invocations of GS primitives: `GS_On()`, `GS_Off()`, `Execute()`, `GS_Open()`, `GS_Close()`, `GS_Barrier()`, etc. The system allows for gathering the data needed for performance metrics such as the amount of data sent, time of data transmission and process identifiers. The OCM-G

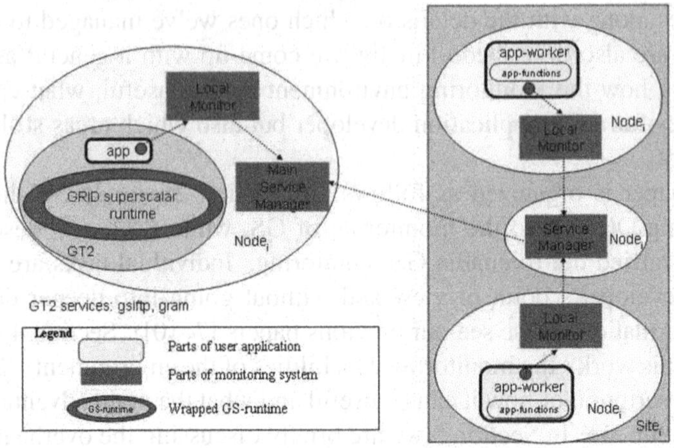

Figure 1. Monitoring of GS–based applications - architecture

concept allows to control the amount and frequency of monitored data sent from the monitored application to the monitoring system. To avoid unnecessary traffic and overhead, the monitoring data is sent to the monitor only if is explicitly required.

To allow the system under discussion to monitor GS–based applications, some specific start-up steps have to be performed:

- the OCM-G should be initialized from within the application code
- *OCM-G Main Service Manager* (MSM) should be up and running
- An application should be started (this step should be performed with additional parameters pointing to the MSM. During this step, the *Service Manager* (SM) and the *Local Monitor* (LM) are created automatically, if needed, by the application process, or the process can connect to SMs and LMs that have already been created beforehand.
- Now, any component that can communicate using the OMIS interface [2] can connect to the *Main Service Manager*, subscribe to the required probes and receive the monitored events of interest, to make decisions, e.g. about migrating the application to another Grid node if necessary.

To enable the intercepting of calls to GS run-time primitives, we need to instrument the GS run-time library. We are going to use a tool provided by the OCM-G distribution that performs instrumentation of application libraries in order to trigger the events related to *enter/exit* to library functions. The developer must provide a library and so-called instrumentation description file that specifies which functions inside the library should be instrumented. The description file also specifies for each instrumented function, which of its parameters should be sent to the monitor when a function is called. We also take into consideration adapting the existing instrumentation tool for dynamic libraries.

Distributed and parallel applications usually consist of concurrently executed processes. In order to identify which processes belong to the same application, the OCM-G introduces the application name as an `Id`. In order to be registered in the OCM-G monitoring system, each process must be run with the application name and with the address of the MSM. Usually, it can be done by passing all this information through an application command line. The GS also uses the application name to bind distributed parts of the application. The part that resides on a client machine and acts as a front-end of the application for the user is called *master*, and parts that are executed on the computational Grid are called *workers*. GS supports application deployment process with a set of tools provided with GS distribution that make it almost automatically. A single code line that is responsible for a process registration into the OCM-G must be inserted into the master as well into the worker programs. Next, both programs must be compiled using the OCM-G wrapper script that links with additional OCM-G related objects and libraries.

An application prepared in this way can be controlled and observed using the OCM-G. The inserted instrumentation code sends all required monitoring data to the monitor. All these operations are completely transparent to the user application and performed without any changes to the original GS runtime source code which was made available by the end of our research, so within our research we assume that the GS is available as a binary code only.

A separate issue is the performance measurements and visualization of GS applications. In contrast to message-passing applications for which the G-PM was developed where the set of application processes is static or quasi static, GS applications feature a great number of worker processes which are started and die when their goal is fulfilled. This implies a hard challenge for G-PM to provide an up-to-date list of the currently running processes. Another issue is visualization: while standard profiling displays still work for GS, time-lined visualization needs to completely change its semantics rather towards aggregated metrics. Solutions to the above and some other issues are discussed below.

3. Implementation efforts to enable GS monitoring

In this section we present the changes applied to GS, OCM-G and G-PM that were required for this integration. We start from the low-level ones (GS modification needed to let it communicate with the OCM-G) and end by describing the changes to the front-end G-PM.

3.1 GRID superscalar function instrumentation

In order to make the GRID superscalar function invocations visible in the OCM-G monitoring system, these methods need to be instrumented. OCM-G provides the `cg-ocmg-libinstr` tool that was used during this task. This tool needs to be provided with a library to instrument and a so called description file, which explains how each function should be instrumented. We have created two description files, one for each of the GS static libraries. Thanks to this, we have successfully instrumented the following GRID superscalar methods: `GS_{On,Off}()` - the main GS routine that starts/ends the GRID superscalar environment has been instrumented with the code allowing the master application to automatically register in OCM-G, `IniWorker()/EndWorker()` - this function starts/ends worker application execution, it has been instrumented in a manner similar to `GS_On()` - when a worker is created it registers in OCM-G; the other instrumented functions include:

- `GS_{Open, Close}()`,
- `GS_{Begin, Barrier, Speculative_End}()`,
- `DoSubmit()`,
- `FindBetterEstim()`,
- `GS_Internal_Throw()`,
- `GS_System()`,
- `UpdateLists()`, and
- `WriteCheckpoint()`.

One of the challenges that we had to overcome here was a problem with the library names. It turned out that the `cg-ocmg-libinstr` tool, when instrumenting code, creates variables that are named after the library names. But a variable name cannot contain a dash ('-'), which caused the tool to fail. Creating differently named aliases to the libraries solved the case.

In order to ease the process of library instrumentation, we also created a script (`gs_lib_instr.sh`) which finds the GS libraries (along with their respective description files), creates their backup copies and instruments them.

3.2 Execution script

In order for any application to be able to register in OCM-G, it should be passed some command line parameters: the identifier of the monitor and application name. These parameters needed to be passed to worker applications to allow them to register in the monitoring system. The main challenge here was that the environment executes workers automatically and so the user has no access to their command line arguments.

To overcome this problem we created a special script (`monGS`) through which all the GS applications that are to be monitored should be invoked. For example, to enable the monitoring of application `SampleApp`:

```
./monGS ./SampleApp --ocmg-appname myApp --ocmg-mainsm
    959c635d:8a44
```

This script is responsible for passing the command line parameters to the worker applications where they are used to register in OCM-G.

3.3 G-PM core modifications

The G-PM tool was created with MPI applications in mind, where the number of processes is practically constant and once all of them have registered in OCM-G, there aren't any more expected. So the tool waited for a given number of processes to register and then attached to all of them (to be able to process monitoring data of their execution).

In a GRID superscalar environment the situation is completely different, because the number of processes to be created is not known in advance. A call to a grid-enabled function creates a new worker process. Therefore not only is this number hard to determine but also a process lifetime is difficult to predict. In different parts of the program new workers can be created whilst others might have already long been terminated: here there are no fixed rules.

To be able to handle such dynamic changes we introduced to G-PM the following mechanism: at the beginning of its runtime, the tool creates a request in OCM-G to be always notified, whenever a new process registers in the monitoring system (see Fig. 2). In such a case this new process gets temporarily suspended, which enables G-PM to attach to it and wake it up again. Owing to this approach, the G-PM tool is able to gather performance data about all of the GS application processes.

3.4 New GS-oriented metrics

For the newly instrumented functions, G-PM has been provided with their respective "count" and "delay" metrics. "Count" metrics represent the number of times a given function has been invoked, whilst "delay" metrics - the amount of time the function execution took. It is through these metrics that GS

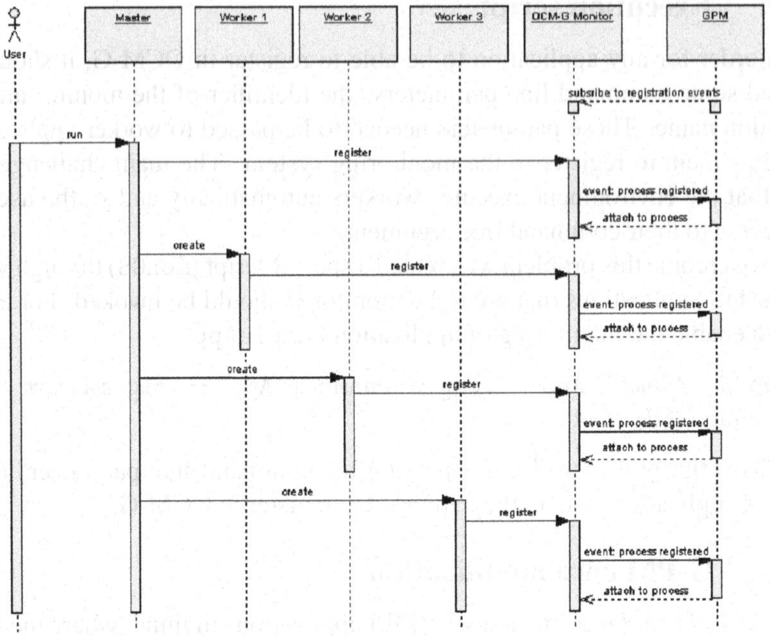

Figure 2. The GS-adapted mode of attaching G-PM to processes

application execution can be observed and interpreted (see an example in Fig. 3).

3.5 GS-enabled Space-Time visualization mode

The Space-Time visualization mode that was recently created for G-PM was different than the other modes in the fact that instead of getting data from the monitor by sending requests to OCM-G, it parsed and analyzed the output of the `cg-ocmg-tracer` tool. We decided to modify this mode to make it work as all other ones, because `cg-ocmg-tracer` was designed only to gather information about MPI-related events in an application's execution which made it inadequate for GS needs. The changes involved removing the parsing logic from Space-Time and attaching the modified visualization logic to one of the standard data models. The new version of Space-Time is presented in Fig. 4.

As can be seen, the mode has been stripped of its ability to show data transfers between individual processes, but this part of the visualization is not as important in the context of GRID superscalar as it is for MPI. The new version of Space-Time can be used just as any other mode, to visualize the values of chosen metrics.

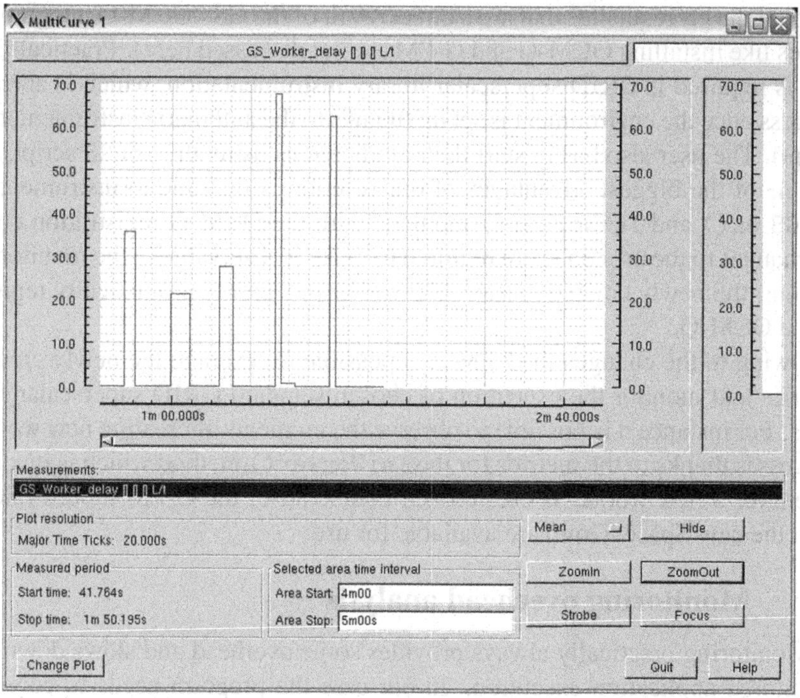

Figure 3. G-PM: Measuring worker execution time in a TSP application

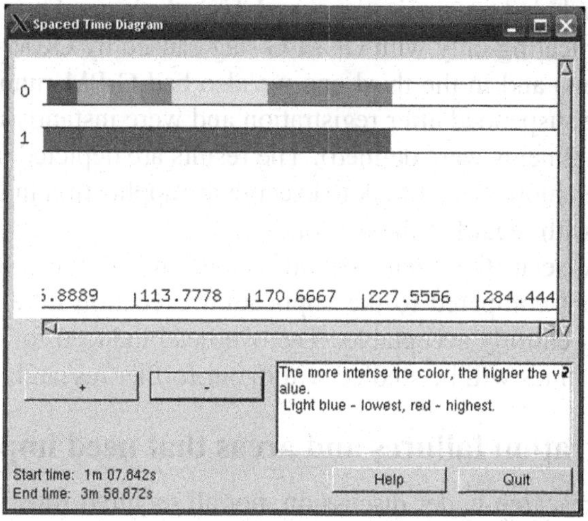

Figure 4. New *function-specific* Space-Time visualization mode

4. Capabilities of the monitoring environment

The GS application developer is given a powerful monitoring tool. It is worth noting that the prerequisites for using it are quite little (we are taking into account the prerequisites that are a direct result of the GS - OCM-G integration, issues like installing OCM-G and G-PM are not discussed here). Practically all that is required is GRID superscalar library instrumentation, which is an easy process once the environment is set up (thanks to the automatic instrumentation script). The user also has to start their applications using the `monGS` script.

One of the biggest advantages of our solution is that due to instrumenting the `GS_On()` and `IniWorker()` methods with the OCM-G registration code, no changes to the user code are required to make it observable in the monitoring system: the newly created master and worker processes automatically register in the OCM-G.

Owing to the changes in G-PM it is possible to leverage the newly created metrics and monitor the execution of chosen standard GRID superscalar routines. For instance it is possible to observe the moments of creating new worker processes thanks to the metrics for the `IniWorker()` method which is invoked whenever a new worker is created. Of course all of the G-PM modes (along with the new Space-Time) are available for use.

5. Monitoring overhead analysis

Monitoring practically always provides some overhead and slows down the monitored application execution. In our case the program needs to communicate with OCM-G and this procedure does entail delay. To measure it, we ran the application `Simple.c` shown above in a couple of different scenarios. The first one included no monitoring (no delay), the second one was the application communicating only with OCM-G (lag caused by OCM-G registration and notifications) and in the third one we also had G-PM running, so all the processes were suspended after registration and were instantly awoken by the tool (no measurements were defined). The results are depicted in Fig. 5. They show how much more time it took to execute the application in the second and third scenario with regard to the first one.

As it can be seen, the delay is really small and in our case was at most a couple percent compared to the application execution time. We consider this kind of lag entirely acceptable. The overhead induced for a much bigger number of machines will be studied within our further research.

6. Integration failures and areas that need improvement

Within the research under discussion, not all required functions have been successfully instrumented. For instance it was not possible to instrument the `Execute()` method, due to the fact that it has a variable number of parameters. In this case it was not possible to use the standard OCM-G instrumentation technique implemented in the `cg-ocmg-libinstr` tool. According to

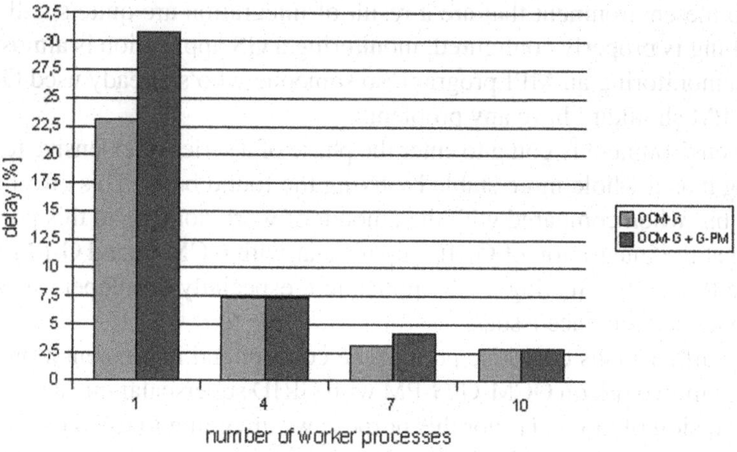

Figure 5. Delay caused by performance monitoring

our research, instrumenting this routine would involve some hardware-specific assembler coding which would be non-portable.

Another feature we were also planning but so far have not created is a completely new process-specific Space-Time display. This means we would see a separate visualization bar for each new process, which would be very interesting in terms of GRID superscalar, because it would allow to exactly determine the actions that took place in each of the processes. This would also require the Space-Time window to grow during application lifetime (because space for the new bars is needed). In the end in many applications the list of bars would grow to be quite large, but the result would be worth it.

Another area in need of improvement is the amount of tests performed on the environment. So far it has been used for quite simple monitoring scenarios and more extensive tests are still required. It would be very useful to try to monitor multi-process applications in a truly distributed environment. Some bugs discovered during the on-going testing should also be fixed.

7. Summary

The work on the integration OCM-G into GRID superscalar necessitated extensions to the internal mechanisms of the system, including communication. Nevertheless the OCM-G preserved its way of providing monitoring services for GUI or automatic tools through the well-tested interface OMIS. The final conclusions that we can come up with are quite optimistic. The GRID superscalar developer is provided with not only a way of monitoring a GS application during its lifetime but also a helpful tool for presenting the gathered monitoring data in a meaningful graphical manner. The additional costs of setting up the environment that are a result of integration are quite small. Once everything is properly configured, monitoring a GS application is almost identical to monitoring an MPI program, so someone who's already used OCM-G and G-PM shouldn't have any problems.

The environment is going to enter the phase of a series of extensive tests and making it as a whole more stable by fixing the found bugs. This effort should not be big when compared with the amount of work done up to this point. We hope that the integration of GRID superscalar with OCM-G and G-PM will be of help to anyone creating a GS application, especially developers striving to overcome performance issues.

Our further plans comprise porting the concept and implementation results of integration work on OCM-G/G-PM with GRID superscalar into a new GCM-based version of GS [11]. For this purpose we are going to use the experience gained when working on J-OCM [12], a Java-oriented version of the OCM.

Acknowledgments

This research is partly funded by the EU IST FP6-0004265 CoreGRID project and by the Ministry of Science and Technology of Spain (TIN-2004-07739-C02-01).

References

[1] Badia, R.M., Labarta, J., Sirvent, R., Pérez, J.M., Cela, J.M., and Grima, R. *Programming Grid Applications with GRID superscalar.* Journal of Grid Computing, vol. 1, 2003, pp. 151-170.

[2] Ludwig, T., Wismüller, R., Sunderam, V., and Bode, A. *OMIS – On-line Monitoring Interface Specification (Version 2.0).* Shaker Verlag, Aachen, vol. 9, LRR-TUM Research Report Series, (1997) `http://wwwbode.in.tum.de/Λomis/OMIS/Version-2.0/version-2.0.ps.gz`

[3] Globus Project homepage `http://www.globus.org/`

[4] EU IST CrossGrid project page `http://www.eu-crossgrid.org/`

[5] Balis, B., Bubak, M., Funika, W., Wismüller, R., Radecki, M., Szepieniec, T., Arodz, T., Kurdziel, M. *Grid Environment for On-line Application Monitoring and Performance Analysis.* Scientific Pogrammning, vol. 12, no. 4, 2004, pp. 239-251.

[6] Wismüller, R., Bubak, M., Funika, W. *High-level application-specific performance analysis using the G-PM tool.* Future Generation Comp. Syst. 24(2), pp. 121-132 (2008)

[7] Badia R.M., Bubak, M., Funika, W., and Smetek, M. *Performance Monitoring of GRID superscalar applications with OCM-G.* In: Sergei Gorlatch, Marco Danelutto (Eds.), Proceedings of the CoreGRID Workshop "Integrated Research in Grid Computing", Pisa, Italy, November 28-30, 2005, pp. 229-236, TR-05-22, University of Pisa, 2005

[8] Badia R.M., Sirvent R.,Bubak M., Funika W., Klus C., Machner P. and Smetek M. *Performance monitoring of GRID superscalar with OCM-G/G-PM: integration issues.* In:

S. Gorlatch, M. Bubak, and T. Priol (Eds.), Achievements in European Research on Grid Systems, CoreGRID Integration Workshop 2006, October 19-20, Krakow, Poland, Springer, 2008, pp. 193-205

[9] Badia R.M., Sirvent R., Bubak M., Funika W., Machner P. *Performance monitoring of GRID superscalar with OCM-G/G-PM: tuning and improvements*. In Proc. of CoreGRID Integration Workshop 2007, 12-14 June 2007, Heraklion, Greece, Springer, 2008 (to be published)

[10] Badia R.M., Sirvent R., Bubak M., Funika W., Machner P. *Performance monitoring of GRID superscalar: visualization modes*. In Proc. CoreGRID Integration Workshop 2008, 2-4 April 2008, Hersonissos, Greece, pp. 266-274, Heraklion, Crete University Press, 2008

[11] Tejedor, E. and Badia, R.M. *A Component-Based Integrated Toolkit*. In CoreGRID Workshop on Grid Programming Model, Grid and P2P Systems Architecture, Grid Systems, Tools and Environments, Heraklion, Crete (Greece), June 2007.

[12] Funika, W., Godowski, P., Pegiel, P., and Bubak, M. *Towards User-Defined Performance Monitoring of Distributed Java Applications*. In Proc. of e-Science 2006, Second IEEE International Conference on e-Science and Grid Computing, Dec. 4-6, 2006, Amsterdam, 2006

AUTHORIZING GRID RESOURCE ACCESS AND CONSUMPTION

Michal Jankowski
Poznań Supercomputing and Networking Center, Poznań, Poland
jankowsk@man.poznan.pl

Erik Elmroth
Department of Computing Science and HPC2N, Umeå University, Sweden
elmroth@cs.umu.se

Norbert Meyer
Poznań Supercomputing and Networking Center, Poznań, Poland
meyer@man.poznan.pl

Abstract The tasks to authorize users access to grid resources and to authorize their regulated consumption is studied and some key functionality is identified. A novel authorization infrastructure is proposed by combining the Virtual User System (VUS) for dynamically assigning local pool-accounts to grid-users and the SweGrid Accounting System (SGAS) for grid-wide usage logging and real-time enforcement of resource pre-allocations.

Keywords: authorization, access control, resource usage, resource allocation, grid economy, SGAS, VUS

1. Introduction

The process of granting users access to grid resources and to authorize their resource consumption in large-scale grids with thousands of users is a complex process. This contribution investigates two vital parts of this process, namely to grant users access to resources without having to á priori open individual user accounts on all grid resources and to perform real-time regulation of the users' resource utilization based their grid-wide pre-allocation and previous consumption. An integrated solution for both problems is proposed by concerted usage of two existing tools.

The two problems are examined in some detail in Section 2. One conclusion is that the authorization process is complex and varying for different usage scenarios. However, by a clear separation of concerns, it is possible to identify well-defined tasks that ideally should be handled by equally well separated components, easily used in concert with other tools, e.g., in accordance with the fundamentals of Service Oriented Architectures (SOA) in general and the grid eco-system approach [20, 7]in particular.

In Section 3, we review two existing technologies for dynamically assigning temporary local user accounts to grid users (VUS - The Virtual User System) and for performing real-time enforcement of grid-wide resource pre-allocations and usage logging (SGAS - The SweGrid Accounting System). Section 4 illustrates how these two solutions can be used in concert, providing key authorization support for a very common usage scenario in academic large-scale grid environments.

Discussions about possible future extensions and some conclusions are given in Section 5 and and Section 6, respectively, followed by acknowledgments and references.

2. Authorization for Grid Resource Usage

Authorization of grid resource usage include authorization of both resource access and resource consumption. Compared to traditional authorization problems, the distributed nature of grids gives additional complexity to the problem. In the following, we introduce some important aspects of these problems.

2.1 Authorizing resource access

Authentication, authorization of resource access, and closely related user management are crucial from the point of view of security of any computing system. The authentication and authorization are the must, eccept free services with anonymous access, that usually are rather simple ones and offer only limited functionality (like read-only data access). Also in a strictly commercial usage scenario, in which anyone who is able to pay is allowed use a complex service, there is at least a need to identify the user.

In the large, distributed, multi-institutional, and complex environment like the Grid, authorization and user management are even more challenging. Problems like managing a global base, mapping global user accounts to local accounts, defining authorization policies for lots of entities (users and services) arise.

The paper [8]provides a definition of the Virtual Organization as a set of individuals or institutions defined by "what (resource) is shared, who is allowed to share, and the conditions under which sharing occurs". This concept allows for easier decentralization of user management (each VO is responsible for managing some group of users). On the contrary, in the classical solution each computing node must store authorization information locally for each user (e. g. in Globus grid-mapfile), an approach which obviously is not scalable and brings a nightmare of synchronization problems. However, in usage scenarios where the mapping to user accounts is not static (i.e., virtual accounts or a similar solution is used), this decentralization requires proper and safe mapping of the grid user to a local account.

Independently of the resource owner's level of trust to the VO, he or she should retain the ultimate control of the local resource. E.,g. the resource owner should be able to define privileges for the members of VOs and to ban single, unwanted users. In order to realize this, the security policy should be combined from two sources: the VO and the resource provider. Another requirement is fine grained authorization [14], that allows limiting user access rights to specific resources. The authorization decision must depend on privileges granted to the user by the VO and it can possibly be over-ruled by the provider. More requirements are described in [4].

Of course, the required model of authorization depends on the application, so that, the authorization system must be quite flexible. This many different aspects of the authorization problem has lead to many different solutions and a variety of security tools and services. For instance, there is a number of services that expose the VO part of the security policies: VOMS [2], VOIS [12], CAS [17]. On the other hand, there are several tools for authorization and mapping the users: VUS (described below), LCAS/LCMAPS [1]and others.

2.2 Authorizing resource consumption

In addition to authorizing a user access to a resource, there is often a need to also authorize the actual usage consumption.

Authorization based on usage quantities is directly or indirectly an authorization based on the users ability to "pay" for the usage. In academic environments, users are commonly assigned pre-allocations (quota) of resources, often simply in terms of a certain number of computer hours (per month, per year, etc) on a particular resource or set of resources. The ability to "pay" is in this case a question of determining if the user has already spent his or her pre-allocation or if there is still quota left for running another job. In grid economies not based on pre-allocations, e.g., based on real cost compensation, the corresponding authorization must be based on the user's real ability to pay.

These two scenarios can be generalized in a number of ways, e.g., depending on the type of grid economy considered. Independently if the economy is based on real or virtual money, the price setting may be dynamic and the mechanism for this may, e.g., include negotiation before resource allocation [16, 3]or analysis of the fraction of resource utilization during the computation

[15]. In either case, there is a need for tools to authorize the actual resource utilization before (and sometimes even during) the utilization of the resource.

There may also be a need to authorize the execution based on other aspects of the "size" of the job to be executed. Often, this is a question of how large number of processors a job may utilize, how many hours a job may run, or a combination of these two, although other parameters such as usage of memory, disk, software, etc, may be taken into account. This type of authorization is most often only a question of enforcement of basic policies defining the types of jobs that are allowed to run during different times of the day or week. However, it may also be of interest to apply different policies depending on the privileges of the user or user group. For example, it is often relevant to take into account the total number of jobs currently submitted or running by a certain user or user group. Notably, support for this type of policy enforcement is common in state-of-the-art batch systems, but for a truly distributed grid, there is a need for similar type of support for grid-wide policy enforcement, or more specifically, local enforcement of local and global policies based on local and grid-wide usage information.

To conclude, there are a number of different aspects to cover when authorizing resource consumption. The fact that these authorization aspects can be required in a large number of different combinations is a good argument for developing these authorization mechanism as small separate components, designed for use in concert.

3. Existing Technologies

In the following, we introduce two existing systems, designed to solve some of the authorization problems presented in Section 2.

3.1 The Virtual User System (VUS)

The Virtual User System (VUS) [12],[13],[11]is an extension of the service that runs users' jobs (e. g., Globus GRAM, gLite Computing Element, etc.). VUS allows jobs to execute without having a personal user account on a site. Instead of personal user accounts for each grid user, there is a pool of so called virtual accounts dynamically allocated to the users. The user-account mapping mechanism assures that only one user is mapped to a particular account at any given time, so that, the jobs of different users are properly isolated. An unused account may be automatically allocated to another user. This allows minimizing overhead related to creating and maintaining user accounts.

The history of account allocations is stored in the VUS database. The database can store any standard and non standard accounting data and any logging information in the global user context. In that way, tracking of user activities is possible, despite the fact that a user is not permanently mapped to any local account. This is of course crucial from a security point of view.

There are groups of virtual accounts on each computing site. Each group consists of accounts with different privileges, so the fine grain authorization is achieved by selecting an appropriate group by the authorization module of VUS. The authorization module is pluggable and may be easily extended by implementing new plugins. The list of authorization plugins is configurable by the administrator. The mechanism is designed to make it possible to combine authorization policies of a VO and of a resource provider. For example, some plugin may authorize based on the VO membership of the user. The VO manager decides on membership and the resource manager decides if the VO is authorized and which group is associated to the VO. Another plugin may refuse users appearing on a list of banned users. In this way, the resource provider has enough administrative power while part of this power and many of the administrative work is delegated to the VO manager.

VUS is designed for authorization of resource access. It both makes a decision about the authorization (tells if the user is allowed or not) and enforces this decision (by assigning the user an account with pre-defined privileges). Note, that the "resource" is in fact the computing site as the whole, access to its "sub-resources" (queue, CPU, disc space, files, etc.) may be limited only by setting privileges and quota limitations to the local account. This approach does not take into account any grid-level limitations like global access control lists or global quota. Such an approach is connected to the localization of VUS in the grid architecture and the difference between authorization of resource access and consumption.

3.2 The SweGrid Accounting System (SGAS)

The SweGrid Accounting System (SGAS) [9, 19]includes a set of tools designed for capacity allocation between user groups in collaborative grid environments by coordinating the enforcement of grid-wide usage limits. In a typical usage scenario, users or projects are granted grid-wide usage limits (resource pre-allocations), e.g., by a VO allocation authority. The pre-allocations are to be used grid-wide, with no pre-defined usage limit on individual resources.

SGAS provides a Bank [6]where bank accounts are used to keep the balance of the usage corresponding to the pre-allocation. The accounting is done in terms of an abstract currency called "Grid Credits". For improved flexibility, the process of determining the cost for using a particular resource is separated from the Bank, i.e., the Bank is totally agnostic to the mapping between resource usage and Grid Credits.

The Bank provides support for reserving Grid Credits before actually charging the account. The typical usage for this feature is for the resource to reserve a sufficiently large amount in the Bank before a job is allowed to start. After job completion, the exact amount (no larger than the reserved amount) is charged. Using this feature, resources can employ real-time quota enforcement by denying resource access if the account does not have sufficient amount of Grid Credits for the reservation. However, the resource can also be configured for soft (as opposed to strict) enforcement, by allowing jobs to run without sufficient Grid Credits, e.g., with lower priority.

For very large grids or for minimizing the risk of reducing the resource utilization due to total Bank outage, the Bank can be separated into different branches. This feature is facilitated through an implementation of a general Name Service for Web Services, which is a the key component, giving the virtual Bank very close to perfect scaling.

SGAS also includes a logging and usage tracking service (LUTS), for storing information about each individual resource utilization. The information is stored in the Usage Record format proposed by OGF-UR [21]. The logging of usage data is not time critical for the job execution and can for improved efficiency be done in batches for multiple completed jobs at regular intervals or when a certain number of jobs are completed.

The Bank and the LUTS are independent services developed using the Globus Toolkit 4 (GT4), although they can be used from resources running any middleware, given that they can access GT4 services. For integration on particular resources, SGAS provides a Job Account Reservation Manager (JARM) as a single point of integration. The JARM performs all communication with the Bank (i.e., bank account reservations and charging) and the LUTS (i.e., logging of usage data). The JARM needs to be customized to the grid resource manager used on the resource. It has already been integrated in the GT4 GRAM and the NorduGrid/ARC Grid Manager [9]. SGAS is included in the GT4 as a tech preview component. For independent accounting system comparisons, praising the SGAS approach, see [18, 10].

4. VUS-SGAS Integration

This section describes how VUS and SGAS can be used in concert for coordinated authorization of resource access and resource consumption. The architecture of our approach is illustrated on Fig. 1. The modules presented in the figure are described below together with an outline of the job submission and execution process.

In the typical grid scenario, the user is a member of some Virtual Organization. This means in practice, that some facilities (services) for authorization of

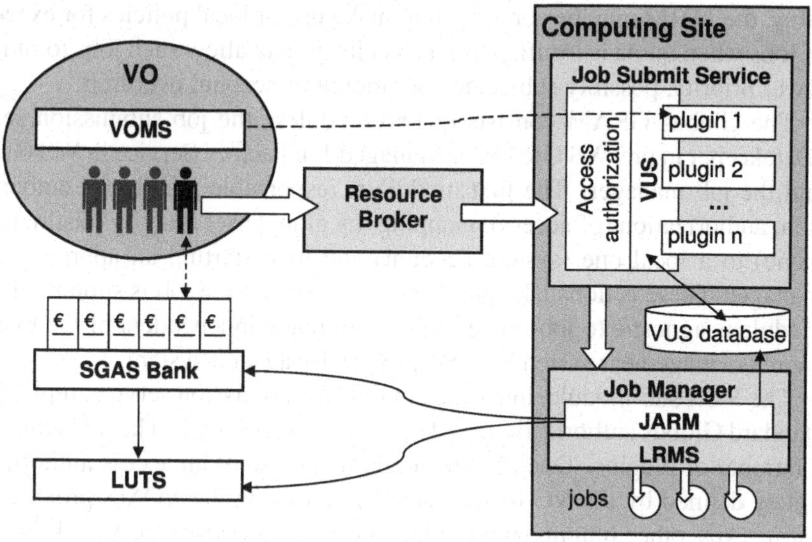

Figure 1. VUS-SGAS integration architecture.

the VO members are needed for the VO (database of its members, authorization service, etc.).

The figure includes a VOMS [2]for authorization of resource access, although any other service providing similar functionality may be used. In order to authenticate based on VO membership and the role of the user, the VOMS signs a proxy certificate for the user, which is used in the authorization process on the resource.

Another service is needed in order to support authorization of resource consumption, such as an SGAS Bank. The Bank is initiated with pre-allocated usage quotas by a Bank administrator, and it provides information about the quotas remaining based on the grid-wide resource usage of the Bank account holder, as described in Section 3.2.

The job submission process is initiated by the user submitting a job, typically via a resource broker, that selects the most appropriate resource for the job at a given time. On the resource, the job is received and managed by a Globus GRAM. In our architecture, the SGAS JARM intercepts the call, and requests Bank account reservation (Hold) of an appropriate amount of Grid Credits. The amount of credits for the reservation is determined from the user's specified maximum execution time. The conversion from execution time to Grid credits is done by the JARM based on the resource cost plan. If the request is successful, the job specification is passed to the GRAM, otherwise it is filtered out, i.e., defined as unauthorized to the requested resource consumption. Notably, the JARM may be configured to make use of local policies for execution of jobs when quota is insufficient. Typically, it may allow such jobs to run with lower priority, possibly subject to the amount of account overdraft.

The Globus GRAM consists of two modules: the job submission service (Gatekeeper in pre-WS GRAM or Managed Job Factory Service in WS GRAM) and the job manager. The first module is responsible mainly for authentication, authorization (of access), mapping the global user identity (distinguished name) to a local one (system account) and then starting an appropriate job manager. These actions take place only once, while the job is submitted. This module is agnostic to job-related information and independent of the local resource management system (LRMS), typically a batch system.

The VUS sub-module, integrated in the job submission service, replaces the standard Globus authorization, as described in Section 3.1. The VUS may have a number of plugins. One plugin should make use of an access authorization policy defined by the VO of the user (by analyzing the VOMS proxy certificate). Any other plugins authorizing access to the resource may be applied according to the local security policy. The last plugin maps the user to an account and stores the mapping in the VUS database. Note, that the account is allocated to the user provided that both types of the authorization have been successful, so that a user account at the resource is not wasted if the job is not allowed to run, e.g., due to Bank account overdraft.

The job specification is passed to the job manager, which is LRMS-specific and able to analyze the job description. Once started, the job manager controls the job through communication with the batch system. After job completion, JARM collects the accounting data, calculates the actual cost and charges the user's Bank account.

The VUS database is capable of storing both standard and non standard accounting metrics and allows defining static prices for a resource unit. The JARM makes use of this price information together with the user-specified predicted maximum execution time and the LRMS accounting data when estimating the expected cost for the execution and for computing the real cost of the job, respectively. Any accounting or logging information may be stored in the database during the execution or anytime later.

The SGAS LUTS may be used for Grid-wide tracking of resource usage. It allows secure publication of the accounting data in the format of OGF Usage Records [21]. The JARM enters this information in the LUTS upon retrieval from the LRMS or after retrieved it from the VUS database for collecting the usage data. Notably, the logging in the LUTS need not be done in real time. On the contrary, it may for performance reasons be done in batches for multiple jobs at a time.

As the job is completed and the temporary user account is no longer used (for some configurable time), it may be released and mapped to another user later on. The accounts are released on demand - when there is no free account for the user, the procedure of releasing accounts is started. This procedure may also be performed periodically.

It may be important in some situations and for some users, to grant access independently of their remaining grid-wide quota, and to allow the job to run without charging the cost to the grid-wide bank. For example, a resource provider may want to give access free of charge to the users from his own organization. Such a feature may be implemented either by a modification of the JARM or by including a VUS plugin that can chose between a JARM-enabled and a JARM-free job submission. Notably, such modification would not have to affect the logging in the VUS of local resource usage.

5. Limitations and Future Extensions

For truly large-scale grids, the SGAS LUTS could benefit from being distributed in the same way as the Bank. Such a development is straight-forward, utilizing the same generic Name Service as for the distributed Bank.

In some situation, it may also be beneficial to have bank accounts organized hierarchically. For example, if a group is given a resource pre-allocation from an outside authority, it could be beneficial for the group to have instruments to easily partition and even re-distribute this grant among the group members. Currently, such arrangements can be realized by having the external authority performing the resource allocation on a per-user basis. For improved flexibility for the groups and reduced burden on the external authority, a hierarchical bank structure, e.g., based on the hierarchical share-policy trees in [5], would be beneficial. For this usage scenario, the hierarchical Bank would also need support for delegating (to "group leaders") the right to perform certain account administration tasks.

For use in hierarchical or overlapping grids, there may be an interest to perform some usage logging (but normally not all) in multiple SGAS LUTSes, maintained by different organizations. As a support for this, the development of an SGAS LUTS federation tool has recently been initiated.

The scope of this paper does not include the problem of synchronization of the authorization between the broker and the computing site. In other words, the broker should be able to state if the user will be able to run the job on the site before the job is actually submitted there. For that purpose, it should perform exactly the same authorization. In general, the broker cannot read the site configuration, but it may "ping" the site to check if the user is allowed to access the resource. For the broker to assure that jobs will not be denied due to Bank quota overdrafts, the Bank reservation process can be modified so that the broker performs the reservation and only leaves to the resource to perform the post execution charging and logging of the job. The general design of SGAS already allows this usage scenario, although it has so far not been used in practice, since the process where the bank performs both reservation and charging makes the accounting operations more transparent in the job submission process.

6. Concluding Remarks

We have presented a novel approach to Grid job authorization for large-scale grids with thousands of users. By combining established technologies for dynamically assigning grid users virtual user accounts on individual computers (with VUS) and grid wide accounting and resource allocation enforcement (with SGAS) we obtain concerted authorization for resource access and resource consumption. Notably, despite the focus on large-scale grids, the proposed solution leaves the resource owner with ultimate control over the resource. We also remark that the solution is highly flexible and allows for policy customization, also for rare cases where there is not need for access control (e.g., applications allowing anonymous access) or control of the degree of consumption (e.g., for users with unlimited, flat-rate usage agreements).

7. Acknowledgments

This work has been supported by the EU CoreGRID NE (FP6-004265), EU BalticGrid NoE (FP6-026715) and The Swedish Research Council (VR) under contract 621-2005-3667. The research has been conducted using the resources of the High Performance Computing Center North (HPC2N). Finally, we acknowledge the anonymous referees for providing valuable feedback.

References

[1] http://www.dutchgrid.nl/datagrid/wp4/lcmaps/.

[2] R. Alfieri, R. Cecchini, V. Ciaschini, L. Dell'Agnello, A. Frohner, A. Gianoli, K. Lorentey, and F.Spataro. VOMS: an Authorization System for Virtual Organizations. In *1st European Across Grids Conference*, Santiago de Compostela, February 13–14 2003.

[3] R. Buyya and S. Vazhkudai. Compute power market: Towards a market-oriented grid. In *The First IEEE/ACM International Symposium on Cluster Computing and the Grid (CCGrid 2001)*, May 2001.

[4] J. Denemark, M. Jankowski, K. Ales, L. Matyska, N. Meyer, M. Ruda, and P. Wolniewicz. Best practices of user account management with virtual organization based access to grid. In Roman Wyrzykowski, Jack Dongarra, Norbert Meyer, and Jerzy Wasniewski, editors, *Parallel Processing and Applied Mathematics*, volume 3911 of *LNCS*, pages 633–642. Springer-Verlag, 2006.

[5] E. Elmroth and P. Gardfjäll. Design and Evaluation of a Decentralized System for Grid-wide Fairshare Scheduling. In *e-Science 2005: First International Conference on e-Science and Grid Computing*, pages 221–229, Washington, DC, USA, 2005. IEEE Computer Society.

[6] E. Elmroth, P. Gardfjäll, O. Mulmo, and T. Sandholm. An OGSA-Based Bank Service for Grid Accounting Systems. In *Applied Parallel Computing*, Lecture Notes in Computer Science, pages 1051–1060. Springer-Verlag, 2006.

[7] E. Elmroth, F. Hernandez, J. Tordsson, and P-O. Östberg. Designing service-based resource management tools for a healthy Grid ecosystem. In *Parallel Processing and Ap-*

plied Mathematics, volume 4967 of *Lecture Notes in Computer Science*, pages 259–270. Springer-Verlag, 2008.

[8] I. Foster, C. Kesselman, and S. Tuecke. The Anatomy of the Grid: Enabling Scalable Virtual Organizations. *International Journal of Supercomputer Applications*, 15(3), 2001.

[9] P. Gardfjäll, E. Elmroth, L. Johnsson, O. Mulmo, and T. Sandholm. Scalable Grid-wide capacity allocation with the SweGrid Accounting System (SGAS). *Concurrency Computat.: Pract. Exper.*, To appear, 2008.

[10] M. Göhner, M. Waldburger, F. Gubler, G.D. Rodosek, and B. Stiller. An Accounting Model for Dynamic Virtual Organizations. Technical Report No. 2006.11, University of Zürich, Department of Informatics, November 2006.

[11] M. Jankowski and N. Meyer. Dynamic User Management in the BalticGrid Project. In Paul Cunningham and Miriam Cunningham, editors, *Expanding the Knowledge Economy: Issues, Applications, Case Studies*, volume 4 of *Information anc Communication Technologies and the Knowledge Economy*, pages 1401–1406, Amsterdam, 2007. IOS Press.

[12] M. Jankowski, P. Wolniewicz, and N. Meyer. Virtual User System for Globus based grids. In *Cracow Grid Workshop '04 Proceedings*, Cracow, 2004.

[13] M. Jankowski, P. Wolniewicz, and N. Meyer. Practical Experiences with User Account Management in Clusterix. In *Cracow Grid Workshop '05 Proceedings*, Cracow, 2005.

[14] K. Keahey, V. Welch, S. Lang, B. Liu, and S. Meder. Fine-grain authorization policies in the grid: design and implementation. In *1st International Workshop on Middleware for Grid Computing*, 2003.

[15] K. Lai, L. Rasmusson, E. Adar, S. Sorkin, L. Zhang, and B. A. Huberman. Tycoon: an Implemention of a Distributed Market-Based Resource Allocation System. Technical report, HP Labs, Palo Alto, CA, USA, December 2004.

[16] J. Li and R. Yahyapour. Negotiation strategies for grid scheduling. In *Advances in Grid and Pervasive Computing*, volume 3947 of *Lecture Notes in Computer Science*, pages 42–52. Springer-Verlag, 2006.

[17] L. Pearlman, V. Welch, I. Foster, C. Kesselman, and S. Tuecke. A community authorization service for group collaboration. pages 50–59, 2002.

[18] C-P. Rückemann, W. Müller, and G. von Voigt. Comparison of Grid Accounting Concepts for D-Grid. In *Proc. Cracow Grid Workshop 06, Cracow*, October 2006.

[19] T. Sandholm, P. Gardfjäll, E. Elmroth, L. Johnsson, and O.Mulmo. A service-oriented approach to enforce Grid resource allocations. *International Journal of Cooperative Information Systems*, 15(3):439–459, 2006.

[20] The Globus Project. An "ecosystem" of Grid components. http://www.globus.org/grid_software/ecology.php. September 2007.

[21] Usage Record WG (UR-WG). https://forge.gridforum.org/projects/ur-wg/, January 2008.

ALL-IN-ONE GRAPHICAL TOOL FOR THE MANAGEMENT OF A DIET GRIDRPC MIDDLEWARE

Eddy Caron, Frederic Desprez, David Loureiro
ENS Lyon, Universit de Lyon, LIP UMR 5668,
CNRS-ENS-Lyon-UCBL-INRIA
46 Allee d'Italie, 69364 Lyon Cedex 07. France
Eddy.Caron@ens-lyon.fr
Frederic.Desprez@ens-lyon.fr
David.Loureiro@ens-lyon.fr

Abstract Grid middleware are the link between large scale (and distributed) platforms and applications. Managing such a software system and the grid environment itself can be a hard task when no dedicated (and integrated) tool exist. Some can be used through nice graphical interfaces, but they are usually dedicated to one or some limited tasks. They do not fulfill all the needs of a grid end-user who wants to deploy grid applications easily and rapidly.

The aim of this paper is to present the case study of an all-in-one software system, designed for the management of a grid middleware and gathering user-friendly graphical interfaces answering to the various needs of end-users. Moreover the software system eases the use of the grid by avoiding the scripting layer under a nice GUI enabling the user a faster and more efficient use of the grid environment. By this means we demonstrate how the DIET Dashboard fulfills all the needs of a unified tool for grid management. This paper gives a comparison with existing and well-known tools dedicated to some specific tasks such as grid resources management, grid monitoring, or middleware management.

Keywords: Grid middleware, Grid management, Grid monitoring, Deployment, Workflow management.

1. Introduction

Large problems ranging from huge numerical simulations to large scale data processing can now be solved through the Internet using grid middleware software systems. Several approaches exist for porting applications to grid platforms. Examples include classical message-passing, batch processing, web portals, and GridRPC systems. This last approach implements a grid version of the classical Remote Procedure Call (RPC) model. A more sophisticated extension of this includes high level scheduling mechanisms and data management. Thus clients spread over the Internet submit computation requests to a scheduler that locates one or more servers available on the grid using some performance measure.

The aim of the DIET [1] (**D**istributed **I**nteractive **E**ngineering **T**oolbox) project is to develop a set of tools to build, deploy, and execute computational server daemons. It focuses on the development of scalable middleware with initial efforts concentrated on distributing the scheduling problem across multiple agents. DIET consists of a set of elements that can be used together to build applications using the GridRPC paradigm. This middleware is able to find an appropriate server according to the information given in the client's request (e.g. problem to be solved, size of the data involved), the performance of the target platform (e.g. server load, available memory, communication performance) and the local availability of data stored during previous computations. The scheduler is distributed using several collaborating hierarchies connected either statically or dynamically (in a peer-to-peer fashion). Data management is provided to allow persistent data to stay within the system for future re-use. This feature avoids unnecessary communications when dependencies exist between different requests.

In a grid environment, we need several complex tools for the management of resources, grid middlewares, and client/server applications. Most grid software systems use command-line interfaces without any Graphical User Interface (GUI). For the creation of a tool dedicated to the management of grid middleware and grid environments, different functions are mandatory. We can consider three main graphical interfaces for such framework: one for resource management, one for grid monitoring, and one for the management of the grid middleware. DIET Dashboard[2] answers to the need of an unified set of tools providing the user with a complete, modular, portable, and powerful way to manage grid resources of the applications that run on it.

The goal of this paper is to show the various aspects to be taken into account for the design of a graphical tool for grid middleware management and how it

[1] `http://graal.ens-lyon.fr/DIET`
[2] `http://graal.ens-lyon.fr/DIET/dietdashboard.html`

can ease the interaction with a grid by avoiding the scripting layer. Thus we designed a tool to make the grid as user-friendly as possible, in order to simplify its use. Many GUI tools dedicated to grid management exist but they are all targeting one or two tasks. The aim of the DIET Dashboard is to provide an all-in-one and flexible software that gathers these tools in an efficient manner. We give a comparison with existing tools dedicated to some specific tasks such as grid resources management, grid monitoring, or middleware management. By this way we demonstrate how the DIET Dashboard fulfilled all the needs of an unified tool making it easy to manage a grid middleware on grid platforms.

The rest of the paper is organized as follows. In Section 2, we briefly review existing works on graphical tools for the grid. Sections 3 and 4 describes the architectures of DIET and DIET Dashboard. Section 4.1 presents the features related to the grid resources management of DIET Dashboard. Section 4.2 presents the features of DIET Dashboard related to grid monitoring. Section 4.3 describes how it can manage the DIET grid middleware. To illustrate the use the DIET Dashboard, we present an experiment in Section 5. Finally, Section 6 concludes the paper.

2. Related Work

In this paper we focus on graphical tools designed for grid environments. Here we will give a description of the three main families of tools dedicated to grid middleware software systems and grid environments.

The first family concerns graphical tools for cluster resource management. They provide a Graphical User Interface (GUI) to check all information from batch schedulers. For example, QMON [16], the GUI designed for N1 Grid Engine from SUN, can examine the properties of any queue on the grid (running, disabled, suspended, etc.). A second graphical menu provides a job submission interface with all the options available. A third interface monitors the jobs status (running, suspended, deleted, pending, etc.).

To illustrate the second family, we can consider Ganglia [12], the graphical tool designed for grid monitoring. Based on a protocol using announces, this tool monitors a cluster or a set of clusters using XML, XDR and RRDtool to represent, retrieve and display the data. For each node Ganglia provides instantaneous information and history about the load, memory, I/O, etc. through a web interface.

The third family concerns tools designed for grid middleware software systems. Many tools exist for the visual specification and execution of scientific workflows as Kepler [1], Taverna [14], SGSDesigner [10], ScyFlow [13], or GridNexus [4]. For example, GridNexus is a graphical system for the creation and the execution of scientific workflows in a grid environment. The user can assemble complex processes involving data retrieval, analysis and visualization by building a directed acyclic graph in a visual environment. Future works talk about the use of GridNexus to help creating and deploying new grid services in addition to scripting existing services. This project plans to develop a generic module to provide interactive feedback while executing a workflow.

Graphical tools mentioned here are all designed with a specific aim. DIET Dashboard combines workflow management, resources reservation, resources mapping, automatic configuration, visualization, and deployment tools in one integrated graphical application.

3. DIET Architecture

The DIET component architecture is structured hierarchically for an improved scalability. Such an architecture is flexible and can be adapted to diverse environments including arbitrary heterogeneous computing platforms. The DIET toolkit [7] is implemented in CORBA and thus benefits from the many standardized, stable services provided by freely-available and high performance CORBA implementations. CORBA systems provide a remote method invocation facility with a high level of transparency. This transparency should not affect the performance substantially, as the communication layers in most CORBA implementations are highly optimized [8]. These factors motivate their decision to use CORBA as the communication and remote invocation fabric in DIET.

The DIET framework comprises several components. A **Client** is an application that uses the DIET infrastructure to solve problems using an RPC approach. Clients access DIET through various interfaces: web portals or programs using C, C++, or Java APIs. A **SeD**, or server daemon, acts as the service provider, exporting a functionality through a standardized computational service interface. A single SeD can offer any number of computational services (depending on the capacity of the machine). A SeD can also serve as the interface and execution mechanism for either a stand-alone interactive machine or a parallel supercomputer (or cluster) using an interface with a batch scheduler. The third component of the DIET architecture, **agents**, facilitate the service location and invocation interactions between clients and SeDs. Collectively, a hierarchy of agents provides higher-level services such as scheduling and data management. These services are made scalable by distributing them across a hierarchy of agents composed of a single **Master Agent (MA)** and several **Local Agents (LA)**. Figure 1 shows an example of a DIET hierarchy.

4. DIET Dashboard

When the goal is to monitor a grid, or deploy a grid middleware on it, several tasks are involved.

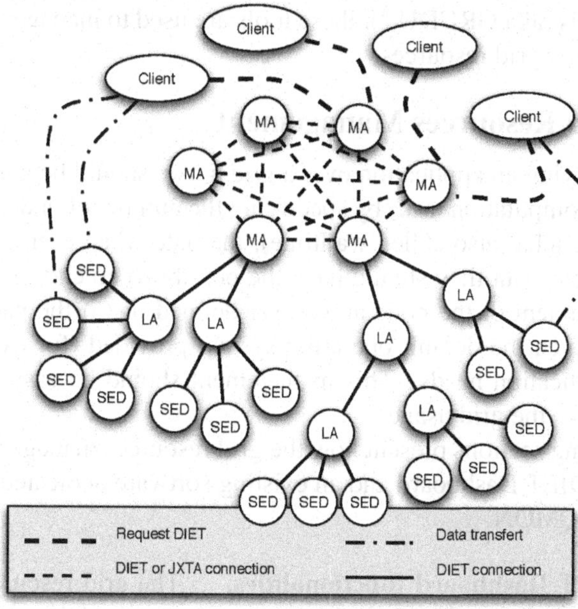

Figure 1. DIET hierarchical organization.

- Managing the resources of a grid: allocating resources, deploying nodes with several operating systems, etc.
- Monitoring the grid: getting the status of the clusters (number of available nodes in each state, number and main properties of each job, Gantt chart of the jobs history), the status of the jobs (number, status, owner, walltime, scheduled start, Ganglia information of the nodes) running on the platform, etc.
- Managing the grid middleware software system within a grid environment: designing hierarchies (manually or automatically by matching resources on patterns), deploying them directly or through workflows of applications, etc.

The DIET Dashboard provides tools trying to answer these needs with an environment dedicated to the DIET GridRPC middleware. It consists of a set of graphical tools that can be used separately or together. These tools can be divided in three categories:

1 Workflow tools: including workflow designer and workflow log service.

2 DIET tools: including tools to design and deploy DIET applications.

3 Grid tools (aka GRUDU [3]): these tools are used to manage, monitor and access user grid resources.

4.1 Grid Resources Management

When deploying an application over a grid a user should be able to allocate resources for computation tasks by specifying the number of nodes needed, the duration of the jobs (also called walltime), the date when each job will start, their priority, etc. But they should have the possibility to choose between the default environment of the node and a user-defined one if the parallel implementation or even the default operating system provided (for example) does not fit the application needs. This management should be easy to realize in order to improve the grid usage.

The following sections present how the grid resources management was designed in the DIET Dashboard and an existing software dedicated to Sun Grid Engine called QMON.

4.1.1 DIET Dashboard functionalities. The grid resources management is realized inside GRUDU, the grid resources module of DIET Dashboard. GRUDU can be easily configured to use different batch schedulers, or different grids. GRUDU can be used inside DIET Dashboard, but also in a standalone mode for users that just want to monitor, manage, or realize reservations on the grid.

Grid'5000[4] [3] project aims at building a highly reconfigurable, controlable and monitorable experimental Grid platform gathering 9 sites geographically distributed in France featuring a total of 5000 processors. The main purpose of this platform is to serve as an experimental testbed for research in grid Computing.

To allocate resources on Grid'5000, the resource tool offers a user-friendly interface allowing the selection of the number of nodes needed at each site, and the definition of the date, walltime of reservation and the queue where the job will be started. The user can select a job type (for example, `deploy` if you plan to change the operating system) for the reservation itself and launch a script on the reserved resources (see Figure 2). Concerning the clusters, the OAR batch scheduler[5] [5] uses properties for the reservations (for example, to select nodes with Myrinet interfaces) and the allocation tool provides an interface for the definition of these properties.

[3] http://graal.ens-lyon.fr/GRUDU
[4] https://www.grid5000.fr
[5] http://oar.imag.fr/

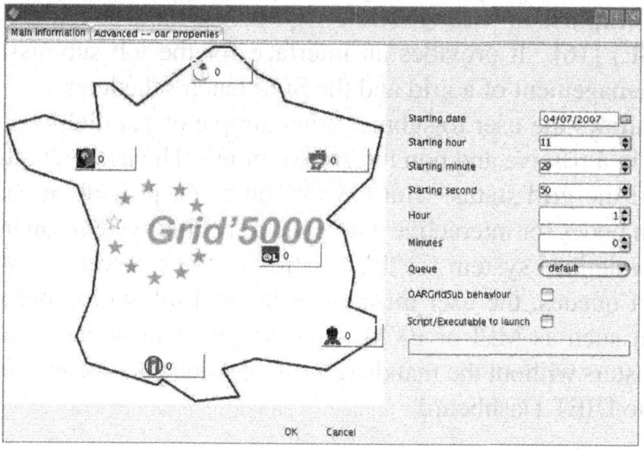

Figure 2. Resources allocation

To manage resources, the user can deploy images on nodes with the operating system needed for the computations. The resources tool also provides a GUI for the deployment of images over Grid'5000 clusters through Kadeploy[6] [9]. (The deployment through Kadeploy allows the user to have its own operating system that he/she can tune and configure as he/she wants.) The nodes and the images (if the user plans to deploy on different clusters, one image per cluster) needed for the experiment (see Figure 3).

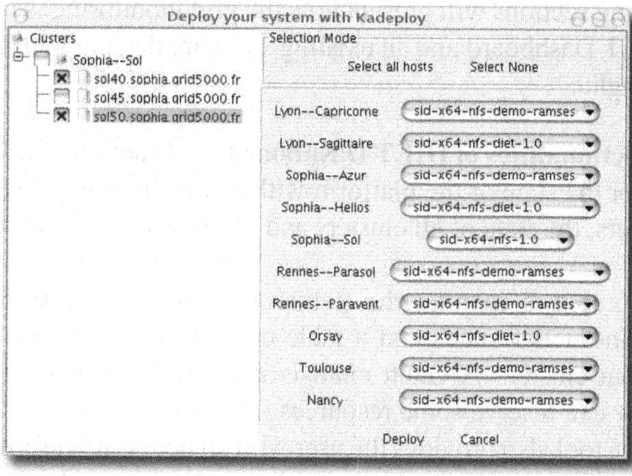

Figure 3. Image deployment through KaDeploy.

[6] `http://kadeploy.imag.fr/`

4.1.2 Comparison with QMON. QMON is the GUI to the N1 Sun Grid Engine (SGE) [16]. It provides an interface for the job submission and the resources management of a grid and the SGE batch scheduler.

QMON allows the user to submit either simple or parallel jobs on queues[7] that are run in a passive and non interactive mode. The users can then monitor the jobs and the grid status. But QMON does not provide an access to the computation nodes for interactive work, and a specific system can not deployed to get a user-defined system for the duration of the reservation. Moreover, to use different queues, the user must use a parallel job with a defined parallel environment such as MPI or PVM, whereas different nodes can be used on different clusters without the mandatory use of some parallel environment with OAR and the DIET Dashboard.

4.2 Grid Monitoring

Grid monitoring is important for a default user before he reserved resources, but also after he has reserved resources. Before submitting any job to a grid, the user should be aware of the available nodes considering their states (free/already used/dead). Whenever there is not not enough resources, the user should be able to know when these will available for computation. After having successfully submitted some jobs, the user should have some interface to get the information about his jobs but also the other jobs running on the grid. Even if sometimes more information could be interesting for expert users, too lower level information could be unusable for the default user who only wants to perform computations on some resources for a given period of time.

The following sections will present how the grid monitoring is implemented within the DIET Dashboard and an existing software dealing with the monitoring called Ganglia.

4.2.1 Functionalities of DIET Dashboard. Thanks to the resource tool we can monitor the state of the platform with charts presenting the load of the different clusters, the state of all clusters and all the users' jobs on the grid (see Figure 4).

We are also able to monitor the status of a particular cluster with charts summarizing the nodes states and a table composed of the jobs (running or waiting) on that cluster. A Gantt chart is also available helping the user to define when he can reserve some resources.

The resource tool also provides the user with all necessary information about every job that are present on a cluster, with, among others, the job Name, the job State, the job hosts, etc.

[7] A QMON queue corresponds to a cluster in the DIET Dashboard for the batch scheduler OAR.

Finally a plugin generates instantaneous data and history concerning the main metrics (the CPU load, the disk/memory/swap used, the in/out bytes, etc.) of the user reserved nodes with information taken from the Ganglia data.

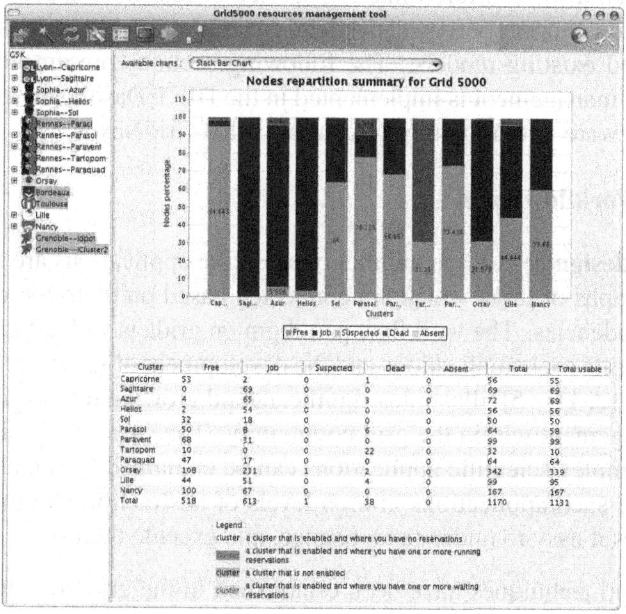

Figure 4. Grid'5000 grid status.

4.2.2 Comparison with Ganglia. Ganglia is a scalable distributed monitoring system for high-performance computing systems such as clusters and grids. Ganglia provides resources usage metrics (memory, CPU, jobs...) for individual sites or whole grids. These are low level and can be used to monitor the hardware of sites of whole grids.

But Ganglia does not provide information of higher level such as the node states, the available resources of clusters or the information about the jobs existing in the clusters. From an user point of view that needs to reserve resources and realize some computations on that nodes, the information about the jobs and the clusters in DIET Dashboard can be sufficient, whereas the ones from Ganglia can be useless because of a too lower level for a standard use. These informations are to be considered as a complement to the monitoring part of the DIET Dashboard (and it is moreover the purpose of a plugin as described in Section 4.2.1).

4.3 Grid Middleware Management

When using a tool managing grids and grid middleware such as DIET, a user expects features such as the design a hierarchy of middleware elements, the remote deployment of locally created hierarchies, or the discovery of online existing and usable services for further use in workflows. Others functionalities can also be offered like log service or real-time execution for running workflows, or resources dependent generation of hierarchies according to predefined existing models. The following sections present how the grid middleware management is implemented in the DIET Dashboard as well as an existing software with monitoring features called GridNexus.

4.3.1 Workflow tools.

Workflow designer A large number of scientific applications are represented by graphs of tasks which are connected based on their control and data dependencies. The workflow paradigm on grids is well adapted for representing such applications and the development of several workflow engines [2, 11, 15] illustrates significant and growing interest in workflow management within the grid community. The success of this paradigm in complex scientific applications can be explained by the ability to describe such applications in high levels of abstraction and in a way that makes it easy to understand, change, and execute them.

Several techniques have been established in the grid community to define workflows. The most commonly used model is the graph and especially the Directed Acyclic Graph (DAG). Since there is no standard language to describe scientific workflows, the description language is environment dependent and usually XML based, though some environments use scripts. In order to support workflow applications in the DIET environment, we have developed and integrated a workflow engine. Our approach has a simple and a high level API, the ability to use different advanced scheduling algorithms, and it should allow the management of multi-workflows sent concurrently to the DIET platform.

In this context, a workflow designer was developed to help users to design workflow applications but also to execute them. Figure 5(a) shows an overview of this tool, where they can have a description of the available services (discovered with online mode) and design a workflow by a drag and drop mechanism. The user does not need to know details about the requested services neither to define them. Once the workflow designed, one can either save it to an XML format supported by the DIET workflow engine or execute it directly. In the second case, the workflow input must be defined.

The XML representation of designed workflows describes required tasks and data dependencies. A task is a DIET service and a data dependency is a link between two parameters. The workflow designer checks and guarantees data type compatibility between source and target ports of each created link.

The workflow description level used here is known as "abstract description". This level of description does not include any runtime information but is sufficient for the workflow execution. DIET hierarchy and workflow engine manage automatically and transparently the user tasks scheduling and execution.

Workflow log service To improve workflow monitoring, we propose a tool dedicated to workflow monitoring that displays the real-time execution processes of different workflows. This graphical tool has two major roles: first it is a central event service that receives and handles the events related to tasks execution progression. Secondly it provides a graphical representation of workflow state. This tool, shown in Figure 5(b), displays the different workflows after they start their execution. Each node of the workflow can be in one of the following states: "waiting", "running", or "done".

4.3.2 DIET tools. A DIET platform can be represented by a hierarchy of agents and servers. Designing and deploying such a hierarchy of distributed and heterogeneous elements can be a hard task for the end user. In our previous works [6], we have defined a XML format to describe DIET platforms. This format describes a DIET hierarchy but also the information about used resources and environments.

To deploy DIET hierarchies on a grid environment the DIET Dashboard provides two methods:

In two steps: First the user creates by hand his DIET hierarchy with the DIET designer. Instead of manipulating complex XML files, the user simply adds Local Agents or Server Daemons to the Master Agent or already added Local Agents. Concerning the Server Daemons you can define the binary to launch, the input parameters etc. This level describes only the application level, and the obtained application description can be extended with runtime information. The main frame of the DIET designer is presented in Figure 6.

To extend this application level hierarchy the user should use the DIET mapping tool (see Figure 7). This tool allows the user to map the allocated Grid'5000 resources to a DIET application. For each Grid'5000

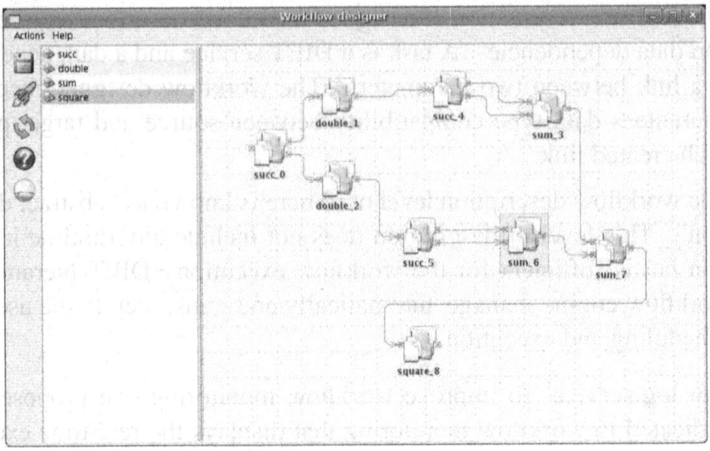

(a) Workflow designer

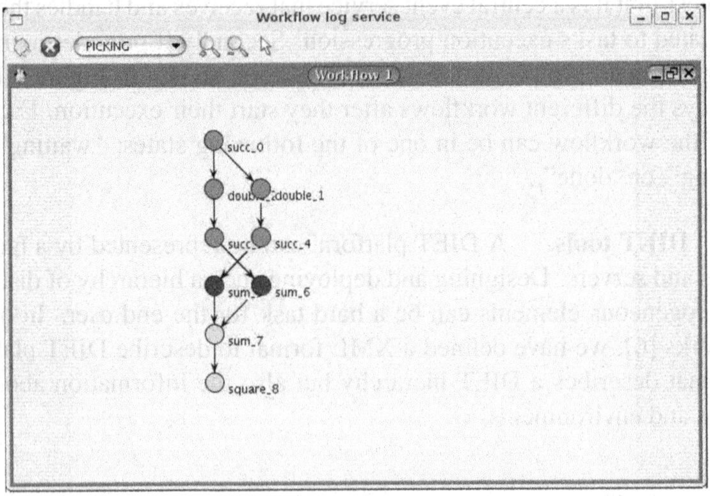

(b) Workflow log service

Figure 5. Workflow tools.

site, the nodes (or hosts) are used in a homogeneous manner but the user can select a particular host if needed.

in one step: The XMLGoDIETGenerator builds a GoDIET XML file that can be used with the DIET deployment tool from a compact description and a reservation directory. For large experiments, writing the GoDIET file by hand is time consuming and if the user should redo this experiment with a different set of machines, the GoDIET file will be generated according to the available resources.

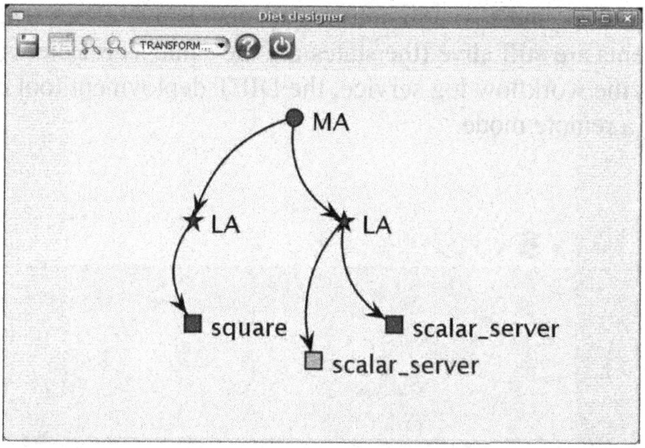

Figure 6. DIET designer.

The way hierarchies are described (through a framework from which their are created according to the available resources) have also to be the most flexible to let the user write all possible hierarchies. One should notice that the XMLGoDIETGenerator is "resources driven" because the final hierarchy will directly depend on the available resources provided, whereas the ones created with the DIET designer and mapping tools will not change if there is more or less available resources.

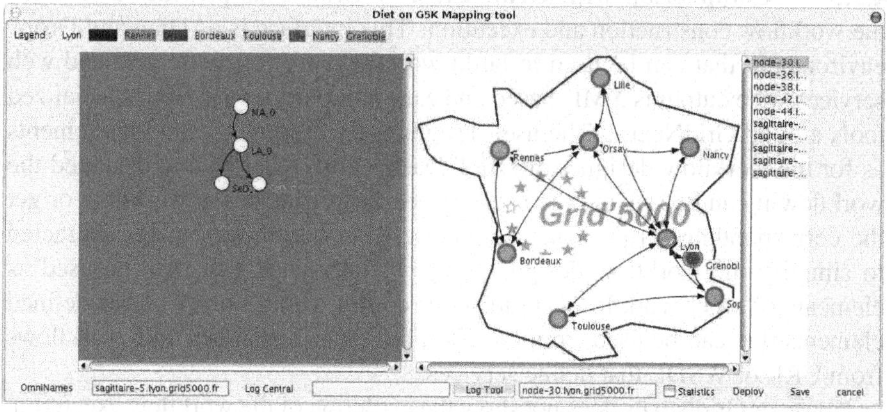

Figure 7. DIET mapping Tool.

When the DIET hierarchies are generated the user can deploy these hierarchies on the grid thanks to the DIET deploy tool (see Figure 8). This tool is a graphical interface to GoDIET. It provides the basic GoDIET operations:

open, launch, stop, and also a monitoring mechanism to check if DIET application elements are still alive (the states are the same as for the workflow log service). As the workflow log service, the DIET deployment tool can be used in a local or a remote mode.

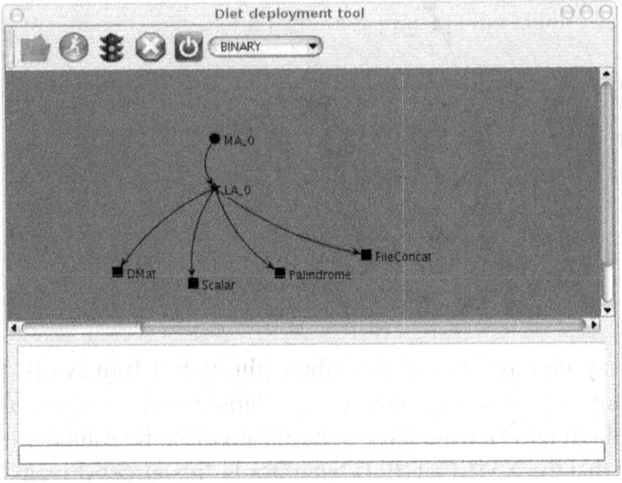

Figure 8. DIET deployment tool.

4.3.3 Comparison with GridNexus. GridNexus provides a GUI for the workflow construction and execution. This interface is a "Drag and Drop" environment that can be used to build workflows from generic grid and web services. The output is XML-based and easy to modify or use from specialized tools around GridNexus. The user designs the workflow by linking elements as for the workflow designer of DIET Dashboard. After having designed the workflow it can be run and the user can see the results of the workflow or get the corresponding script of the workflow. The workflows can be abstracted to simplify the workflow design. These "composites" can then be used as elements of other workflows. GridNexus comes with a library of pre-defined elements that can be used from the GUI, but we can also generate workflows from URL of WSDL that define services.

However GridNexus does not show the evolution of the workflow execution, and it does not provide some log functions in order to prevent from services failures or anything else. Moreover GridNexus does not discover online services but the user should provide him the services which could be complicated for the end-user that might not know where those services are located. Finally GridNexus only manages workflows of tasks, and does not allow the user to design and execute her/his own hierarchies of elements, in order to later execute clients (the ones that are not workflows of executions) on computations nodes.

5. Experiments

An experiment has been realized to test the capabilities of DIET and DIET Dashboard for a large number of machines. This experiment has been realized on Grid'5000, and the chosen application was cosmological computations. For this experiment, the entire Grid'5000 platform was reserved [8] which gave us 12 clusters used on 7 sites for a duration of 48 hours. Finally 979 machines were used with an user-defined environment containing all the needed software for the experiment. Figure 9 gives a bar chart representing the occupation of the cluster with the jobs for the experiment, taken from the resources tool of the DIET Dashboard.

The aim of the experiment was also to start the largest machines reservation over the grid, for the deployment of the largest DIET hierarchy in order to execute the maximum number of cosmological application jobs. The MPI code executed by the DIET servers called RAMSES[9] [17] was developed in Saclay (DAPNIA/CEA) to study large scale structures and galaxies formation. This code is a grid-based hydro solver with adaptive mesh refinement.

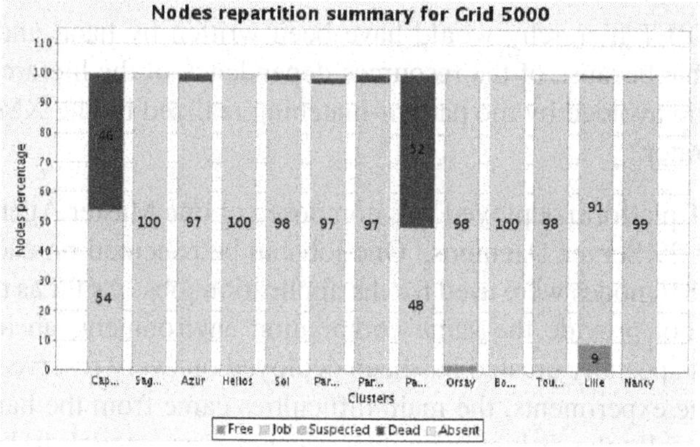

Figure 9. Chart representing the occupation of the different clusters and the node repartition between the different job states (Free/Job/Dead/Absent).

Thanks to GRUDU, reservations were done at the grid level and not on each cluster in 20 seconds. To get an user-defined environment on each machine,

[8] among the uncrashed nodes.

[9] `http://irfu.cea.fr/Projets/COAST/ramses.htm`

GRUDU was able to realize the deployment of every machines of the 12 clusters involved at the same time in roughly 25 minutes. Finally the DIET hierarchy was created through the use of the XMLGoDIETGenerator in 5 seconds and deployed through the DIET Deploy tool and GoDIET in 23 seconds.

If theses tasks would have been done without GRUDU:

- the reservation would have been realized with `oargridsub` (a non-graphical utility dedicated to OAR) by hand by reserving every nodes of each cluster at a time.

  Here is a dummy example of `oargridsub` command:

```
oargridsub
cluster1:rdef="nodes=2",cluster2:rdef"nodes=1",cluster3:rdef="nodes=1",
cluster4:rdef="nodes=2",cluster5:rdef"nodes=1",cluster6:rdef="nodes=1",
cluster7:rdef="nodes=2",cluster8:rdef"nodes=1",cluster9:rdef="nodes=1",
cluster10:rdef="nodes=2",cluster11:rdef"nodes=1",cluster12:rdef="nodes=1",
-s '2007-09-07 16:00:00'
-w '0:10:00'
-p ~/runhpl/runhpl
```

- The use of an user-defined environment would have been impossible without KaDeploy, it would have taken the same amount of time per cluster and not for all of them, and the configuration of the deployment would have been more difficult because of several conditional choices.

- The DIET hierarchy would have been written by hand and not easily readable because of the resources-dependency of the hierarchy description file avoided by the pattern-matching realized by the XMLGoDIETGenerator.

The DIET platform deployed was composed of one Master Agent, 12 Local Agents, and 29 Server Daemons. One job can be executed on each SeD at a given time. 816 nodes were used for the application jobs. As far as the different clusters do not provide the same compilation environment, an image of an environment specially created has been deployed on every reserved nodes.

During the experiments, the main difficulties came from the hardware limitations (typically the disk space which was not large enough to backup data, or some no well defined permissions of /tmp directories on some clusters), and not from DIET or the DIET Dashboard that allowed a good dispatching of the middleware requests and the fast and efficient management of these hardware problems.

6. Conclusion

With the development of grid technologies and the availability of large scale platforms, it becomes mandatory to manage grid applications efficiently and

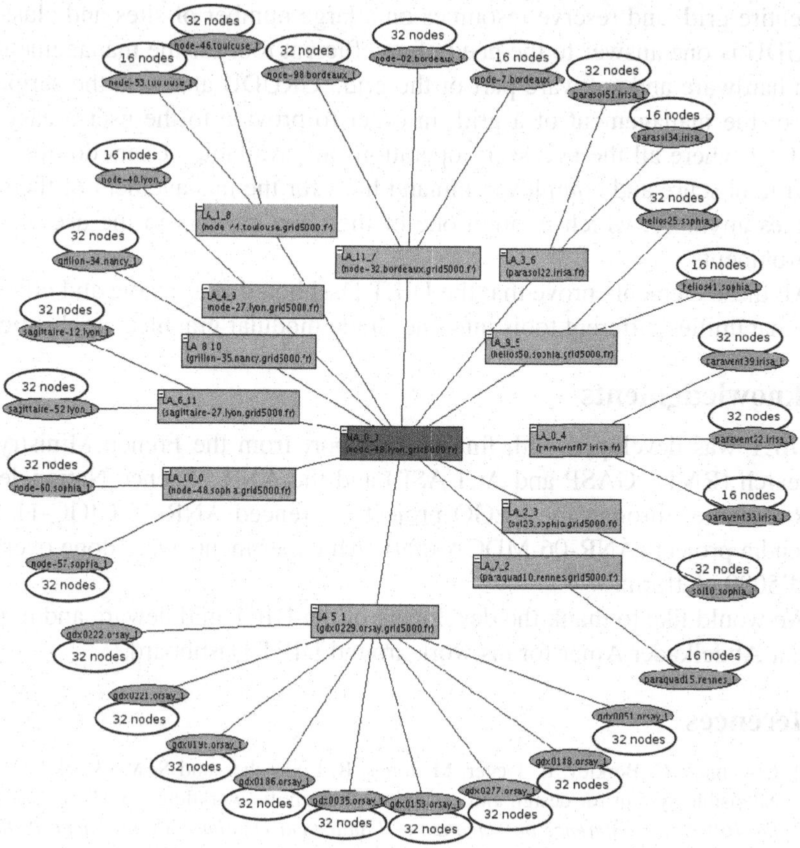

Figure 10. DIET hierarchy deployed during the experiment.

easily. In this paper, they have presented the DIET Dashboard environment which is a complete, modular, portable, and powerful set of tools dedicated to a grid middleware. With this tool, a non-expert user can manage grid resources, monitor the grid itself and manage the grid middleware by designing its grid applications or using workflows and then deploying these grid applications over the grid platform.

The DIET Dashboard offers a large number of modules, created to answer the different needs of tools appearing in a grid context. The software architecture design of DIET Dashboard makes its extensible (modules can easily be added to the core of the application).

The performance of the DIET Dashboard and GRUDU (the tool dedicated to the grid management) have been tested through the experiment realized on

Grid'5000. This experiment showed that the resources tool is able to monitor the entire grid, and reserve resources on a large number of sites and clusters. GRUDU is one answer to the need of an efficient tool for the management of both hardware and software part of the grid. GRUDU abstracts the scripting part of the management of a grid, in order to provide to the user a easy-to-use GUI where all the necessary operations are available. Users do not need to write obscure and complex command lines for the management of their resources anymore, which is often one of the main barriers in the use of grid environments.

All these elements prove that the DIET Dashboard is as stable and efficient tool that unifies different tools into one single modular graphical application.

Acknowledgments

DIET was developed with financial support from the French Ministry of Research (RNTL GASP and ACI ASP) and the ANR (Agence Nationale de la Recherche) through the LEGO project referenced ANR-05-CIGC-11 and Gwendia project (ANR-06-MDCA-009). All experiments were done over the Grid'5000 platform.

We would like to thank the developers of the DIET middleware and in particular Abdelkader Amar for his work around DIET Dashboard.

References

[1] I. Altintas, C. Berkley, E. Jaeger, M. Jones, B. Ludascher, and S. Mock. Kepler: An extensible system for design and execution of scientific workflows. In *Proceedings of the 16th Intl. Conference on Scientific and Statistical Database Management(SSDBM)*, Santorini Island, Greece, June 2004.

[2] K. Amin, G. von Laszewski, M. Hategan, N.J. Zaluzec, S. Hampton, and A. Rossi. GridAnt: A Client-Controllable Grid Workflow System. *hicss*, 07:70210c, 2004.

[3] R. Bolze, F. Cappello, E. Caron, M. Daydé, F. Desprez, E. Jeannot, Y. Jégou, S. Lanteri, J. Leduc, N. Melab, G. Mornet, R. Namyst, P. Primet, B. Quetier, O. Richard, E. Talbi, and I. Touché. Grid'5000: a large scale and highly reconfigurable experimental grid testbed. *International Journal of High Performance Computing Applications*, 20(4):481–494, November 2006.

[4] J.L. Brown, C.S. Ferner, T.C. Hudson, A.E. Stapleton, R.J. Vetter, T. Carland, A. Martin, J. Martin, A. Rawls, W. J. Shipman, and M. Wood. Gridnexus: A grid services scientific workflow system. *International Journal of Computer Information Science (IJCIS)*, 6(2):77–82, June 2005.

[5] N. Capit, G. Da Costa, Y. Georgiou, G. Huard, C. Martin, G. Mounié, P. Neyron, and O. Richard. A batch scheduler with high level components. In *Cluster computing and Grid 2005 (CCGrid05)*, 2005.

[6] E. Caron, P.K. Chouhan, and H. Dail. GoDIET: A deployment tool for distributed middleware on grid'5000. In IEEE, editor, *EXPGRID workshop. Experimental Grid Testbeds for the Assessment of Large-Scale Distributed Apllications and Tools. In conjunction with HPDC-15.*, pages 1–8, Paris, France, June 19th 2006.

[7] E. Caron and F. Desprez. DIET: A Scalable Toolbox to Build Network Enabled Servers on the Grid. *International Journal of High Performance Computing Applications*, 20(3):335–352, 2006.

[8] A. Denis, C. Perez, and T. Priol. Towards high performance CORBA and MPI middlewares for grid computing. In C.-A. Lee, editor, *Proc. of the 2nd International Workshop on Grid Computing*, number 2242 in LNCS, pages 14–25, Denver, Colorado, USA, November 2001. Springer-Verlag.

[9] Y. Georgiou, J. Leduc, B. Videau, J. Peyrard, and O. Richard. A tool for environment deployment in clusters and light grids. In *Second Workshop on System Management Tools for Large-Scale Parallel Systems (SMTPS'06)*, Rhodes Island, Greece, 4 2006.

[10] A. Gómez-Pérez and R. González-Cabero. SGSdesigner: a graphical interface for annotating and designing semantic grid services. In *WWW '06: Proceedings of the 15th international conference on World Wide Web*, pages 867–868, New York, NY, USA, 2006. ACM Press.

[11] D. Hull, K. Wolstencroft, R. Stevens, C. Goble, M. R. Pocock, P. Li, and T. Oinn. Taverna: a tool for building and running workflows of services. *Nucleic Acids Res*, 34(Web Server issue), July 2006.

[12] M. L. Massie, B. N. Chun, and D. E. Culler. The ganglia distributed monitoring system: design, implementation, and experience. *Parallel Computing*, 30(7):817–840, July 2004.

[13] K.M. McCann, M. Yarrow, A. De Vivo, and Piyush Mehrotra. Scyflow: an environment for the visual specification and execution of scientific workflows. *Concurrency and Computation: Practice and Experience*, 18(10):1155–1167, 2006.

[14] T.M. Oinn, M. Addis, J. Ferris, D. Marvin, M. Senger, R. M. Greenwood, T. Carver, K. Glover, M.R. Pocock, A. Wipat, and P. Li. Taverna: a tool for the composition and enactment of bioinformatics workflows. *Bioinformatics*, 20(17):3045–3054, 2004.

[15] G. Singh, E. Deelman, G. Mehta, K. Vahi, M.-H. Su, B. G. Berriman, J. Good, J.C. Jacob, D.S. Katz, A. Lazzarini, K. Blackburn, and S. Koranda. The pegasus portal: web based grid computing. In *SAC '05: Proceedings of the 2005 ACM symposium on Applied computing*, pages 680–686, New York, NY, USA, 2005. ACM Press.

[16] Sun Microsystems. *Sun Grid Engine — Administration and User's guide*, 2002. Version 5.3.

[17] R. Teyssier. Cosmological hydrodynamics with adaptive mesh refinement: a new high resolution code called ramses, 2001.

AN EFFICIENT PROTOCOL FOR RESERVING MULTIPLE GRID RESOURCES IN ADVANCE

Jörg Schneider, Julius Gehr, Barry Linnert
Technische Universitaet Berlin, Germany
{komm,jules,linnert}@cs.tu-berlin.de

Thomas Röblitz*
Zuse Institute Berlin, Germany
roeblitz@zib.de

Abstract We propose a mechanism for the co-allocation of multiple resources in Grid environments. By reserving multiple resources in advance, scientific simulations and large-scale data analyses can efficiently be executed with their desired quality-of-service level. Co-allocating multiple Grid resources in advance poses demanding challenges due to the characteristics of Grid environments, which are (1) incomplete status information, (2) dynamic behavior of resources and users, and (3) autonomous resources' management systems. Our co-reservation mechanism addresses these challenges by probing the state of the resources and by enhancing a two-phase commit protocol with timeouts. We performed extensive simulations to evaluate communication overhead of the new protocol and the impact of the timeouts' length on the scheduling of jobs as well as on the utilization of the Grid resources.

Keywords: Grid resource management, advance co-reservation, flexible status probing, two-phase commit with timeouts

1. Introduction

Over the last decade, Grid computing has evolved from providing basic methods to access distributed heterogeneous compute resources to a research discipline that addresses the demanding needs of both scientific and commercial applications. Scientific simulations and large-scale data analyses often involve complex workflows which require the co-allocation of multiple re-

*This work was partially funded by the German Ministry for Education and Research under grant 01AK804C and by the Institute on Resource Management and Scheduling of the EU Network of Excellence CoreGRID (Contract IST-2002-004265).

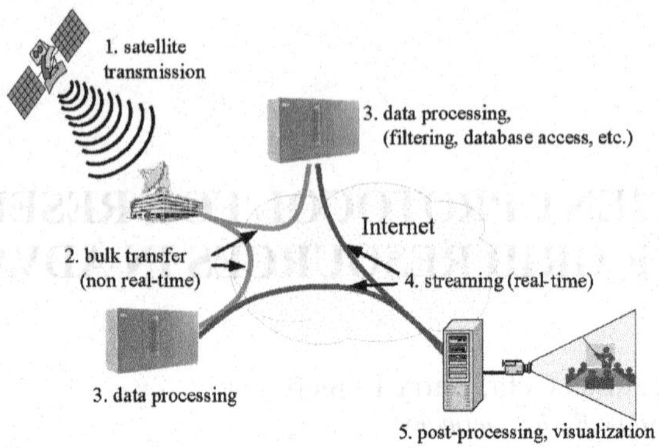

Figure 1. Example: Grid application with time-dependent tasks.

sources. For example, Fig. 1 illustrates a tele-immersion application, which requires different resources such as compute clusters, network links and visualization units. Co-allocating multiple resources can be implemented by different means. First, the resources' management systems coordinate the allocation of resources to a distributed application, i.e., without the need of a higher-level Grid broker. Second, a higher-level Grid broker coordinates the allocation of the resources. In this model, delivering end-to-end quality-of-service (QoS) guarantees to distributed applications necessitates the use of *advance reservations*, because Grid resources are autonomously managed. Autonomous management means, that a Grid broker has only limited control over the start time of a job. While this is sufficient for many single-resource applications, delivery of QoS guarantees to distributed multi-resource applications may be very difficult if not impossible.

In this paper, we follow the second approach, that is reserving multiple resources in advance. In particular, we propose a protocol which (1) reduces the number of trials until a co-reservation is admitted, (2) provides means to reduce the impact of the reservation process to concurrent job submissions and (3) implements an *all-or-nothing* semantics for acquiring co-reservations.

We assume that the capacity of *resources* is space-shared among simultaneously active requests. Furthermore, the resources' local management is planning-based, i.e., it accepts requests starting in the future and guarantees that these requests are allocated the needed capacity. *Co-reservation requests* consist of multiple parts each specifying an earliest start time, a duration, a latest end time and a needed capacity. Different parts of a co-reservation request may require resources of different type and different capacities. The relationship between the parts are specified with temporal and spatial constraints.

The first step in reserving is to filter the existing resources with the static requirements of a request, e.g., the operating system of a machine or the available interfaces to a storage server. The resulting set of *resource candidates* is the input to the mechanism we propose here. Our protocol is composed of three main steps:

1 Determine co-reservation candidates by probing the future status of resources.

2 Gather preliminary reservations for each part of a co-reservation candidate.

3 Commit the preliminary reservations.

A *co-reservation candidate* is a set of tuples each describing a time slot at a certain resource. A time slot is defined by a begin time, an end time and a capacity. Also, a tuple associates evaluation metrics with each time slot such as cost. These performance metrics may be used to select a co-reservation candidate for further processing. While selecting a candidate is an interesting research topic by itself it is beyond the scope of this paper. In the evaluation, we simply used the candidate with the earliest time slots. Note, since the preliminary reservations expire after some timeout, they do not need to be canceled if the whole transaction fails.

The remainder of this paper is structured as follows. In Section 2 we discuss related work. The multi-resource reservation protocol we propose is presented in Section 3. The benefits of the probe messages and the timeouts are evaluated through extensive simulation in Section 4. We conclude in Section 5.

2. Related Work

As described, elaborated resource allocation mechanisms are a key requirement to enable complex applications in the Grid. Grid brokers relying on batch management systems at the local resources will only implement co-allocations at a high cost [9]. If the local resource manager already supports advance reservations, the Grid broker has to submit such reservations in a coordinated manner in order to allocate the requested resources. Several protocols have been proposed for this task, all using the basic concept of a two-phase commit. In the first phase, each required resource is preliminarily reserved. If this was successful for each resource these reservations will be committed. In the literature [1, 3, 5, 6, 7, 14], this protocol is usually applied on exactly named resources. In our approach, the co-allocation request specifies the type of the resource only. Thus, our Grid broker may automatically try multiple combinations of resources until the requested preliminary reservations are obtained.

Kuo and Mckeown [6] present a two-phase commit protocol and show that in all cases only valid final states will be reached. They discuss possible economic models to deal with preliminary reservations. The protocol also supports timeouts for the preliminary reservations. But the impact of timeouts on the resource utilization and the processing of the workload was only stated and not empirically analyzed.

Czajkowski et al. [3] propose a reservation protocol where the application itself or a co-allocation agent on behalf of the application manages the co-allocation. The authors extended the two-phase commit protocol such that the application can dynamically modify the reservation. For example, the application was enabled to give up a reservation only if it could get another reservation.

Brandic et al. [1] developed a two-phase commit protocol to ensure a requested quality-of-service. The protocol is employed between a Grid user and the Grid broker. The Grid broker will produce a QoS offer consisting of a predicted execution time, an allocation for all needed resources, and a prize based on an economic model. The user confirmation of such an offer equals the commit in the two-phase commit protocol. The offer is valid for a limited time only, but the actual impact of this timeout is not evaluated.

Haji et al. address the issues of the two-phase commit protocol with restricted knowledge [5]. They propose a mechanism to monitor all suitable resources until the preliminary reservation will be carried out. The local resource management systems of the selected resources will inform the Grid broker on each state change. The monitored resources must provide detailed information on their status which contradicts the information hiding aspect of the Grid. Additionally, the protocol operates with immediate reservations only.

The HARC co-scheduler [7] uses Gray and Lamport's Paxos Commit Protocol, a generalization of the two-phase commit protocol. Using this protocol, the commit process may succeed if multiple participants fail or are temporarily unavailable. The HARC co-scheduler requires detailed information about the timetables of the requested resources.

The MetaScheduling Service [14] uses a negotiation protocol for co-allocations. In a first step each resource is asked for the earliest possible start time. This step is repeated using the latest start time as a new lower bound until all resources return the same time. The subsequent steps implement the two-phase commit protocol. The resources are selected by the user before the negotiation begins. Our proposed probe requests works similarly to the first step, but the probe responses contain multiple possible start times in the whole requested time frame.

In the context of transactions the two-phase commit is a fundamental technique for processing distributed transactions. Various approaches extended the basic two-phase commit such that it could also be applied in distributed systems without a central coordinator, i.e., by introducing an additional phase to elect a coordinator [13].

3. The Reservation Protocol

The reservation protocol must cope with the specific characteristics of Grid environments, which are (1) incomplete status information, (2) dynamic behavior of the resources and users, and (3) autonomy of the resources' local management systems. In the theoretic case, that a client would have global information and could control any state change in the resources, it could simply request the reservation of multiple available resources. In a realistic scenario, however, a client neither has global information nor does he or a broker fully control the resources. Hence, a client does not know a-priori, which resources are available. The reservation protocol, we propose, approaches this problem by specifying three methods tailored at the level of information a client possesses and by defining the relationships between these methods. Here a client is any participant who is requesting some service. For example, a user sending a request to a broker, or a broker sending a request to a resource. The participants can compose a multi-level hierarchy, which is common in economic environments. For the sake of simplicity, we will limit the discussion to three levels: clients, broker and resources.

3.1 Building Blocks of the Protocol Phases

The protocol involves the three phases: (1) probing, (2) gathering preliminary reservations and (3) committing. The corresponding methods and the level of information to which they are applicable are summarized in Table 1. Figure 2(a) shows symbols for each phase. While the upper row illustrates the interaction for sending a request, the lower shows symbols for transmitting the response messages. In the following sections, these symbols are used to compose protocol instances.

Table 1. Protocol methods for different levels of status information.

Method	Description	Level of information (X)
probe	Resources are asked to provide information about their current and future state.	low (0)
reserve	A preliminary reservation is requested. The request can be given with fixed or ranged values.	high for fixed request parameters, medium for flexible request parameters (1)
commit	A previously admitted preliminary reservation is committed.	highest (2)

Probing phase. The purpose of the probing phase is to gather detailed information about the state of a resource. If a component receives a probe request it determines reservation candidates. Each reservation candidate is defined by a

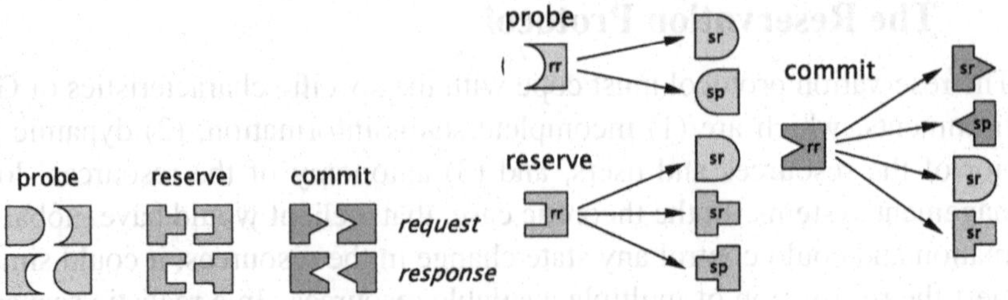

(a) Symbols representing message exchanges for the three protocol phases: *probing, gathering preliminary reservations* and *committing*.

(b) Rules for composing protocol methods to protocol instances. Symbol labels: sr - send request, rr - receive request, sp - send response (cf. Sect. 3.1 for a detailed description of the methods).

Figure 2. Method symbols and rules for composing protocol instances.

start time, an end time and a quality-of-service level which satisfy the bounds of the flexible request. Each reservation candidate is associated with a number of evaluation metrics. The used evaluation metrics only depend on what a client is requesting and what a service provides. Typical, evaluation metrics are cost, utilization, makespan, etc. [12].

Gathering preliminary reservations. Preliminary reservations are like normal reservations except that they need to be confirmed until a given time. Before that time, a resource may not allocate the reserved capacity to any other request. Canceling a preliminary reservation (or simply not confirming it) does not impose any cost to the client. Similar to a probe request a reservation request may be given with flexible parameters. Flexibility enables a broker to negotiate the exact parameters. Note, this is not only beneficial for the client side, but also for the resources, which can express their preferences. In a scenario with fixed parameters, a resource can only grant or deny a request.

Committing phase. In the committing phase, a client confirms the preliminary reservations it will use. This phase is essential to implement an all-or-nothing semantics in a Grid environment. A client will only start committing reservations if it has received preliminary reservations for all request parts. Because a resource must not allocate the capacity of granted preliminary reservations to any other request, it is interested in receiving a confirmation or cancellation as soon as possible.

3.2 Rules for Composing Protocol Instances

A client may possess different levels of information. Consequently, a reservation process can be initiated with each of the three methods. The rules for composing protocol instances only limit the actions of a service receiving a request of a client. Figure 2(b) illustrates these rules using the symbols introduced in Sect. 3.1.

The service receiving a request corresponding to the information level X may only issue requests of the same or a lower level of information $Y \leq X$ (cf. Table 1). For example, if a broker receives a reserve request, it can only issue probe or reserve requests to resources. Only the sender of a request may switch to a method corresponding to a higher level of information.

3.3 A Protocol Instance for Grid Environments

In many Grid environments, the three main parties involved in job management are the clients, a broker and the resources. Here we present a protocol instance that is adopted to such situations. Figure 3 provides an overview of the interactions of a client with the broker and of the broker with the resources.

The interactions of the components are as follows:

1 *Client Request.* The client sends a reserve request to a broker.

2 *Probe Request.* The Grid broker sends a probe request to all suitable resources specifying the constraints given by the user.

3 *Probe Response.* The requested local resource management systems (RMS) estimate whether the request could be fulfilled. Each RMS constructs a number of reservation candidates matching the requirements, i.e., containing specific values for the number of CPUs, the start time, or the required bandwidth. Each reservation candidate is further rated with respect to how well it fits into the known workload of the resource.

4 *Reservation.* Using the information from the probe responses, the Grid broker can now calculate a co-reservation candidate. The allocation takes into account the user given requirements and the scheduling strategy of the Grid broker, but also the preferences given by the local resource management systems (the rating associated with each reservation candidate). All selected resources of this co-reservation candidate are now asked for a preliminary reservation.

5 *Reservation Granted* or *Reservation Failed.* The local resource manager tries to incorporate the reservation into their schedule and informs the Grid broker about the result of the operation. Additionally, a timeout period will be negotiated until which the preliminary reservation will be held up.

6a. *Reservation Commit.* After the required resources are preliminarily reserved, the Grid broker commits all reservations. Figure 3 shows an optional step, in which the broker presents the preliminary reservation to the client and lets the client make a final decision.

6b. *Reservation Rollback.* If a single reservation fails, all former successful reservations will be canceled and a new co-reservation candidate without the failed resource will be calculated. The processing continues with step 4.

6c. *Timeout.* If the Grid broker does not respond within a given time, the local resource management system cancels the preliminary reservation.

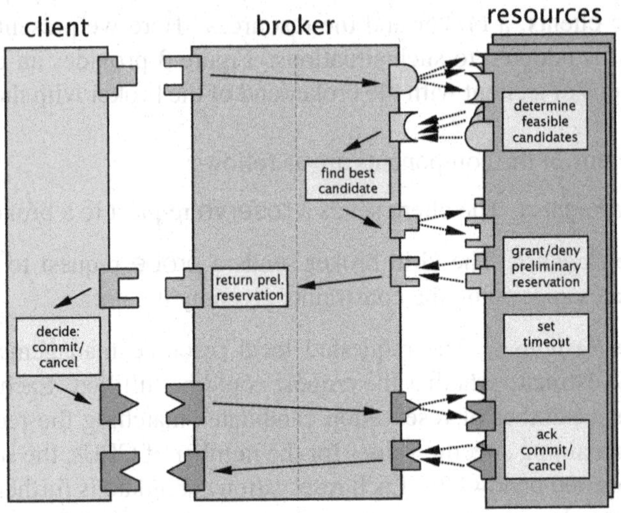

Figure 3. Example instance of the protocol with three parties – a client, a broker and multiple resources. Solid arrows indicate one control flow. Dotted arrows show the message flow between the broker and the resource.

Using a probe request, the Grid broker is now able to create a set of resources to request, which will – with a high probability – accept the reservation. Note, whether a resource accepts a reservation, depends on the current status of the resource, which may have changed between the probe request was processed and the subsequent reservation request. In general, probing will reduce the number of reservation requests send out until one succeeds. By answering a probe request, a resource provides more detailed information about its current status than what can be derived from standard resource monitoring services [4, 8]. However, each resource can decide on its own how much information it will make available. For example, it could only send back a few reservation candidates despite that more would be free. This can be used for enforcing local scheduling policies and may prevent Grid brokers from reconstructing the precise local utilization.

3.4 Trade-offs for Choosing Commit Timeouts

The moment a resource grants a preliminary reservation it also sets off a timeout until which it will keep the reservation and waits for a commit message. In this section, we discuss the trade-offs for choosing timeout values. Analytically, a timeout is composed of two distinct parts: the *technical* part and the *negotiation* part. The technical part is calculated as the round-trip time of the messages between the broker and the resources as well as between the user and the broker. Let N be the number of parts of a co-reservation request and r the message round-trip time. Depending on the communication scheme between the broker and the resources – sequential or parallel – the technical part of the timeout T_t must not be less than $(N + 1)r$ or $2r$, respectively. If a resource sets off a timeout smaller than T_t, it can not receive a commit message before the timeout expires. Note, for the sake of simplicity, we ignored message handling times in the above formulas.

The negotiation part is composed of two parts. The first part is caused by the broker performing re-negotiation and gathering alternative reservations if some of the original candidates were denied. The second part is due to a client, which may want to evaluate the gathered preliminary reservations. For example, a client could query competing Grid brokers, check the available budget or receive a clearance from the accounting. Choosing a value for those parts depends on many parameters, in particular the current workload of the resources, their reservation policies and the co-reservation requests. While the first part can be evaluated through extensive parameter studies, the second part is very difficult to model. Therefore, the experimental evaluation (cf. Sect. 4) focuses on the first part.

Enabling the user to manually influence the booking process, also requires a fault-tolerant booking protocol. Users may simply forget to cancel reservations or may not being able to do so (e.g., due to system crashes, network failures, etc.). In the travel business, advance reservations are often combined with a refund policy such that the client has to pay only a small fee if the reservation is canceled. In economics research, this is known as the "no show"-problem [11]. In online shopping, recent studies [10] show that only a small percentage of customers finally submit an order after filling up the virtual shopping cart. Usually they leave the web site without clearing the shopping cart. Clearly, there is a trade-off between the time of a customer to commit his decision and the costs of a provider whose resources are blocked until the timeout expires.

Figure 4 illustrates the trade-offs for choosing timeout values. At each level in the resource management hierarchy, the service in the role of the provider – the actual resource (solid curve in Fig. 4a) or the Grid broker (dashed curve in Fig. 4b) – favors a short timeout. When the reservation is not committed or canceled before the timeout expires, the system's performance may be unnec-

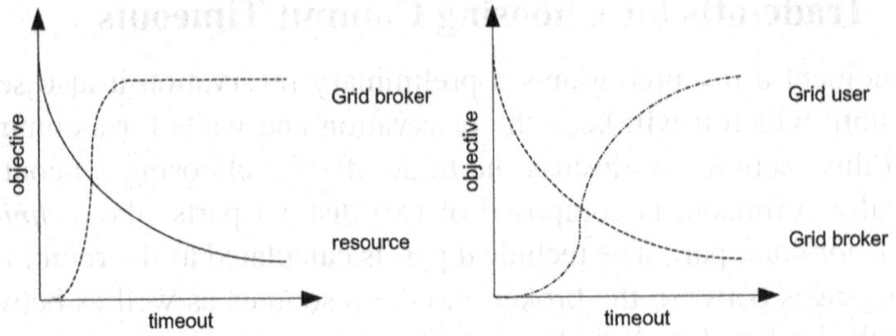

(a) Lower level (without human interaction): A Grid broker in the role of a client. A resource in the role of a provider.

(b) Higher level (with human interaction): A user in the role of a client. A Grid broker in the role of a provider.

Figure 4. The trade-off between the objective and timeout value for negotiation partners in the Grid resource management hierarchy.

essarily degraded. In other words, the longer a resource provider must hold up a eventually canceled preliminary reservation, the smaller will be the objective of the provider. Performance degradation can be measured by the number of rejected requests due to blocked resources and by the resource utilization. In contrast, the service in the role of the client – the Grid broker (dashed curve in Fig. 4a) or the Grid user (dash-dotted curve in Fig. 4b) – prefers a long timeout. Note, the different shapes of the clients' curves. A program serving as Grid broker may require smaller timeouts to reach a certain objective than a human being. Thus, the whole processing of co-reservation requests should be carried out with as less as possible human interaction.

4. Experimental Evaluation

We evaluated the common protocol instance for Grid environments described in Sect. 3.3 by means of parameter sweep simulations. In particular, we analyzed the impact of the probing phase and the length of the timeouts. In the following, we describe the simulated infrastructure, the workload, the user behavior, the metrics used for evaluation and present the results in detail.

4.1 Simulated Infrastructure and Workload

The simulated hardware infrastructure consists of eight parallel machines with homogeneous processors (512, 256, 256, 128, 128, 96, 32 and 32). For the sake of simplicity, the simulations were made using a simple synthetic job and user interaction model. Each job was assumed to be reserved in advance with the advance booking period being exponentially distributed. Job durations and requested processors were uniformly distributed over the interval $[1250, 3750]$

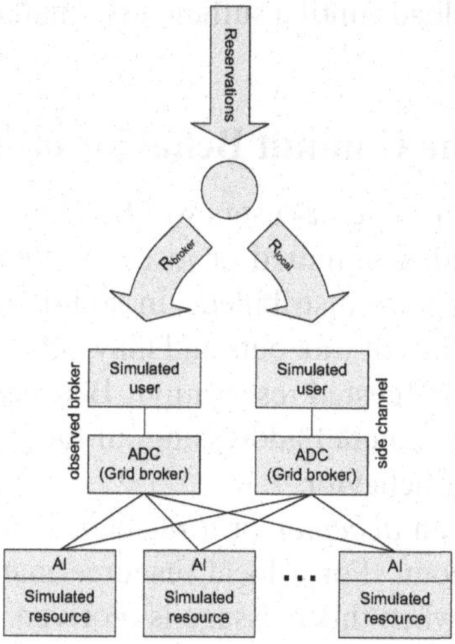

Figure 5. The simulation setup in the experimental evaluation.

and $[1, 10]$, respectively. The inter-arrival time was used to model various load situations.

To compare the performance of the proposed protocol, we used two implementations of the Grid broker – one without (version A) and one with probing (version B). In the implementation without probing, the broker tries to reserve without sending probe messages. It just uses the information about those jobs which were submitted through the broker itself, thereby simulating the problem of missing information about the status of resources. That is, the broker has no information about the jobs which were submitted by other brokers. Figure 5 shows the simulation setup. The left path is used for the measurement of different performance metrics. The right path is used to inject the workload which is not under the control of the evaluated broker. The components Administrative Domain Controller (ADC) and Adaptive Interface (AI) are part of the Virtual Resource Manager (VRM) [2] which we used for the simulations. The ADC serves as a Grid broker, while the AI may interface with different local resource management systems (LRMS). For the evaluation, we used a simple planning-based scheduler for compute resources as LRMS.

The generated workload R was divided into two sets: the set of jobs submitted to the improved broker R_{broker} and the set of jobs submitted via the side channel broker R_{local}. The jobs where randomly assigned to one of these sets preserving a given ratio $\frac{|R_{broker}|}{|R|}$ and a uniform distribution over the simulation time. Each parameter set – number of jobs, timeouts, acceptance ratios – was tested with several workloads until a sufficiently small confidence interval was reached.

4.2 Modeling the Commit Behavior of Users

Modeling the behavior of actual users would require to describe how many reservations are canceled, committed or just forgotten and how the response times (cancel or commit) are distributed. In addition, users may adapt their behavior to specific settings of timeouts and may behave differently depending on the properties of the requested reservation. Because, only few information is available for defining a model addressing all these issues, we used a very simple model of the user behavior.

A user can either be an *accepter* or a *rejecter*. An accepter would send a commit within the timeout. For a local resource management system, however, it does not matter when this message is received. Hence, we assume that it is send immediately after the reservation was preliminarily booked. A rejecter might send a cancel within the timeout or will not send any message at all. The later is the worst case from the point of view of the local resource management system. Hence, we assume that a preliminary reservation of a rejecter is automatically canceled in case of its timeout.

Thus the only variables in our user model are the number of accepters and the number of rejecters. In the evaluation, we used a set of accepters $R_{accepter}$ with a fixed number of $10,000$ co-reservations and a fixed inter-arrival time distribution. For each evaluated accepter-rejecter-ratio $ratio_i$, a corresponding set $R_{rejecter,ratio_i}$ containing $10,000/ratio_i$ co-reservations requests was generated. These requests were automatically canceled when the timeout expired.

4.3 Metrics

We used different metrics for evaluating the impact of the probing and the committing phases.

Metrics for the probing phase. The purpose of the probe messages is to minimize the communication needed to negotiate the terms of a reservation. Hence, we measured for each request the total number of messages n_{probe} exchanged between the broker and the resources. Because the negotiation for a complex workflow application involves more resources than a simple job, the communication cost for probing C_{probe} is defined as

$$C_{probe} := \frac{n_{probe}}{n_{jobs}} \tag{1}$$

where n_{jobs} is the numbers of sub-jobs. We also measured the impact of the probing on the number of actual reservation attempts r. The more the probe messages improve the knowledge of the status of the resources, the less reservation attempts should be necessary.

Metrics for the committing phase. We evaluated the timeout settings by measuring the impact of the workloads on the acceptance rate α defined as

$$\alpha := \frac{|R_{accepted}|}{|R_{accepter}|} \tag{2}$$

with $R_{accepted}$ being the set of reservations that are accepted and committed and $R_{accepter}$ the set of reservation requests for which a user will accept the obtained preliminary reservations.

4.4 Results for the Probing Phase

Figure 6b shows the number of reservation attempts (vertical axis) over different numbers of $\frac{|R_{broker}|}{|R|}$-ratios (horizontal axis). The higher the ratio, the more reservations are submitted at the evaluated broker or in other words the less status information was missing. All experiments were performed with an inter-arrival time of 20 time slots. The worst case in terms of reservation attempts is if all co-reservation candidates fail to be reserved. Therefore, the diagram shows individual graphs for successful and unsuccessful co-reservations. The graphs demonstrate that the probing phase significantly reduces the number reservation attempts for both successful and unsuccessful requests. Only in the case of $\frac{|R_{broker}|}{|R|} = 100\%$, i.e., all requests are submitted via the evaluated broker, the broker (version B) using the knowledge on previous reservations needs less co-reservation candidates than the probing broker (version A).

Figure 3b, shows the number of reservation attempts (vertical axis) over the inter-arrival time of jobs (horizontal axis). Smaller inter-arrival times correspond to higher load. For these experiments, the workload was evenly split, such that 50% of the requests were send to the evaluated broker and 50% were sent to the side channel. The graphs show that, the higher is the load (small inter-arrival times), the more does probing reduce the number of reservation attempts. For larger inter-arrival times, probing does not yield an improvement.

Figure 7a shows the total normalized number of exchanged messages between a broker and the resources C_{probe} (vertical axis) over different numbers of $\frac{|R_{broker}|}{|R|}$-ratios (horizontal axis). The graphs show that, for most ratios, the total normalized number of messages is higher for the broker employing the proposed protocol both for successful and unsuccessful requests. This is due to the additional probe messages. In our evaluation, each resource receives a probe message. Thus, eight probe messages were sent out for each sub-job of a co-reservation request (our simulation environment consists of eight resources, cf. Sect. 4.1). In contrast, the broker not using the probing mechanism (version

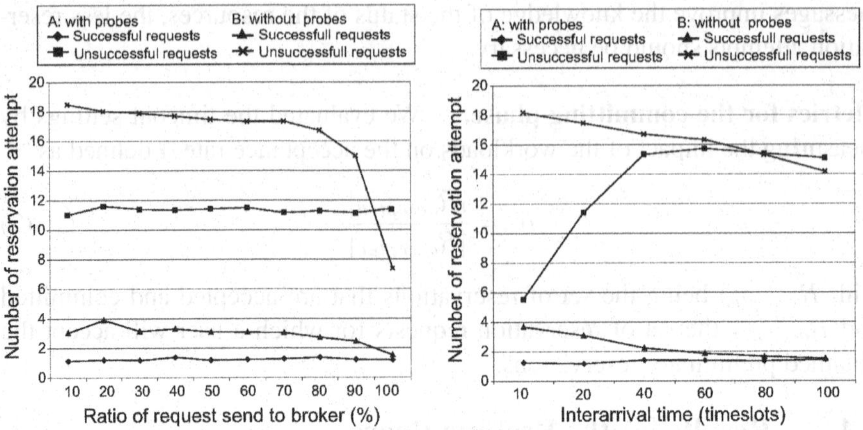

(a) Reservation attempts for different $\frac{|R_{broker}|}{|R|}$ ratios.

(b) Reservation attempts for different load situations.

Figure 6. Comparison of the protocols with and without probing.

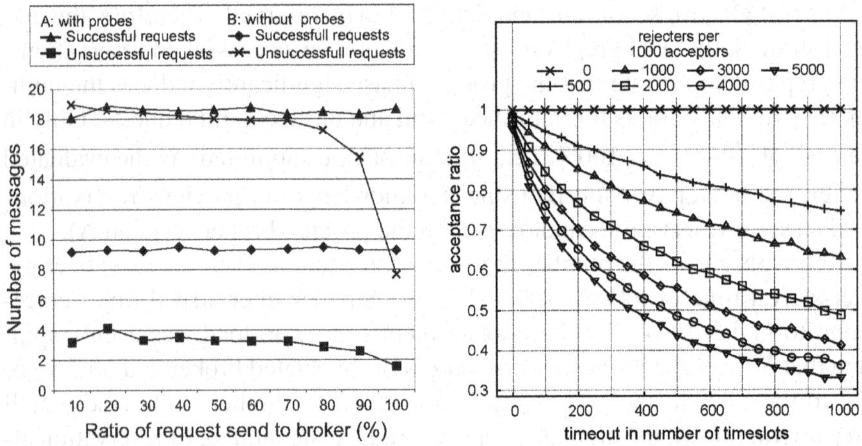

(a) The total number of messages.

(b) The average acceptance rate α for all jobs.

Figure 7. Comparison of the protocols with and without probing. Acceptance rate for all jobs.

B), only sends the reservation request. However, the results for the probing protocol may be improved by sending probing messages in parallel, resulting in a smaller overhead.

4.5 Results for the Committing Phase

The simulated hardware infrastructure as well as the synthetic job and user interaction model was same as in the experiments evaluating the probing mechanism (cf. Sect. 4.1 and Sect. 4.2). In contrast to the evaluation of the probing mechanism, we did not distinguish between local and Grid jobs as both suffer from unnecessary blocked resources in the same way. Hence, the number of jobs submitted via the side channel (cf. Fig. 5) were set to zero.

Figure 7b shows the acceptance rate (vertical axis) over the timeout (horizontal axis). Different curves represent rejecter-accepter-ratios (depicted by the number of rejecters per 1,000 accepters). The timeout is measured in number of time slots. The graphs show that, the smaller the number of rejecters, the smaller the impact of the timeout on the acceptance rate. This graph can be used to calculate timeouts dynamically based on the estimated rejecter-accepter-ratio and the target acceptance rate. For example, if we expect one rejecter per accepter and the target acceptance rate is approx. 0.8 the timeout needs to be set at about 300 time slots (cf. to curve "1,000").

5. Conclusion

In this paper, we presented an enhanced approach for reserving multiple Grid resources in advance. Most existing reservation protocols implement a two-phase commit. Applied to scenarios including complex workflows or multi-site applications these protocols may lead to a high number of requests by a Grid broker trying to allocate resources. The lack of knowledge about the availability of the resources causes this high number of requests. In contrast to these approaches, our reservation protocol implements a probe phase to gather the availability information and try only co-reservation candidates with a high success probability.

We also investigated the impact of timeouts implemented in our reservation protocol as an efficient mechanism to reduce resource wastage due to canceled or not committed reservations. The results of our experiments show a significant impact of the choice of the timeout length on the overall performance of the Grid resource management system. Based on our research the Grid providers and manager is now able to adjust the timeout length to their objectives. By observing the acceptor-rejecter-ratio the timeout may be adapted dynamically.

References

[1] I. Brandic, S. Benkner, G. Engelbrecht, and R. Schmidt. QoS Support for Time-Critical Grid Workflow Applications. In *Proceedings of the 1st International Conference on e-Science and Grid Computing (e-Science 2005)*, pages 108–115, 2005.

[2] L.-O. Burchard, M. Hovestadt, O. Kao, A. Keller, and B. Linnert. The Virtual Resource Manager: An Architecture for SLA-aware Resource Management. In *4th Intl. IEEE/ACM Intl. Symposium on Cluster Computing and the Grid (CCGrid), Chicago, USA*, pages 126–133, 2004.

[3] K. Czajkowski, I. Foster, and C. Kesselman. Resource Co-Allocation in Computational Grids. In *Proceedings of the Eighth IEEE International Symposium on High Performance Distributed Computing (HPDC-8)*, pages 219–228, 1999.

[4] K. Czajkowski, C. Kesselman, S. Fitzgerald, and I. Foster. Grid Information Services for Distributed Resource Sharing. In *Proceedings of the 10th IEEE International Symposium on High Performance Distributed Computing (HPDC-10)*, pages 181–194, 2001.

[5] M. H. Haji, P. M. Dew, K.Djemame, and I. Gourlay. A SNAP-based community resource broker using a three-phase commit protocol. In *18th International Parallel and Distributed Processing Symposium*, pages 56–65, 2004.

[6] D. Kuo and M. Mckeown. Advance Reservation and Co-Allocation Protocol for Grid Computing. In *Proceedings of the 1st International Conference on e-Science and Grid Computing (e-Science 2005)*, pages 164–171, 2005.

[7] J. MacLaren, B. Rouge, and M. Mc Keown. HARC: A Highly-Available Robust Co-scheduler. Technical report, Center for Computation and Technology, Louisiana State University, 2006.

[8] M. L. Massie, B. N. Chun, and D. E. Culler. The Ganglia Distributed Monitoring System: Design, Implementation, and Experience. *Parallel Computing*, 30(7):817–840, July 2004.

[9] H. H. Mohamed and D. H. J. Epema. Experiences with the KOALA co-allocating scheduler in multiclusters. *IEEE International Symposium on Cluster Computing and the Grid (CCGrid 2005)*, 2005.

[10] H. K. Omwando, J. Favier, I. Cremers, and T. van Tongeren. The Best Of Europe's Online Retail. Technical report, Forrester Research, October 2003.

[11] S. Ringbom and O. Shy. Reservations, refunds, and price competition. Technical Report 5/2003, Svenska handelshögskolan, Swedish School of Economics and Business Administration, November 2003.

[12] T. Röblitz, F. Schintke, and A. Reinefeld. Resource Reservations with Fuzzy Requests. *Concurrency and Computation: Practice and Experience*, 18(13):1681–1703, November 2006.

[13] D. Skeen. Nonblocking commit protocols. In *Proceedings of the 1981 ACM SIGMOD international conference on Management of data*, pages 133–142, 1981.

[14] O. Wäldrich, P. Wieder, and W. Ziegler. A Meta-scheduling Service for Co-allocating Arbitrary Types of Resources. In *Proc. of the Second Grid Resource Management Workshop (GRMWS05) in conjunction with the Sixth International Conference on Parallel Processing and Applied Mathematics (PPAM 2005)*, volume 3911 of *LNCS*, pages 782–791. Springer, 2005.

SCALABLE CONCURRENCY CONTROL IN A DYNAMIC MEMBERSHIP – EXPERIMENTAL RESULTS*

Augusto Ciuffoletti
INFN-CNAF, Via Berti Pichat, Bologna, Italy
augusto@di.unipi.it

Ali Asim
University of Paris Sud-XI, Paris, France
Ali.Asim@lri.fr

Abstract We introduce a solution for a concurrency control problem which is frequently encountered in practice: in a dynamic system we want that the load on a centralized resource is uniformly distributed among users, offering a predictable performance as long as it is not overloaded. We propose an original solution based on probabilistic assumptions, and we comment early experimental results.

Keywords: performance stabilization, randomized diffusion, membership management

*This research work is carried out under the FP6 Network of Excellence – CoreGRID project funded by the European Commission (Contract IST-2002-004265)

1. Introduction

Concurrency control is one of the basic building blocks of a distributed system. In this paper we examine a simple yet significant concurrency control instance: each node of the system must be enabled to execute a *critical operation* at approximately regular intervals, and we want the lapse between two successive executions to be decoupled from the size of the system.

We may find several use cases for this kind of concurrency control, even when we restrict our scope to the management of a Grid infrastructure: for instance, access to a global resource registry (the kind of problems otherwise solved using Distributed Hash Tables [5]), or execution of bulk data transfers [13] from data repositories. As a general rule, all applications for which a globally available resource, whose capacity we expect to grow with system size, can take advantage of such kind of concurrency control.

We describe how token circulation, a technique that is traditionally used to enforce mutual exclusion, can be extended to cover this case of concurrency control, and present experimental results that prove its effectiveness.

2. Multiple tokens randomly moving

The circulation of a unique token whose presence enables the execution of the *critical operation* is a traditional topic of applied and theoretical research [6, 12]. However, the circulation of a unique token does not guarantee that each node is enabled periodically when the system size chages, since the *return time*, the lapse between two successive visits of the token to a given node, clearly depends on the size of the system.

The presence of several tokens is a less investigated technique [9, 3] which is suitable for our problem statement. Considering a constant and uniform *token latency*, the lapse between the receive of a token and its forward the the next node, one solution consists in changing the number of tokens linearly with system size. This is a quite original approach, and we found no bibliography on this subject.

In order to apply such technique, we apparently need to know a local estimate of system size: this is a quite intriguing research problem [2]. We explore an alternative which consists in using the feedback that we obtain from the observed *return times*; using that feedback we locally control token generation or removal. We expect that this form of closed loop control stabilizes the number of tokens so that each node is visited by a token with the required frequency. Such technique relies on the assumption that *token latency*, the interval between two successive token passing operations, is a stationery process.

Notably, the token circulation technique makes reference to a topology (by default circular), that guides the token across the system. The maintenance of an overlay ring on the fabric of the distributed system is a well studied topic;

however, the extension of known solutions to systems of thousands of nodes with unreliable links is problematic.

An alternative, which is valid when considering as the underlying fabric a full mesh topology like the transport level of the Internet, is to use a random walk approach: at each step the token is forwarded to another node selected at random in the distributed system [7, 11].

Such a technique introduces a further problem, since each node needs to access the directory of system nodes to select the next destination for a token. For the sake of reliability, we exclude the presence of a centralized registry, but we assume that each node collects a significant fraction of node identifiers. The resulting topology approximates a full mesh, since each node will be adjacent only to the peers listed in the local directory. However, theoretical analysis of random diffusion processes [8, 10] ensures that in such case the random walk process is similar to the case of a full mesh.

The collection of a membership directory may introduce scalability problems: our solution consists in piggybacking to each token the notice of recent join and leave events. This limits the response to the *churm*, the process of join and leave events, of our membership.

The availability of a directory of the membership is also required to ensure some security: when a node receives a token from a peer, it should be able to check whether the sender is included in the membership. In our solution we envision the storage of authenticated public keys in the directory: keys are used to produce a signature of each received token, before it is forwarded to the next peer.

Summarizing, our solution will feature the following techniques:

- a feedback mechanism that regulates the number of tokens is used to ensure the frequency of token arrival events on each node
- tokens are forwarded randomly based on the local knowledge of the membership
- each token is signed using sender's certificate
- each token carries recent membership changes observed by the sender.

2.1 Regulation of the number of tokens

Each node measures the lapse from last token passing operation, and computes an Exponentially Weighted Moving Average (EWMA) using successive values. The EWMA returns a robust estimate of the average *interarrival time* of a token on a given node.

Comparing the EWMA with the desired *interarrival time* the node is able to trigger compensating actions, that have the effect of optimizing the number of tokens in the system:

- the observation of an interarrival time longer than $k_{max} * \overline{t_{wait}}$ reflects in the generation of a new token;
- the observation of an interarrival rate shorter than $\overline{t_{wait}}/k_{max}$ reflects in enqueuing the token until that time;
- token overflowing the capacity c of the queue are removed from the system

The token buffering in the input queue smooths the variation of the number of tokens in the system: simply removing early tokens has been observed to induce a slower convergence.

The convergence of the above rules to the desired interarrival time depends on the distribution of the interarrival times for the specific system. It is possible to prove that the system converges to the desired value if, when the number of tokens ensures the requested interarrival time, the two events of token generation and removal have identical probabilities.

The parameters k_{max} and c should be computed so to satisfy such a requirement, but this cannot be done analytically. Therefore we opt for a first hit approximation suitable for an asymmetric distribution of interarrival times, the right queue being significantly longer than the left one.

In our experiment we used $k_{max} = 3$ and $c = 2$: such parameters showed to be somewhat conservative, since average interarrival time is better than expected, at the expenses of the number of circulating tokens.

2.2 Local registry management

When a node passes the token to another node, it includes in the token a list of recently observed join and leave events. The capacity of this list is a system-wide constant: we used the value of 10. Each element in the list contains the identifier of a node, and its certificate. Let us follow step by step a token passing event, starting from the send event.

The node that forwards a token piggybacks to the token its signature, computed on the whole token using its personal certificate. Starting from the first retry, the node sends also its certificate and, after some unsuccessful retries, it selects another peer.

Upon receiving a token, the node first verifies whether the peer is in the local directory, and if the signature matches with the certificate. If either test fails, the token is silently discarded, assuming that a safe peer will resend the same token together with its certificate. If the token contains a certificate, this is verified using the public key of the certification authority, and the signature is checked. If either test fails, the token is silently discarded.

The final step consists in updating the registry with the updates recorded in the token, and merging the update list with the local update list. Once the critical activity controlled by the token is complete, the token is forwarded to another peer.

A join event fits smoothly in the above schema. The joining node obtains two input parameters: one personal certificate released by a well known Certification Authority (CA), and the address of another node in the system.

Using this information the node generates a new token, indicating itself as a joining member in the update list. The token is signed using the certificate, and sent to the contact peer. It is to be noted that the token generation event is expected to induce the eventual removal of a token.

The leave operation is managed similarly: upon leaving, a node produces a token with a leave event recorded in the update list. Failure detection is managed likewise, although the protocol is resilient to the presence of crashed nodes in the membership. In both cases the certificate of the failed node is permanently invalidated: in case of restart the node will need a new certificate.

We assume the presence of unique CA, whose public key is available to all nodes in the system, in charge of producing the certificates. The interplay between the CA and the generic node falls outside the scope of this paper.

3. Experimental results

We notice that our solution features many decisions points that are resolved using probabilistic assumptions: we were not able to assess its validity in theory, and we attempted a experimantal validation using a prototype implementation run on a testbed of 191 nodes.

The protocol implementation counts approximately 200 Perl lines. Since we were mostly interested in system dynamics, we opted for two simplifications: we did not implement authentication and the leave event.

The former simplification is meant to have a small impact on the significance of our protoytpe: in a separate paper [4] we address experimental results for an authenticated token passing protocol, and the impact of signing/checking is minimal

The prototype has been run on a testbed on the development infrastructure Grid5000 [1]. Grid5000 is a research project of the French Government. The aim of this project is to develop a Grid platform where researchers and scientists perform large scale experiments. Seventeen French national laboratories are involved in this research project. The major funding agencies for Grid5000 include, the *Ministeŕe de l'Education, de la Jeunesse et de la Recherche*, ACI Grid, INRIA, CNRS and some universities in France.

Grid5000 provides a very configurable and controllable environment for the experiments. It also provides the necessary software tools for the reservation of resources, deployment of experiments, for the monitoring and collection of results. Users can tailor the environment according to the particular nature of

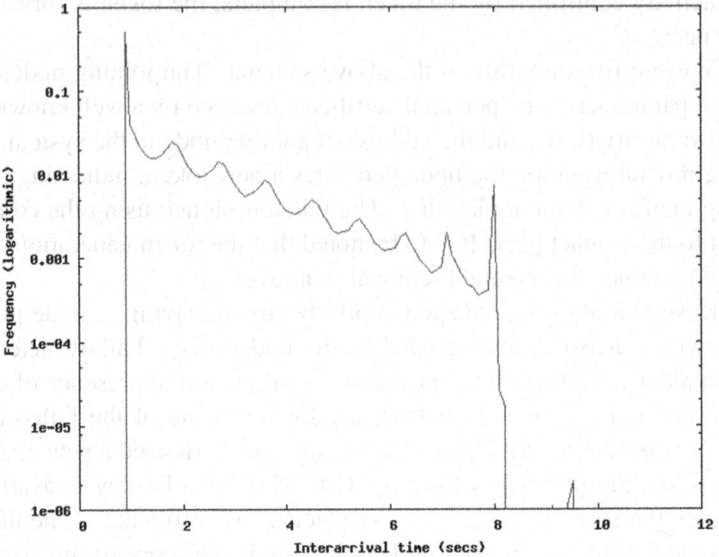

Figure 1. Frequency distribution of token interarrival time on nodes (log scale on y)

their experiments and data. To make the resource utilization optimal, the nodes on the Grid5000 can be shared between the users at the CPU and core level. Work is in progress to connect the Grid5000 with the Grid networks in other countries like Netherlands and Japan.

From the user viewpoint Grid5000 works much like a 70's batch system: a submitted job is run when resources are available. This fact motivated the adoption for our experiment of quite low time constants, in order to have a significant result after a minimum time. We opted for an expected *token latency* of 30 msecs, roughly corresponding to a token passing operation, thus obtaining very fast running tokens, and a target *token receive interarrival time* of 2.63 seconds. The size of the system was variable, and here we report an experiment with a number of nodes that gradually reaches 191 nodes. The duration of the experiment was set to 150 minutes: during the first 30 minutes the nodes grow from one to 191. With such settings, we want to observe the behavior of the system during a quite fast *power on* transient, and during a period of stability. Using an approximated model, not illustrated in this paper, we expect two tokens running in the system.

In order to assess the validity of our algorithm, we examine three quantities that give an idea of the dynamics of the system: the *token receive interarrival time* at each node, the number of tokens simultaneously circulating in the system, the time to diffuse the notice of a join to all nodes.

The distribution of the interarrival time is in figure 1. The plot shows a peak at the minimum value, corresponding to $\overline{t_{wait}}/k_{max} = 0.88secs$, indicating that tokens are usually enqueued before use: the "waving" trend of the plot has a similar reason.

The frequency of interarrival times drops exponentially (note the logarithmic scale on the y axis), and the probability of a interarrival time longer than 3 seconds is less than 1 percent: interarrival time shows an average of 1.71 seconds, instead of the target 2.63.

In figure 2 we see the dynamic variation of tokens during the experiment. It is quite evident the initial transient, during which the size of the system gradually grows from 0 to 191 nodes: the number of tokens follows a linear slope, and stabilizes to approximately 50 tokens, significantly more than expected.

Such a mismatch between the expected value and the experimental result is mainly due to the value of the parameters that control the token generation and removal rules, namely c and k_{max}: these parameters should be selected so that, when the number of tokens in the system is optimal for the target interarrival time, the probability of removing a token is equal to the probability of adding one. This fact would ensure that the number of tokens is in equilibrium when the number of tokens is optimal.

The evaluation of control parameters is difficult: although Internet performance is sufficiently uniform in time and space, the extremely randomized design of our token exchange protocol makes impossible to compute in advance the right value. An experimental tuning is therefore needed, but the robustness of the protocol ensures that the same values can be used in many different environments.

In our case, we used *first guess* values for our experiments: with the experience gained, we will refine the value of such parameters for next experiments.

Finally, we analyze figure 3 that helps evaluating the suitability of our protocol for broadcasting information to each node in the system. We recall that, for the correct operation of our protocol, we only need that most of the nodes, not necessarily all, receive a join update: the above results confirm this as a matter of fact, but leave a question mark on the time that is needed to inform *each* node about a join event.

Such results can be hardly checked against known theoretical results about the *cover time* of a random walk [10]: we recall that broadcasting is managed by a finite length list appended to the token, that several tokens are simultaneously running, and that each node merges its local event list with the one of the received token, before forwarding it.

Figure 3 shows that the broadcast time is quite long, with an average of 25 minutes. Depending on the application this time may be of interest.

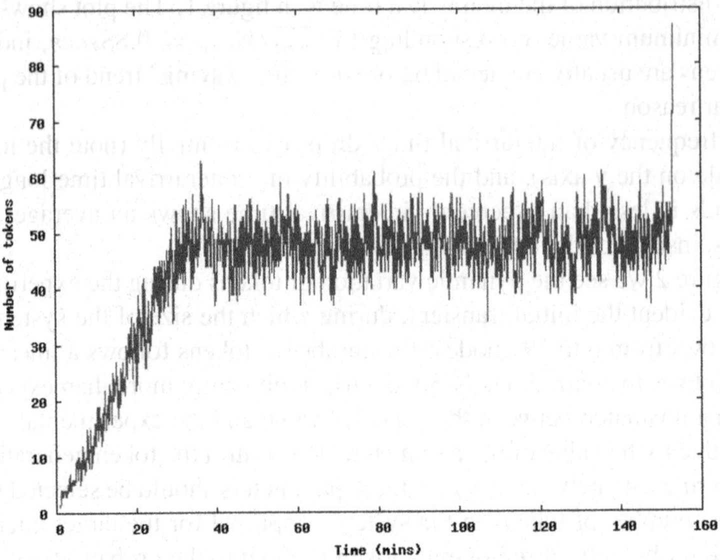

Figure 2. Variation of the number of tokens during the experiment

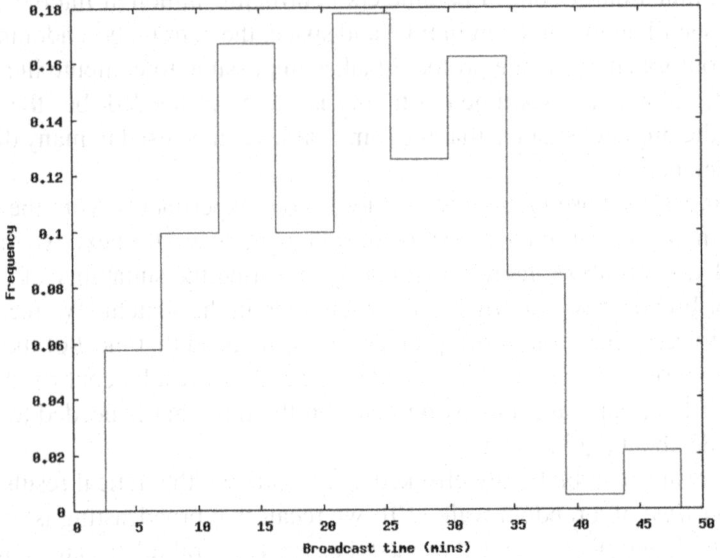

Figure 3. Frequency of broadcast times for join events

4. Conclusions and future works

The solution we propose makes extensive use of *probabilistic* assumptions: therefore many performance parameters are characterized by distributions, not by deterministic values. In order to validate its operation we implemented a simplified version of the algorithm and we used Grid5000 as a testbed.

It is to be noted that the results in this paper come from one of the first experiments: more experiments are scheduled in the short term.

From the results available so far we understand that the algorithm, although probabilistic in nature, has a quite predictable behavior: the interarrival time of tokens is quite concentrated in time, its distribution falls exponentially, and is near to the requirements. An inside look at the engine shows that the number of tokens in fact follows the size of the system, with a quite fast response to variations. However, the number of tokens is higher than expected, and tokens are short lived: this is a matter for future investigation. Membership changes propagate and eventually reach all nodes in the system.

References

[1] Raphael Bolze, Franck Cappello, Eddy Caron, Michel Daydé, Frédéric Desprez, Emmanuel Jeannot, Yvon Jégou, Stephane Lantéri, Julien Leduc, Noredine Melab, Guillaume Mornet, Raymond Namyst, Pascale Primet, Benjamin Quetier, Olivier Richard, El-Ghazali Talbi, and Touche Iréa. Grid'5000: a large scale and highly reconfigurable experimental grid testbed. *International Journal of High Performance Computing Applications*, 20(4):481–494, November 2006.

[2] Javier Bustos-Jimenez, Nicolas Bersano, Elisa Schaeffer, Jose Miguel Piquer, Alexandru Iosup, and Augusto Ciuffoletti. Estimating the size of peer-to-peer networks using Lambert's W function. In *Proceedings of the CoreGRID Integration Workshop 2008*, pages 51–62, Hersonissos, Greece, April 2008.

[3] Nimmagadda Chalamaiah and Badrinath Ramamurthy. Multiple token distributed loop local area networks: Analysis. In *5th International Conference On High Performance Computing*, pages 400 – 407, December 1998.

[4] Augusto Ciuffoletti. Secure token passing at application level. In *1st International Workshop on Security Trust and Privacy in Grid Systems*, page 6, Nice, September 2007. submitted to FGCS through GRID-STP.

[5] Frank Dabek, M. Frans Kaashoek, David Karger, Robert Morris, and Ion Stoica. Wide-area cooperative storage with CFS. In *Proceedings of the 18th ACM Symposium on Operating Systems Principles (SOSP '01)*, Chateau Lake Louise, Banff, Canada, October 2001.

[6] Edsger W. Dijkstra. Self-stabilizing systems in spite of distributed control. *Communications of the ACM*, 17(11):643–644, 1974.

[7] Schlomi Dolev, Elad Schiller, and Jennifer Welch. Random walk for self-stabilizing group communication in ad-hoc networks. In *Proceedings of the 21st Simposium on Reliable Distributed Systems (SRDS)*, Osaka, Japan, October 2002.

[8] Feige. A tight lower bound on the cover time for random walks on graphs. *RSA: Random Structures and Algorithms*, 6, 1995.

[9] M. Flatebo, A.K. Datta, and A.A. Schoone. Self-stabilizing multi-token rings. *Distributed Computing*, 8(3):133–142, 1995.

[10] L. Lovasz. Random walks on graphs: a survey. In D. Miklos, V. T. Sos, and T. Szonyi, editors, *Combinatorics, Paul Erdos is Eigthy*, volume II. J. Bolyai Math. Society, 1993.

[11] Bernard Thibault, Alain Bui, and Olivier Flauzac. Topological adaptability for the distributed token circulation paradigm in faulty environment. In Jiannong Cao, editor, *Second International Symposium on Parallel and Distributed Processing and Applications – Hong Kong (China)*, number 3358 in Lecture Notes in Computer Science, pages 146–155. Springer, 2004.

[12] S. Tixeuil and J. Beauquier. Self-stabilizing token ring. In *Proceedings of the Eleventh International Conference on System Engineering (ICSE'96)*, Las Vegas, USA, July 1996.

[13] B. Volckaert, P. Thysebaert, M. De Leenheer, F. F. De Turck, B. Dhoedt, and P. Demeester. Network aware scheduling in grids. In *Proc. of the 9th European Conference on Networks and Optical Comm unications*, page 9, Eindhoven, The Netherlands, Jun 2004.

IMPROVING THE PEER-TO-PEER RING FOR BUILDING FAULT-TOLERANT GRIDS*

Boris Mejias, Donatien Grolaux, Peter Van Roy
Universite Catholique de Louvain, Belgium
{bmc|ned|pvr}@info.ucl.ac.be

Abstract

Peer-to-peer networks are gaining popularity in order to build Grid systems. Among different approaches, structured overlay networks using ring topology are the most preferred ones. However, one of the main problems of peer-to-peer rings is to guarantee lookup consistency in presence of multiple joins, leaves and failures nodes. Since lookup consistency and fault-tolerance are crucial properties for building Grids or any application, these issues cannot be avoided. We introduce a novel relaxed-ring architecture for fault-tolerant and cost-efficient ring maintenance. Limitations related to failure handling are formally identified, providing strong guarantees to develop applications on top of the relaxed-ring architecture. Besides permanent failures, the paper analyses temporary failures and broken links, which are often ignored.

Keywords: Peer-to-peer, relaxed-ring, fault-tolerance, lookup consistency, ring maintenance.

*This research is mainly funded by EVERGROW (contract number:001935) and SELFMAN (contract number: 034084), with additional funding by CoreGRID (contract number: 004265).

1. Introduction

Classical approaches for building Grid systems using resource and service discovery are mainly centralised or hierarchical. Since centralised networks present the weakness of having single point of failure, peer-to-peer networks are gaining popularity as an alternative decentralised choice. Building decentralised applications requires several guarantees from the underlay peer-to-peer network. Fault-tolerance and consistent lookup of resources are crucial properties that a peer-to-peer system must provide. Structured overlay network providing a Distributed Hash Table (DHT) using Chord-like ring topology [10] are a popular choice to solve the requirements of efficient routing, lookup consistency and accessibility of all resources. But all these properties are compromised in presence of failure or high churn (multiple peers joining or leaving in very short time).

The benefits of using peer-to-peer systems have been already stated in previous CoreGRID results [12, 11], but the problems related to fault-tolerance has not been deeply addressed. A high level approach is proposed in [2], where the failure detection and self-organisation of the network is entirely delegated to the peer-to-peer system. Since this work addresses these issues precisely at the low level, it can be seen as a complementary result.

Despite the self-organising nature of the ring architecture, its maintenance presents several challenges in order to provide lookup consistency at any time. Chord itself presents temporary inconsistency with massive peers joining the network, even in fault-free systems. A stabilisation protocol must be run periodically to fix these inconsistencies. Existing analyses conclude that the problem comes from the fact that joins and leaves are not atomic operations, and they always need the synchronisation of three peers. Synchronising three peers is hard to guarantee with asynchronous communication, but this is inherent to distributed programming.

Existing solutions [7–8] introduce a locking system in order to provide atomicity of join and leave operations. Locks are also hard to manage in asynchronous systems, and that is why these solutions only work on fault-free systems, which is not realistic. A better solution is provided by DKS [5], simplifying the locking mechanism and proving correctness of the algorithms in absent of failures. Even when this approach offers strong guarantees, we consider locks extremely restrictive for a dynamic network based on asynchronous communication. Every lookup request involving the locked peers must be suspended in presence of join or leave in order to guarantee consistency. Leaving peers are not allowed to leave the network until they are granted with the relevant locks. Given that, peers crashing can be seen as peers just leaving the network without respecting the protocol of the locking mechanism breaking the guarantees of the system. Another critical problem for performance is presented when a peer crashes while some joining or leaving peer is holding its lock. Then, locks in a distributed system can hardly present a fault-tolerant solution.

We have developed an algorithm that only needs the agreement of two nodes at each stage, which is easier to guarantee given point-to-point communication. This decision leads us to a relaxed-ring topology, simplifying the joining algorithm and becoming fault tolerant to permanent or temporary failures of nodes, and also to broken links, which are often ignored by existing approaches.

The following section describes the relaxed-ring architecture and its guarantees. We continue with further analysis of the topology and its fault tolerant behaviour, ending with conclusions.

2. P2PS's relaxed-ring

The relaxed-ring topology is part of the new version of P2PS [4], which is designed as a modular architecture based on tiers. The whole system is implemented using the Mozart-Oz programming system [9], where the lowest level tier implements point-to-point communication between peers. Some layer upper to this one, we implement the maintenance of the relaxed-ring topology, which is the focus of this paper. This layer can correctly route lookup requests providing consistency. Other layers built on top of this one are in charge of providing efficient routing, reliable message sending, broadcast/multicast primitives and naming services. All these layers provide efficient support for building decentralised systems such as grid based on services architectures like P2PKit [6].

As any overlay network built using ring topology, in our system every peer has a successor, predecessor, and fingers to jump to other parts of the ring providing efficient routing. Ring's key-distribution is formed by integers from 0 to N growing clockwise. For the description of the algorithms we will use event-driven notation. When a peer receives a message, the message is triggered as an event in the ring maintenance tier.

Range between keys, such as $(p, q]$ follows the key distribution clockwise, so it is possible that $p > q$, and then the range goes from p to q passing through 0. Parentheses '()' excludes a key from the range and square brackets '[]' includes it.

2.1 The relaxed-ring

As we previously mentioned, one of the problem we have observed in existing ring maintenance algorithms is the need for an agreement between three peers to perform a join/leave action. We provide an algorithm where every step only needs the agreement of two peers, which is guaranteed with a point-to-point communication. In the specific case of a join, instead of having one step involving 3 peers, we have two steps involving 2 peers. The lookup consistency is guaranteed between every step and therefore, the network can still answer lookup requests while simultaneous nodes are joining the network. Another relevant difference is that we do not rely on graceful leaving of peers, because anyway, we have to deal with leaves due to network failures.

Our first invariant is that *every peer is in the same ring as its successor.* Therefore, it is enough for a peer to have connection with its successor to be considered inside the network. Secondly, the responsibility of a peer starts with the key of its predecessor plus 1, and it finishes with its own key. Therefore, a peer does not need to have connection with its predecessor, but it must know its key. These are two crucial properties that allow us to introduce the relaxation of the ring. When a peer cannot connect to its predecessor, it forms a branch from the *"perfect ring"*. Figure 1 shows a fraction of a relaxed ring where peer k is the root of a branch, and where the connection between peers h and i is broken.

Having the relaxed-ring architecture, we introduce a new principle that modifies the routing mechanism. The principle is that *a peer can never indicate another peer as responsible for a key*. This implies that even when the successor of a peer seems to be the responsible of a key, the request must be forwarded to the successor. Considering the example in figure 1, h may think that k is the responsible for keys in the interval $(h, k]$, but in fact there are three other nodes involved in this range. Note that the forwarding of a lookup request can be directed forward of backward with respect to the key distribution. It has been proved that this modification to the usual routing mechanism does not creates cycles and always converge.

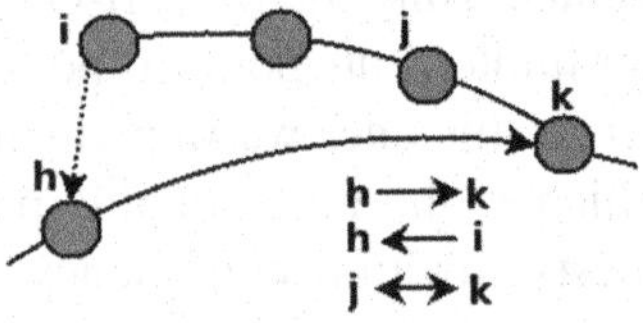

Figure 1. The relaxed-ring architecture

Before starting the description of the algorithms that maintain the relaxed-ring topology, we first define what do we mean by lookup consistency.

Def. *Lookup consistency implies that at any time there is only one responsible for a particular key k, or the responsible is temporary not available.*

When a new peer wants to join the ring, first, it gets its own identifier from a random key-generator. At this starting point, the node does not have a successor (*succ*), then, it does not belong to any ring, and it does not know its predecessor (*pred*), so obviously, it does not have responsibilities. Having an access point, that can be any peer of the ring, the new peer triggers a lookup request for its own key in order to find its best successor candidate. This is quite usual procedure for several Chord-alike systems. When the responsible of the key contacts the new peer, it begins the join algorithm that will be discussed in the next section.

2.2 The join algorithm

As we have previously mentioned, the relaxed-ring join algorithm is divided in two steps involving two peers each, instead of one step involving three peers as in existing solutions. The whole process is depicted in figure 2, where node q joins in between peers p and r. When peer r replies the lookup request to q, and q send the $join$ message to r triggering the joining process.

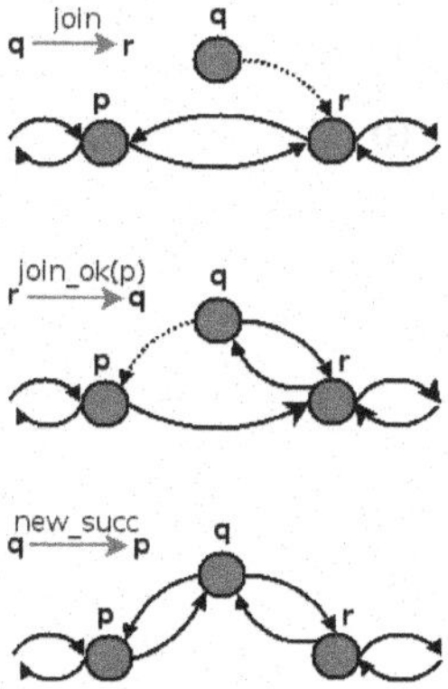

Figure 2. The join algorithm.

The first step is described in algorithm 1, and following the example, it involves peer q and r. This step consists of two events, $join$ and $join\_ok$. Since this event may happen simultaneously with other joins or failures, r must verify that it has a successor, respecting the invariant that every peer is in the same ring as its successor. If it is not the case, q will be requested to retry later.

If it is possible to perform the join, peer r verifies that peer q is a better predecessor. Function $betterPredecessor$ just checks if the key of the joining peer is in the range of responsibility of the current peer in the case of a regular join. If that is the case, p becomes the old predecessor and is added to the $predlist$ for resilient purposes. The $pred$ pointer is set to the joining peer, and the message $join\_ok$ is send to it.

It is possible that the responsibility of r has changed between the events $reply\_lookup$ and $join$. In that case, q will be redirected to the corresponding peer with the $goto$ message, eventually converging to the responsible of its key.

When the event $join\_ok$ is triggered in the joining peer q, the $succ$ pointer is set to r and $succlist$ is initialised. The function $getLast$ returns the peer with the last key found clockwise, and removes it from the set. It returns nil if the set is empty. After $succlist$ is initialised, q must set its $pred$ pointer to p acquiring its range of responsibility. At this point the joining peer has a valid successor and a range of responsibility, and then, it is considered to be part of the ring, even if p is not yet notified about the existence of q. This is different than all other ring networks we have studied.

Note that before updating the predecessor pointer, peer q must verify that its predecessor pointer is nil, or that it belongs to its range of responsibility. This second condition is only used in case of failure recovery and it will be described in section 3. In a regular join, $pred$ pointer at this stage is always nil.

Algorithm 1 Join step 1 - adding a new node

```
upon event ⟨ join | i ⟩ do
    if succ == nil then
        send ⟨ try_later | self ⟩ to i
    else
        if betterPredecessor(i) then
            oldp := pred
            pred := i
            predlist := {oldp} ∪ {predlist}
            send ⟨ join_ok | oldp, self, succlist ⟩ to i
        else if (i < pred) then
            send ⟨ goto | pred ⟩ to i
        else
            send ⟨ goto | succ ⟩ to i
        end if
    end if
end event

upon event ⟨ join_ok | p, s, sl ⟩ do
    succ := s
    succlist := {s} ∪ sl \ getLast(sl)
    if (pred == nil) ∨ (p ∈ (pred, self)) then
        pred := p
        send ⟨ new_succ | self, succ, succlist ⟩ to pred
    end if
end event

upon event ⟨ goto | j ⟩ do
    send ⟨ join | self ⟩ to j
end event
```

Once q set $pred$ to p, it notifies p about its existence with message new_succ, triggering the second step of the algorithm.

The second step of the join algorithm basically involves peers p and q, closing the ring as in a regular ring topology. The step is described in algorithm 2. The idea is that when p is notified about the join of q, it updates its successor pointer to q (after verifying that is a correct join), and it updates its successor list with the new information. Functionally, this is enough for closing the ring. An extra event has been added for completeness. Peer p acknowledges its old successor r, about the join of q. When $join\_ack$ is triggered at peer r, this one can remove p from the resilient $predlist$.

If there is a communication problem between p and q, the event new_succ will never be triggered. In that case, the ring ends up having a branch, but it is still able to resolve queries concerning any key in the range $(p, r]$. This is because q has a valid successor and its responsibility is not shared with any other peer. It is important to remark the fact that branches are only introduced in case of communication problems. If q can talk to p and r, the algorithm provides a perfect ring.

Algorithm 2 Join step 2 - Closing the ring

```
upon event ⟨ new_succ | s, olds, sl ⟩ do
    if (succ == olds) then
        oldsucc := succ
        succ := s
        succlist := {s} ∪ sl \ getLast(sl)
        send ⟨ join_ack | self ⟩ to oldsucc
        send ⟨ upd_succlist | self, succlist ⟩ to pred
    end if
end event

upon event ⟨ join_ack | op ⟩ do
    if (op ∈ predlist) then
        predlist := predlist \ {op}
    end if
end event
```

No distinction is made concerning the special case of a ring consisting in only one node. In such a case, $succ$ and $pred$ will point to $self$ and the algorithm works identically. The algorithm works with simultaneous joins, generating temporary or permanent branches, but never introducing inconsistencies. Failures are discussed in section 3. Note that message $upd\_succlist$ is for resilient purposes. It updates the list of successors that will be used for the recovery of a failure detected in the successor. The following theorem states the guarantees of the relaxed ring concerning the join algorithm.

THEOREM 2.1 *The relaxed-ring join algorithm guarantees consistent lookup at any time in presence of multiple joining peers.*

PROOF 1 *Let us assume the contrary. There are two peers p and q responsible for key k. In order to have this situation, p and q must have the same predecessor* j*, sharing the same range of responsibility. This means that* $k \in (j, p]$ *and* $k \in (j, q]$*. The join algorithm updates the predecessor pointer upon events* $join$ *and* $join\_ok$*. In the event* $join$*, the predecessor is set to a new joining* *peer j. This means that no other peer was having j as predecessor because it is a new peer. Therefore, this update does not introduce any inconsistency. Upon event $join\_ok$, the joining peer j initiates its responsibility having a member of the ring as predecessor, say i. The only other peer that had i as predecessor before is the successor of j, say p, which is the peer that triggered the $join\_ok$ event. This message is sent only after p has updated its predecessor pointer to j, and thus, modifying its responsibility from $(i, p]$ to $(j, p]$, which does not overlap with j's responsibility $(i, j]$. Therefore, it is impossible that two peers has the same predecessor.*

3. Failure Recovery

In order to provide a robust system that can be used on the Internet, it is unrealistic to assume a fault-free environment or perfect failure detectors, meaning complete and accurate. We assume that every faulty peer will eventually be detected (strongly complete), and that a broken link of communication does not implies that the other peer has crashed (inaccurate). To terminate failure recovery algorithms we assume that eventually any inaccuracy will disappear (eventually strongly accurate). This kind of failure detectors are feasible to implement on the Internet.

Every node monitors the communication with every peer it is connected to. If a failure is detected, the $crash$ event is triggered as it is described in algorithm 3. The detected node is removed from the resilient sets $succlist$ and $predlist$, and added to a $crashed$ set. If the detected peer is the successor, the recovery mechanism is triggered.

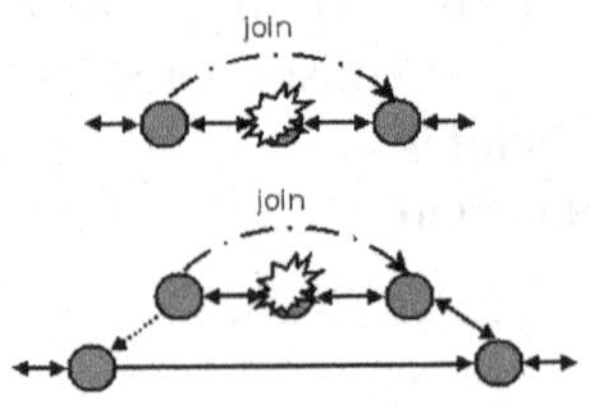

Figure 3. Simple crashes.

The $succ$ pointer is set to nil to avoid other peers joining while recovering from the failure, and the successor candidate is taken from the successors list. The function $getFirst$ is analogue to $getLast$ used in algorithm 1. Note that as every crashed peer is immediately removed from the resilient sets, these two functions always return a peer that appears to be alive at this stage. The successor candidate is contacted using the $join$ message, triggering the same algorithm as for joining. If the successor candidate also fails, a new candidate will be chosen. This is verified in the if condition.

When the detected peer p is the predecessor, no recovery mechanism is triggered because p's predecessor will contact the current peer. The algorithm decides a predecessor candidate from the $predlist$ to recover from the case when the tail of a branch is the crashed peer. We will not explore this case further in this paper because it does not violate our definition of consistent lookup. To solve it, it is necessary to set up a time-out to replace the faulty predecessor by the predecessor candidate.

The *alive* event is triggered when a link recovers from a temporary failure. This can be implemented by using watchers or a fault stream per distributed entity [3]. If the peer is alive, it is enough to remove it from the *crashed* set. This will terminate any pending recovery algorithm.

Algorithm 3 Failure recovery

```
upon event ⟨ crash | p ⟩ do
    succlist := succlist \ {p}
    predlist := predlist \ {p}
    crashed := {p} ∪ crashed
    if (p == succ) ∨ (p == succ_candidate) then
        succ := nil
        succ_candidate := getFirst(succlist)
        send ⟨ join | self ⟩ to succ_candidate
    else if (p == pred) then
        if (predlist ≠ ∅) then
            pred_candidate := getLast(predlist)
        end if
    end if
end event

upon event ⟨ alive | p ⟩ do
    crashed := crashed \ {p}
end event
```

Figure 3 shows the recovery mechanism triggered by a peer when it detects that its successor has a failure. The figure depicts two equivalent situations. Using the *crashed* set, function *betterPredecessor* can check fault status. Since the *join* event is used both for a regular join and for failure recovery, the function will decides if a predecessor candidate is better than the current one if it belongs to its range of responsibility, or if the current *pred* is detected as a faulty peer.

Knowing the recovery mechanism of the relaxed-ring, let us come back to our joining example and check what happens in cases of failures. If q crashes after the event *join*, peer r still has p in its *predlist* for recovery. If q crashes after sending *new_succ* to p, p still has r in its *succlist* for recovery. If p crashes before event *new_succ*, p's predecessor will contact r for recovery, and r will inform this peer about q. If r crashes before *new_succ*, peers p and q will contact simultaneously r's successor for recovery. If q arrives first, everything is in order with respect to the ranges. If p arrives first, there will be two responsible for the ranges $(p, q]$, but one of them, q, is not known by any other peer in the network, and it fact, it does not have a successor, and then, it does not belong to the ring. Then, no inconsistency is introduced in any case of failure.

Since failures are not detected by all peers at the same time, redirection during recovery of failures may end up in a faulty node. Then, the *goto* event must be modified such that if a peer is redirected to a faulty node, it must insist with its successor candidate. Since failure detectors are strongly complete, the algorithm will eventually converge to the correct peer.

Cases hard to handle are broken links and crashes at the tail of a branch. In the case of the broken link (inaccuracy), the failure recovery mechanism is triggered, but the successor of the suspected node will not accept the join message. The described algorithm will eventually recover from this situation when the failure detector reaches accuracy. In the case of the crash of the node at the tail of a branch, there is no predecessor to trigger the recovery mechanism. In this case, the successor could use one of its nodes in the predecessor list to trigger recovery, but that could introduce inconsistencies if the suspected node has not really failed. If the tail of the branch has not really failed but it has a broken link with its successor, then, it becomes temporary isolated and unreachable to the rest of the network. Having unreachable nodes means that we are in presence of network partitioning. The following theorem describes the guarantees of the relaxed-ring in case of temporary failures with no network partitioning.

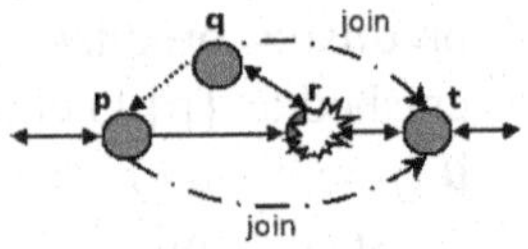

Figure 4. The failure of the root of a branch triggers two recovery events

THEOREM 3.1 *Simultaneous failures of nodes never introduce inconsistent lookup as long as there is no network partition.*

PROOF 2 *Every failure of a node is eventually detected by its successor, predecessor and other peers in the ring having a connection with the faulty node. The successor and other peers register the failure in the* crashed *set, and remove the faulty peer from the resilient sets* predlist *and* succlist*, but they do not trigger any recovery mechanism. Only the predecessor triggers failure recovery when the failure of its successor is detected, contacting only one peer from the successor list at the time. Then, there is only one possible candidate to replace each faulty peer, and then, it is impossible to have two responsible for the same range of keys.*

With respect to network partitions, there are two important cases we want to analyse. The crash of a branch's root, and the isolation of a set of nodes from the rest of the ring. The isolation problem can occur in any system using ring topology, and it can involve consecutive peers or peers distributed all over the ring. Network partitioning introducing temporary uncertainty has been proved by Ghodsi [5], and it is related to the proof provided in [1] about limitations of web services in presence of network partitioning.

Figure 4 depicts a network partition that can occur in the relaxed-ring topology. The proof of theorem 3.1 is based on the fact that per every failure detected, there is only one peer that triggers the recovery mechanism. In the case of the failure of the root of a branch, peer r in the example, there are two recovery messages triggered by peers p and q. If message from peer q arrives first to peer t, the algorithm handle the situation without problems. If message from peer p arrives first, the branch will be temporary isolated, behaving as a network partition introducing a temporary inconsistency. This limitation of the relaxed-ring is well defined in the following theorem.

THEOREM 3.2 *Let r be the root of a branch, $succ$ its successor, $pred$ its predecessor, and $predlist$ the set of peers having r as successor. Let p be any peer in the set, so that $p \in predlist$. Then, the crash of peer r may introduce temporary inconsistent lookup if p contacts $succ$ for recovery before $pred$. The inconsistency will involve the range $(p, pred]$, and it will be corrected as soon as $pred$ contacts $succ$ for recovery.*

PROOF 3 *There are only two possible cases. First, $pred$ contacts $succ$ before p does it. In that case, $succ$ will consider $pred$ as its predecessor. When p contacts $succ$, it will redirect it to $pred$ without introducing inconsistency. The second possible case is that p contacts $succ$ first. At this stage, the range of responsibility of $succ$ is $(p, succ]$, and of $pred$ is $(p', pred]$, where $p' \in [p, pred]$. This implies that $succ$ and $pred$ are responsible for the range $(p', pred]$, where in the worse case $p' = p$. As soon as $pred$ contacts $succ$ it will become the predecessor because $pred > p$, and the inconsistency will disappear.*

Theorem 3.2 clearly states the limitation of branches in the systems, helping developers to identify the scenarios requiring special failure recovery mechanisms. Since the problem is related to network partitioning, there seems to be no easy solution for it. An advantage of the relaxed-ring topology is that the issue is well defined and easy to detect, improving the guarantees provided by the system in order to build fault-tolerant applications on top of it.

4. Conclusion

The amount of Grid systems built on top of peer-to-peer networks is increasing. Since Grid users design their application at a higher level, it is reasonable to assume that failure handling will the delegated to the peer-to-peer system. This is why its crucial to provide a robust fault-tolerant network.

In this paper we have presented a novel relaxed-ring topology for fault-tolerant and self-organising peer-to-peer networks. The topology is derived from the simplification of the join algorithm requiring the synchronisation of only two peers at each stage. As a result, the algorithm introduces branches to the ring. These branches can only be observed in presence of connectivity problems between peers, allowing the system to work in realistic scenarios, providing fault-tolerant ring maintenance.

The guarantees and limitations of the system are clearly identified and formally stated providing helpful indications in order to build fault-tolerant applications on top of this structured overlay network. Having these guarantees, solving issues related to network partitioning become more addressable.

References

[1] Eric A. Brewer. Towards robust distributed systems (abstract). In PODC '00: Proceedings of the nineteenth annual ACM symposium on Principles of distributed computing, page 7, New York, NY, USA, 2000. ACM Press.

[2] Denis Caromel, Alexandre di Costanzo, and Christian Delbé . Peer-to-peer and fault-tolerance: Towards deployment-based technical services. Future Generation Computer Systems, 2007. To appear.

[3] Raphaël Collet and Peter Van Roy. Failure handling in a network-transparent distributed e programming language. In Advanced Topics in Exception Handling Techniques, pages 121-140, 2006.

[4] DistOz Group. P2PS: A peer-to-peer networking library for Mozart-Oz. http://gforge.info.ucl.ac.be/projects/p2ps, 2007.

[5] Ali Ghodsi. Distributed k-ary System: Algorithms for Distributed Hash Tables. PhD dissertation, KTH - Royal Institute of Technology, Stockholm, Sweden, December 2006.

[6] Kevin Glynn. P2PKit: A services based architecture for deploying robust peer-to-peer applications. http://p2pkit.info.ucl.ac.be/index.html, 2007.

[7] Xiaozhou Li, Jayadev Misra, and C. Greg Plaxton. Active and concurrent topology maintenance. In DISC, pages 320-334, 2004.

[8] Xiaozhou Li, Jayadev Misra, and C. Greg Plaxton. Concurrent maintenance of rings. Distributed Computing, 19(2):126-148, 2006.

[9] Mozart Community. The Mozart-Oz programming system. http://www.mozart-oz.org.

[10] Ion Stoica, Robert Morris, David Karger, Frans Kaashoek, and Hari Balakrishnan. Chord: A scalable Peer-To-Peer lookup service for internet applications. In Proceedings of the 2001 ACM SIGCOMM Conference, pages 149-160, 2001.

[11] Domenico Talia, Paolo Trunfio, Jingdi Zeng, and Mikael Heqvist. A peer-to-peer framework for resource discovery in large-scale grids. In Proc. of the 2nd CoreGRID Integration Workshop, pages 249-260, Krakow, Poland, October 2006.

[12] Paolo Trunfio, Domenico Talia, Paraskevi Fragopoulou, Charis Papadakis, Matteo Mordacchini, Mika Pennanen, Konstantin Popov, Vladimir Vlassov, and Seif Haridi. Peer-to-peer models for resource discovery on grids. In Proc. of the 2nd CoreGRID Workshop on Grid and Peer to Peer Systems Architecture, Paris, France, January 2006.

Author Index